Recommendations for *Solid Code*

Solid Code *does a great job of hitting that super har*`          `
the management books and the technology b`    `
model software to security design to defensi`                 `*. show*
you the best practices you can apply to your a`              `*en better.*

—`                   `*Cofounder, Wintellect*

Solid Code *isn't just about code; it imparts the know how to deliver a solid project. This book delivers straightforward best practices, supplemented with case studies and lessons learned, from real products to help guide readers to deliver a perfect project—from design through development, ending with release and maintenance.*

—*Jason Blankman, Software Development Engineer, Microsoft Corporation*

As a software developer of 20 years, there are a few books that I read again every couple of years. I believe that Solid Code *will be one of the books that you will read over and over, each time finding new insight for your profession.*

—*Don Reamey, Software Development Engineer, Microsoft Corporation*

Solid Code *is an invaluable tool for any serious software developer. The book is filled with practical advice that can be put to use immediately to solidify your code base.* Solid Code *should definitely be on your shelf, close at hand, as you'll use it again and again!*

—*John Alexander, Microsoft Regional Director, Managing Partner, AJI Software*

Solid Code *is a must read for any IT professional, especially if you plan on using managed code. The book not only covers engineering best practices but also illustrates them with real test case studies.*

Andres Juarez, Release Manager, Microsoft Corporation

This is a very well-written book that offers best practices in cultivating an efficient software development process by which typical developer mistakes can be avoided. The authors provide practical solutions for detecting mistakes and explain how software development and testing works at Microsoft.

Venkat B. Iyer, Test Manager, Microsoft Corporation

This book is excellent for developers at any level—beginner to experienced. It provides the foundation of great development practices that should be used by any size development team, and even by individual programmers.

John Macknight, Independent Software Developer

Microsoft®

Solid Code

Optimizing the Software Development
Life Cycle

Donis Marshall

John Bruno

PUBLISHED BY
Microsoft Press
A Division of Microsoft Corporation
One Microsoft Way
Redmond, Washington 98052-6399

Library of Congress Control Number: 2008940526

Printed and bound in the United States of America.

1 2 3 4 5 6 7 8 9   QWT   4 3 2 1 0 9

Distributed in Canada by H.B. Fenn and Company Ltd.

A CIP catalogue record for this book is available from the British Library.

Microsoft Press books are available through booksellers and distributors worldwide. For further information about international editions, contact your local Microsoft Corporation office or contact Microsoft Press International directly at fax (425) 936-7329. Visit our Web site at www.microsoft.com/mspress. Send comments to mspinput@microsoft.com.

Acquisitions Editor: Ben Ryan
Developmental Editor: Devon Musgrave
Project Editor: Melissa von Tschudi-Sutton
Editorial Production: nSight, Inc.
Technical Reviewer: Per Blomqvist; Technical Review services provided by Content Master, a member of CM Group, Ltd.
Cover Illustration by: John Hersey

Body Part No. X15-28130

This book is dedicated to my children: Jason, Kristen, and Adam.
Jason is a talented young man, Kristen is now in college,
and Adam (at 11) defeats me in chess regularly.

—Donis Marshall

To Christa, Christopher, and Patrick, this book is for you.
Your love and support inspire me every day.

—John Bruno

Contents at a Glance

Table of Contents

What do you think of this book? We want to hear from you!

Microsoft is interested in hearing your feedback so we can continually improve our books and learning resources for you. To participate in a brief online survey, please visit:

microsoft.com/learning/booksurvey

What do you think of this book? We want to hear from you!

Microsoft is interested in hearing your feedback so we can continually improve our books and learning resources for you. To participate in a brief online survey, please visit:

microsoft.com/learning/booksurvey

Foreword

Software engineering is not engineering. As a software developer, I would love nothing more than to say I am an engineer. Engineers think through and build things that are supposed to work the first time due to careful planning. So having the word "engineer" in my job title would be very cool indeed.

Let's look at what would happen if the normal software engineering approach were applied to aerospace engineering. A plane is sitting at a gate boarding passengers, and an aerospace engineer—on a whim or forced by management—decides to replace the tail section. Because it's just a tail section, let's just rip it off and stick another one on right there at the gate. No problem, we can make it work! If aerospace engineering were approached like software engineering, I think the passengers would stampede to get off that plane as fast as possible. But those are the kind of changes that are made every day in major software projects the world over. The old joke is that "military intelligence" is an oxymoron, but I'd have to say that it fits "software engineering" as well. What makes this even more troubling to me is that software truly rules the world, but the approach nearly everyone takes to making it can in no way be called engineering.

Why is it that I know the physical computer I'm using right now will work, but the program I'm using, Microsoft Word, will screw up the auto numbering of my lists? While my electrical engineering friends will not be happy to hear this, hardware is easy. The electrical engineer has a limited number of inputs to work with, unlike the essentially unlimited number given to software developers.

Management also considers electrical engineering "real engineering," so management gives the appropriate time and weight to those efforts. The software business, as a distinct field, is not a mature industry; it really hasn't been around that long. In fact, I myself am slightly younger than the software business, so my youthful look reveals some of the problem. If I were as old as electrical engineering, I'd be writing this from the grave.

Another difficulty with software development can sometimes be the software developers themselves. Realistically, the barriers to becoming a software developer can be quite low. I'm a prime example: I was working as a full-time software developer before I had a bachelor's degree in computer science. Because I was able to "talk the talk" in interviews, I was given a job writing software. None of my employers really cared about my lack of education because they could hire me cheaper than someone with a degree.

All real engineering fields require you to achieve ambitious certification criteria before you can add the Professional Engineer (PE) designation to your name. There's nothing like that for the software industry. That's due in part to the fact that no one can agree what all software developers should know because of the newness of the industry. In other fields, the PE designation appropriately carries huge weight with management. If a certified engineer says a design won't work, she won't sign off on the plans and the project won't go forward. That forces management to take the planning process much more seriously. Of course, by signing off on a project, the PE acknowledges liability for ethical and legal ramifications should things go wrong. Are you ready to sign off on the ethical and legal liability of your software's design? Until we get our industry to that point, we can't really call ourselves engineers in the traditional sense.

The good news is that even in the nearly 20 years I have been in the software development business I've seen huge changes for the better. Senior management is finally getting the message that software project failures cost companies serious amounts of money. Take a look at Robert Charette's "Why Software Fails" in the September 2005 issue of the *IEEE Spectrum* magazine (*http://www.spectrum.ieee.org/sep05/1685*) for a list of spectacular failures. With the costs so high, some senior management are finally committing real resources to get software projects kicked off, planned, and implemented right the first time. We still have a long way to go, but this buy-in for real planning from management is one of the biggest changes I've seen in my time in the industry.

On a micro level, the best change in software development is that nearly all developers are finally serious about testing their code. Now it's fortunately rare to hear about a developer who throws the code over the wall to the QA group and hopes for the best. This is a huge win for the industry and truly makes meeting schedules and quality gates achievable for many teams. As someone who has spent his career on the debugging and performance-tuning side of the business, I'm really encouraged about our industry becoming more mature about testing. Like all good change, the testing focus starts with the individual and the benefits work their way up the organization.

What's also driving change is that our tools and environments are getting much better. With .NET, we have an easy way to test our code, so that means more people will test. Also, the abstraction layers are moving up, so we no longer have to deal with everything on the computer. For example, if you need to make a Web service call, you don't have to manually open the port, build up the TCP/IP packet, call the network driver, wait for the data to return, or parse the return data. It's now just a method call. These better abstraction layers allow us to spend more time on the important parts of any software project: the real requirements and solving the user's problem.

We still have a long way to go before our field is a real engineering field, but the signs are encouraging. I think a big change will occur when we finally start treating testing as a real profession—one that is equal to or more important than development. While I probably won't see the transition to software engineering before I retire, I'm very encouraged by the progress thus far. Let's all keep pushing and learning so we can finally really be called engineers.

This book, *Solid Code*, is a great step in the direction of treating software as an engineering discipline. Bookstores' programming shelves groan under two types of development books. The first kind is the hand-waving software-management type, and the second is the gritty internals-of-a-technology type; I'm guilty of writing the latter. While those books have their uses and are helpful, the types of books we are missing are the ones that talk about real-world team software development. The actual technology is such a small part of a project; it's the team and process aspects that present the biggest challenges in getting a software project shipped. *Solid Code* does a great job of hitting that super hard middle ground between the management books and the technology books. By covering ideas from how to model software to security design to defensive programming, Donis and John, show you how the best practices you can apply to your development will make it even better. Reading *Solid Code* is like experiencing a great project lead by a top development manager and working with excellent coworkers.

The whole book is excellent; I especially loved the emphasis on planning and preparation. Many of the projects that my company, Wintellect, has had to rescue are the direct result of poor planning. Take those chapters to heart so you'll avoid the mistakes that will cost you tons of money and time. Another problem the book addresses is the tendency to leave performance tuning and security analysis for the very end of the project. As the title of Chapter 4 so succinctly points out, "Performance Is a Feature." The recommendations in those chapters are invaluable. Finally, the book's emphasis on real-world coding and debugging will pay dividends even when the code goes into maintenance mode. Even though I've been working in the field nearly 20 years, I picked up a lot of great ideas from *Solid Code*.

Every developer needs to read this book, but there are others in your company who need to read it as well. Make your manager, your manager's manager, and your manager's manager's manager read this book! The one question I always get from senior managers at any company is, "How does Microsoft develop software?" With the Inside Microsoft sections in most chapters of *Solid Code*, your management will see how Microsoft has solved problems in some of the largest applications in use today. Now start reading! It's your turn to help move our industry into a real engineering discipline!

John Robbins
Co-founder, Wintellect

Acknowledgements

Isaac Newton has been credited with the phrase, "If I have seen further, it is only by standing on the shoulders of giants." That statement is certainly applicable to this book, especially when considering the practices, perspectives, and experiences contained within it. More specifically, those shoulders belong to the many people who have contributed to this project. Although our names adorn the cover, we owe much of the credit to the individuals who have helped bring this book to life. We are grateful for their efforts and support throughout this project, and would like to acknowledge them individually.

For starters, we could not have done it without the team at Microsoft Press. We would like to thank Ben Ryan, Devon Musgrave, and Melissa von Tschudi-Sutton for ensuring a high-quality outcome and keeping the project on schedule. Additionally, we would also like to thank the technical editor Per Blomqvist and copy editor Cindy Gierhart for their invaluable contributions and feedback.

As mentioned, this book includes practices, perspectives, and experiences. Many of these elements would not have been included without the contributions, support, and feedback of the professionals from Microsoft and the industry. Specifically, we would like to thank the contributors and reviewers: Jason Blankman, Eric Bush, Jacob Kim, Don Reamey, Dick Craddock, Andres Juarez Melendez, Eric Schurman, Jim Pierson, Richard Turner, Venkatesh Gopalakrishnan, Simon Perkins, Chuck Bassett, Venkat Iyer, Ryan Farber, and Ajay Jha.

There is also a special acknowledgement for Wintellect. Wintellect is a consulting, debugging, and training firm dedicated to helping companies build better software faster through a concentration on .NET and Windows development. Its services include in-depth, multiday .NET on-site and open enrollment training as well as development and consulting services including emergency debugging. The company also produces Devscovery conferences—three-day multitrack events targeting the intermediate to advanced developer. For more information about Wintellect, visit *www.wintellect.com*.

John Robbins and Jeffrey Richter of Wintellect provided invaluable insights and timely feedback. Thanks!

Donis Marshall   I have written several books. However, this is my first book with a coauthor. I have been left with one important question after the completing the book. Why did I not have a coauthor on earlier book projects? John Bruno was an incredible asset to this project. His broad knowledge and insights have made this book an important read for any technologist in the Windows arena. John also possesses a rare attribute among authors—timeliness.

John Bruno   Writing a book is a commitment that often affects those closest to you. I would like to first thank my wife, Christa, and my two sons, Christopher and Patrick, for their patience, understanding, and sacrifice during the development of this book. Their love and support inspire me to be the best man I can be, everyday. Additionally, I am grateful to Donis Marshall for inviting me to join him on this project. I sincerely appreciate his friendship and the opportunity to work with him on such an important subject. I have been fortunate throughout my life to have known many creative and insightful people. To those of you who have always been there to inspire, encourage, challenge, and support me, I thank you.

Introduction

Software development has evolved greatly over the past several years. Improvements in programming languages and rapid development tooling, like .NET and Visual Studio 2008, have driven the software industry to build higher-quality software, faster, cheaper, and with more frequent upgrades or refreshes. Despite this continued demand for more software and the evolution in tools and processes, building and releasing quality software remains a difficult job for all participants of software projects, especially developers. Fortunately, this title encapsulates the essence of the best-in-class engineering practices, processes, policies, and techniques that application developers need for developing robust code.

Solid Code explores best practices for achieving greater code quality from nearly every facet of software development. This book provides practical advice from experienced engineers that can be applied across the product development life cycle: design, prototyping, implementation, debugging, and testing. This valuable material and advice is further supplemented by real world examples from several engineering teams within Microsoft, including, but not limited to, the Windows Live Hotmail and Live Search teams.

Who Is This Book For?

Solid Code has something for every participant in the software development life cycle. Most specifically, it is targeted toward application developers who are seeking best practices or advice for building higher-quality software. Portions of this book illustrate the important role of the engineering process as it relates to writing high-quality code. Other parts focus on the criticality of testing. However, most of this book focuses on improving code quality during design and implementation, covering specific topics like class prototyping, performance, security, memory, and debugging.

This book targets both professional and casual developers. Readers should have a basic understanding of programming concepts and object oriented programming in C#. There are no skill level expectations. *Solid Code* is about the practical application of best practices for managed code application development. The topics discussed within the book should resonate with managed code developers of all skill levels.

Organization of This Book

Solid Code is organized similarly to the application development life cycle. The chapters are not separated into parts, but rather grouped according to four key principles. These principles are outlined in Chapter 1, "Code Quality in an Agile World", and include: Focus on Design, Defend and Debug, Analyze and Test, and Improve Processes and Attitudes.

- **Focus on Design**   One of the great themes of this book is the importance of thoughtful design as a means to improve overall product quality. To support this theme, practices such as class design and prototyping, metaprogramming, performance, scalability, and security are explored.

- **Defend and Debug**   Although great designs are critical to building a high-quality software application, it is equally important to understand the pitfalls that hinder delivery of bug-free code. Topics such as memory management, defensive programming techniques, and debugging are all discussed in the context of this principle.

- **Analyze and Test**   Even the greatest programmers produce bugs despite following the recommended best practices. Therefore, it is important to discuss code analysis and testing as methods for further improving code quality.

- **Improve Processes and Attitudes**   Beyond best practices, engineering processes and culture can have a great impact on the quality of the work being produced. We explore several key topics for improving the efficiency of the team as well as their passion for quality.

System Requirements

You will need the following hardware and software (at a minimum) to build and run the code samples for this book in a 32-bit Windows environment:

- Windows Vista, Windows Server 2003 with Service Pack 1, Windows Server 2008, or Windows XP with Service Pack 2

- Visual Studio 2008 Team System

- 2.0 gigahertz (GHz) CPU; 2.6 GHz CPU is recommended

- 512 megabytes (MB) of RAM; 1 gigabyte (GB) is recommended

- 8 GB of available space on the installation drive; 20 GB is recommended

- CD-ROM or DVD-ROM drive

- Microsoft mouse or compatible pointing device

The Companion Web Site

This book features a companion Web site that provides code samples used in the book. This code is organized by chapter, and you can download it from the companion site at this address: *http://www.microsoft.com/learning/en/us/books/12792.aspx*.

Find Additional Content Online

As new or updated material that complements this book becomes available, it will be published online to the Microsoft Press Online Developer Tools Web site. This includes material such as updates to book content, articles, links to companion content, errata, sample chapters, and more. This Web site is available at *http://www.microsoft.com/learning/books/online /developer* and it will be updated periodically.

Support for This Book

Every effort has been made to ensure the accuracy of this book and companion content. Microsoft Press provides corrections for books through the Web at the following address:

http://www.microsoft.com/mspress/support/search.aspx

To connect directly to Microsoft Help and Support to enter a query regarding a question or issue you may have, go to the following address:

http://support.microsoft.com

If you have comments, questions, or ideas regarding the book or companion content or if you have questions that are not answered by querying the Knowledge Base, please send them to Microsoft Press using either of the following methods:

E-mail:

mspinput@microsoft.com

Postal mail:

Microsoft Press
Attn: *Solid Code* editor
One Microsoft Way
Redmond, WA 98052-6399

Please note that product support is not offered through the preceding mail addresses. For support information, please visit the Microsoft Product Support Web site at

http://support.microsoft.com

Chapter 1
Code Quality in an Agile World

We are what we repeatedly do. Excellence, therefore, is not an act, but a habit.

—Aristotle

As software developers, we want our products to be excellent. Our desire is to delight our users with bug-free experiences and to ensure the highest quality in the programs we create. Among our peers, we strive to demonstrate our technical prowess with the elegant and stable code we write. Each of us works hard at achieving these goals every day. Our repetitive efforts to develop high-quality software, coupled with our desires to continually improve our methods and practices, solidify our habits as developers. As Aristotle suggests, excellence is achieved through repeated great execution.

Building high-quality software is a difficult job, though. Even the most rudimentary programs will have bugs. Everyone, including the best engineers, put them there. Humans, by nature, are imperfect and occasionally slip up. As we translate human instructions to a software application that we want to do our bidding, mistakes will be made, exceptions will be thrown, and, yes, quality problems will arise.

But it's unfair to pin responsibility for software quality solely on developers. Software engineering is a process involving many participants from different disciplines. At Microsoft, for instance, engineering teams are typically divided into three disciplines: Program Management, Development, and Test. Program Managers ensure that product specifications are precise and well thought out, and they set definitive goals for the quality of the end product. Developers create the most efficient and flexible designs, ensure accuracy of the algorithms, and leverage well-known best practices for code implementation. Testers consider every possible permutation of both code and application behavior and fully examine and exercise each code path of the software. Quality is part of the end-to-end engineering life cycle and therefore is every participant's responsibility. Software development organizations understand this principle and go to great lengths to implement processes and programs to ensure that quality is a core focus for each team member.

Software development processes and methodologies have existed in the industry since the late 1960s. As computing power increased, software programs grew increasingly more complex. This increased complexity in software development, and the relative immaturity of the industry, led to several problems with software projects, including cost overruns, poor-quality software due to lack of formal quality processes, and low maintainability of code. As a result, formal software development processes were born. Their primary goal was to put formal structure around a series of tasks that ultimately led to an improved outcome of the development effort. Simply stated, the goal of having formal engineering processes was to achieve a higher-quality product and a more predictable time to market or deployment. Using a process to ensure the quality of a product is fundamental to delivering nearly any product or service, regardless of industry. Chances are, as software developers, you have experienced one or more different project management methodologies during your career, such as waterfall, agile, or even the Microsoft Solutions Framework (MSF).

Traditional Methods of Software Development

You have probably heard the term "waterfall" applied to the more traditional software development life cycle (SDLC). This term refers to the way each phase of the SDLC cascades steadily downward, as shown in Figure 1-1, through the following sequential phases:

- **Requirements**   A detailed, written description of the software to be built.

- **Design**   The process of planning the implementation details of a software project.

- **Implementation**   The process of coding, testing, and debugging the individual parts of the software being developed.

- **Integration and verification**   The phase when the various portions of the software are being brought together for integration and broader testing.

- **Installation and maintenance**   The end of the SDLC, when the new software is deployed and moves into a cycle of post-release fixes and adjustments.

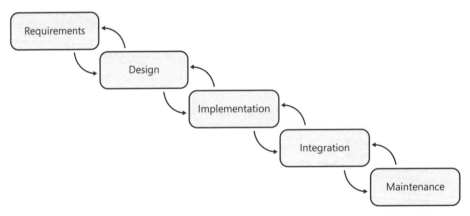

FIGURE 1-1 Traditional software development life cycle.

The model's rigidity requires sequential forward progress through these phases until the software is completed and requires that each phase be completed before the next can begin. Requirements specification must be fully completed before proceeding to design. Once design is completed and a plan is in place for engineers to implement the requirements, coding begins. Integration follows coding, and the various parts of the program are brought together and tested as a complete system. Once integration is complete and the software is deployed, the maintenance phase starts. In each of these phases, a great deal of emphasis is placed on written documentation as well, which tends to make waterfall projects heavyweight.

The waterfall model approaches quality by suggesting that the more time spent analyzing and designing the software, the more likely flaws will be uncovered early in the process and subsequently avoided in the downstream development of the code. Critics argue that this methodology does not work well in practice because critical details of the program or application cannot truly be known until the development team is progressing through implementation. Additionally, since the model is stringent about finalizing specifications before coding begins, there is very limited opportunity for including any early customer or beta tester feedback into the release cycle, which constrains the team in addressing customer needs in a timely manner. Finally, complete end-to-end testing does not occur until late in the cycle, which adds risk to the quality of the application, when integration of critical elements begins.

> **Note**   The "waterfall" methodology is often credited to Dr. Winston W. Royce, based on a paper he authored in 1970 titled "Managing the Development of Large Software Systems." The irony of this accreditation is that Dr. Royce was essentially arguing that the methodology was risky and invited failure. He mentioned how testing at the end of the life cycle, where all critical components of the system are coming together for the first time, was not realistic. He went on to suggest that flaws discovered late in the cycle would lead to inevitable cost overruns due to the high likelihood of subsequent design changes. Although he believed in the conceptual idea of the multiphased life cycle, he desired an evolution to a more iterative approach that would likely achieve a better result than a sequential model.

Proponents and opponents aside, the waterfall method of software project management has provided a framework for many of the derivative models that exist today. Just as the late 1980s and early 1990s saw the evolution of Rapid Application Development methods, in recent years, many organizations have moved toward agile development methodologies, both of which are derivatives of the waterfall methodology. These newer models are much more iterative in their approach to the software development process, and they promote shorter, quicker, more focused release cycles.

Agile Methods of Software Development

The movement toward more lightweight software development methodologies has been attributed to the general dissatisfaction with heavyweight, restrictive methods like waterfall. Several of these lightweight methods began emerging in the mid-1990s and emphasized concepts such as self-organizing teams, face-to-face communication, lightweight documentation, and frequent releases. Eventually, several of these methodologies' creators, including

Kent Beck, Martin Fowler, and Ward Cunningham, formed the Agile Alliance[1] and unified the principles of agile software development with the Agile Manifesto.[2]

Agile methodologies tend to encourage iterative approaches to software development with small, self-organizing teams that work in short, very collaborative release cycles. Quality is paramount in every phase of agile software development, and many of the key principles—such as pair programming, test-driven development, refactoring, and continuous integration—ensure that defects are found and eradicated early and often in the release cycle, unlike in the more traditional methodologies.

There are many different agile methodologies in use today, including but not limited to Scrum, eXtreme Programming (XP), test-driven development (TDD), refactoring, and continuous integration. Additionally, there are plenty of great resources available for understanding the principles and practices within each method (see the booklist in Appendix A). It is worth examining a few of the more popular methods of agile in this chapter, and illustrating which of the principles and practices of each has long been favored to improve the quality of software in Microsoft engineering culture.

Scrum

Scrum is perhaps the best known, or at least the best recognized by name, of the agile methods in use today. At its core, Scrum is not truly a methodology, per se, but rather a framework of practices and defined roles for participants in its processes. Scrum, like most agile methods, encourages small, self-organizing teams that work on a well defined set of development tasks during a short release cycle.

Despite providing a valuable framework for managing the software development process, Scrum itself does little to prescribe any specific methods for managing the quality of the software being developed. This is not necessarily problematic, though, because Scrum pushes accountability to individuals within the Scrum team, which promotes the freedom to implement their own quality practices. Other agile methodologies, however, focus less on project frameworks but are much more prescriptive about specific practices for managing code quality.

Each Scrum project cycle is represented by a *Sprint*, which is a period of time during which development of a set of features is completed. A Sprint begins with a planning period, where Scrum teams commit to a set of features on which they will focus their efforts. The set of features that are selected by the team during this planning period originate from the Product Backlog, which is a prioritized list of all potential features for the software being developed. By the end of the planning period, all features selected from the Product Backlog are entered

---

[1] *http://www.agilealliance.org.*

[2] *http://www.agilemanifesto.org/principles.html.*

and tracked in the Sprint Backlog, which represents the details of the team's specific feature work. Once the Sprint Backlog is defined, the Sprint can begin. Typically, a Sprint will last 30 days, during which time the team meets each day to review work status and help respective team members remain productive. By the end of the Sprint, the set of features previously defined in the Sprint Backlog is completed and usable. This process is illustrated in Figure 1-2.

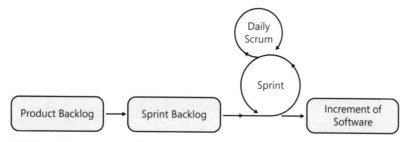

FIGURE 1-2 Scrum process flow.

> **Note** Scrum is a really interesting framework to read about. In addition to some of the colorful terminology for participant roles, such as "pigs" and "chickens," there is a lot of value in the framework Scrum provides. I recommend reading *Agile Project Management with Scrum*, by Ken Schwaber (Microsoft Press, 2004) to learn more.

Scrum is perhaps the most widely used form of agile project management practices within the Microsoft engineering teams. The process Scrum provides for managing work is actually quite effective for small, relatively autonomous feature development teams. Most teams have used Scrum in conjunction with our core engineering practices with great effects.

eXtreme Programming

Unlike Scrum, eXtreme Programming (XP) is not a framework of practices that labels participants or processes with interesting titles or terminology associated with contact sports. XP combines well-defined, valuable set practices into a customer-focused methodology for delivering high-quality software in an iterative manner.

XP proponents assert that ever-evolving software requirements are a natural and desirable part of software development. Rather than attempt to define all requirements in advance of development, XP encourages flexibility in adapting to changing requirements throughout the project cycle. The model relies on a very close working relationship between software developers and their business counterparts, or customers, as shown in Figure 1-3. The XP life cycle is a continuous iteration of feature definition, estimation, feature selection, and feature development. With each project iteration, XP teams become more efficient and effective at delivering solid code with maximum customer impact and within a short development cycle.

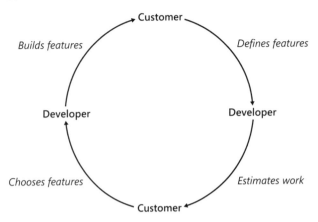

FIGURE 1-3 eXtreme Programming process model.

While the philosophy and practice of XP has been the subject of debate in recent years over such issues as unstable requirements, lack of documentation, and its inability to scale to large teams, several of the practices that XP promotes are quite valuable for managing code quality. Examples of those methods[3] include:

- **Developer testing** Developers continually write, and often start by writing unit tests, which must pass for development to continue.

- **Code refactoring** Developers are always restructuring the system without altering behavior to simplify, reduce duplicity, and add additional flexibility.

- **Pair programming** Developers work in pairs to reduce coding mistakes.

- **Continuous integration** Features are integrated and built every time a key development task is completed.

- **Coding standards** Rules are established that emphasize communication through the code, which developers are required to follow.

These practices are not unique to XP, but they are great examples of quality practices that in many cases transcend other agile methodologies. Several of these methods, such as developer testing, code refactoring, and continuous integration, have been used in practice within Microsoft engineering teams for years and are proven to be quite effective. We will explore these practices within Microsoft engineering teams later in this chapter.

Test-Driven Development

In addition to the agile methods already described, other methods such as test-driven development (TDD) have emerged in recent years. TDD suggests that tests express the require-

---

3   Kent Beck and Cynthia Andres, *Extreme Programming Explained: Embrace Change* (Addison-Wesley Professional, 2004), p. 54.

ments with which the code must comply. This technique requires developers to write an automated unit test before writing feature code. As feature code evolves, automated tests provide immediate feedback to the developer and confirm, through true or false assertions, whether the code is behaving correctly. Because each feature of the software subsequently possesses a corresponding test or set of tests, higher confidence in the quality of the code is often the result.

The TDD process[4] for developing features includes the following steps:

- **Write a test**   Developers are required to first develop a test that maps to the particular feature requirement.

- **Run all tests and see the new test fail**   Assuming that a set of tests exist across the code base, the new test should inevitably fail due to the lack of new feature code.

- **Write code that makes the test pass**   Feature code is developed to meet the requirement of the new test.

- **Run all tests and ensure all succeed**   Once the new feature code has been written, all tests should be executed again to ensure that new tests pass.

- **Refactor code**   Any code written to satisfy the previous steps may not be optimized and should subsequently be refactored to remove duplication or other code bloat.

- **Rinse and repeat**   Continue until there are no other requirements left to implement.

Other agile methodologies encourage developer-written unit tests, but TDD stands apart in its rigid view of testing before coding. TDD provides an interesting value proposition as a process that ensures high code quality; however, it does not provide an end-to-end framework for managing the software development life cycle. The goal of TDD is simply to be a framework for addressing customer requirements with software through an iterative approach to testing and coding.

Agile Practices in Microsoft Engineering Culture

It is no secret that Microsoft is the largest software engineering company in the world. The company does not earn that title by the number of employees alone but rather the incredible number of products that are delivered each year by Microsoft engineers and development teams across the many continents on which the company maintains an engineering presence.

For its size, Microsoft is an incredibly nimble company, and engineering teams are generally very agile in their approach to delivering software products to market. For example, teams in Microsoft's Online Services Division, such as Windows Live, are known to

---

[4]   James W. Newkirk and Alexei A. Vorontsov, *Test-Driven Development in Microsoft .NET* (Microsoft Press, 2004).

deliver major feature updates several times per year to worldwide audiences of hundreds of millions. Consider the size and complexity of products like Microsoft Windows or Microsoft Office. These products require very large, well-coordinated, incredibly precise engineering processes that are highly focused on code quality. Despite the size and complexity of these products, the code base, and the engineering teams, Microsoft still manages to deliver new versions of these products on a fairly frequent basis. (Office releases on average once every two years.) How Microsoft teams accomplish this is based on years of continuous evolution and improvement to engineering practices and automated tooling, which in and of themselves could be the subject of an entire book. However, there are a few of the aforementioned agile practices that are worth mentioning.

> **Note**   For a more in-depth example of how Microsoft teams have continued to evolve engineering practices, I recommend reviewing the Windows Engineering team's blog at *http://blogs.msdn.com/e7/*.

For several years, perhaps a decade or more, Microsoft engineering teams have incorporated several "agile" practices for improving quality. Particularly, most teams incorporate coding best practices, developer-written unit tests, refactoring, and continuous integration practices into their daily software development regimen. Teams like the Office team build and deploy the working product on a daily basis. Code from multiple development teams is continuously integrated and tested using highly tuned, automated build and test systems. The result is a daily version of the complete product that is of dependable quality. As you might imagine, these processes require quite an engineering investment, but the result is a "turn-the-crank" process that is optimized for repeatability and high-quality output. Microsoft Visual Studio offers a great set of tools that enable large and small development teams alike to both automate their build processes using MSBuild and automate test coverage using Visual Studio Team System testing tools (VSTS). Both provide capabilities of running daily builds and suites of automated tests in unattended environments.

Moving Quality Upstream

During each phase of the development life cycle, quality practices guide program managers, developers, and testers toward the best end product they can collectively produce:

- At the beginning of the development life cycle, the focus is on gathering customer insights and feedback, conducting detailed planning, feature specification, and overall system design.

- During the implementation phase of the life cycle, developers focus on applying quality techniques to the code they develop, through use of standards, code sharing and optimization, and unit testing.

- Prior to release, testers perform broad system and integration testing to ensure the end-to-end product is of high quality.

This perspective implies that the integration of quality practices should be pervasive across all phases of the SDLC. This is not always the case, however:

- Waterfall promotes ensuring quality through up-front planning and broad spectrum testing after coding.

- Agile promotes quality in the middle of the life cycle and relies on specific practices to ensure code quality remains high through the entire project.

In waterfall methods, developers write code and hand it off to testers to evaluate that code for defects. In this model, as developers continue to add features and complexity at a rapid rate, the scope and burden of testing the entire application grows significantly. This accumulation of test work late in the project cycle adds risk to the quality of the software and can have a crippling effect on new feature development and long-term maintainability of the system. Simply stated, the more code that is written, the more difficult the software is to test.

> **Note** In *Debugging Microsoft .NET 2.0 Applications* (Microsoft Press, 2006), John Robbins asserts that "feature creep" is perhaps the largest contributor to poor quality in software. Make no mistake; adding features late in the development cycle is a recipe for trouble. However, there will be circumstances where you will succumb to project or business pressures and accept these late additions. It's important to establish strong quality processes for all features, regardless of when you commit to delivering them.

Moving quality practices like testing upstream or earlier in the development life cycle, as agile methods like XP suggest, reduces the risks of releasing bug-ridden software. Additionally, by ensuring that each feature has been verified and tested prior to being checked in to a source tree, the agility of the development team actually increases due to fewer build breaks, lower bug counts, and a more repeatable and stable feature development process. In principle, feature development and coding should only proceed as fast as it can be verified through testing. This allows software development to progress forward at a more consistent and manageable rate, with a higher degree of output quality. This is evident in how agile methods like XP promote inherent testability of code and recommend investments in automated test frameworks like that of VSTS or NUnit for developing and continuously executing suites of automated tests against your code.

Applying quality practices upstream in the development life cycle promotes early discovery of issues in the code, which ultimately increases the ability of software developers to respond to those issues, alter their designs as needed, and meet schedule commitments.

Accountability for quality of the software becomes shared across developers and testers, and the SDLC becomes more agile and predictable. This philosophy not only encourages the tactical application of better quality practices but also promotes a culture of quality within engineering teams. This union of quality and agility is achieved when great engineering practices are combined with a culture of quality and a project delivery rigor and rhythm that best fits your organization's needs.

Inside Microsoft: Windows Live Hotmail Engineering

Windows Live Hotmail is a Web-based e-mail product offered by Microsoft within the Windows Live suite of services. Hotmail is perhaps one of the most well-known of all e-mail services on the Internet and was one of the first free Web-based e-mail services when it launched in 1996. For many years, Hotmail was provided under the MSN brand of services until being rebuilt in managed code and relaunched under the Windows Live brand in 2007. At present, Hotmail is the most widely used Web-based e-mail product in the world and is delivered to more than 250 million users[5] worldwide in more than 35 languages. The key components of the application include Web-based e-mail, calendar, contact management, and instant messaging features.

Since being acquired by Microsoft in 1997, Hotmail has gone through a complete transition, from a Unix-based application to now a managed code application running on Windows Server technologies. It is large, sophisticated, and divided into multiple components including, but not limited to, storage, mail delivery, and Web front-end subsystems. Once deployed, the size of the Web front-end subsystem alone is more than 250 megabytes (MB). This is an indicator of Hotmail's size as an application, but it in no way represents its complexity.

Because it is primarily an e-mail application, Hotmail must be extremely scalable, reliable, secure, and safe from various Internet-based abuse tactics like spam, viruses, and phishing. Users have come to expect a high level of quality from personal information management applications such as Hotmail, and, consequently, competition with rival products to offer first-class mail, calendar, and contact management software is fierce. To maintain its position as a global leader in Web-based communication, Hotmail's engineering processes must ensure timely and repeatable delivery of high-quality, reliable, and scalable application code and infrastructure.

Engineering Principles

The Windows Live Hotmail engineering team has developed a great deal of experience over the years in the delivery of high-quality, reliable, and feature-rich Web applications to

---

5   comScore, Inc., press release, February 5, 2008, *http://www.comscore.com/press/release.asp?press=2196*.

a global audience. As a team, they recognize the depth and complexity of the engineering challenges they face and have spent years perfecting their practices. They adhere to a set of guiding principles that govern how they deliver software to market. These principles include:

Focus on quality of service, performance, and security   Perhaps the most important of all features, the team prioritizes this principle above all others. The culture of the team promotes a high degree of product quality, and the team believes that Hotmail should be a reliable, fast, and secure service for its users. This belief permeates the team's engineering practices from design, coding, and testing through Web site architecture and infrastructure. While many companies strive for a similar culture, the Hotmail team has been able to achieve this by injecting a quality focus into all aspects of its development processes.

Leverage iterative development   All disciplines within the team (which include program management, development, and test) work together to define, develop, and test the software using iterative development methodologies. The Hotmail team has learned from its experience and from the experience of other teams at Microsoft that iterative development improves the quality of the code and reduces bug counts throughout the development cycle while increasing the efficiency of the team. The team employs several tactics to ensure success with iterative development, including keeping iterations short (six to eight weeks), completing features end-to-end prior to starting new features, working in small and autonomous teams, and communicating information about the state of its projects early and often.

Ensure predictable and repeatable processes   Over the years, the Hotmail team has been most successful with its product quality because the team has come to rely on predictable and repeatable processes. For example, common Web server hardware, deployment methodologies, and manageability tools have helped the team gain efficiencies in managing its Web infrastructure, while planning and development processes have helped the team minimize risk to delivery schedules and improve overall delivery quality.

Use common tools, processes, and terminology   As with most teams at Microsoft, the Hotmail team is part of a larger organization of product development teams within Windows Live. For efficiency, these teams share common tools and processes like source control, build processes, and bug-tracking databases. Overall engineering processes and terminology are also consistent across teams, which ultimately helps streamline the software delivery process as well as improve overall communication between teams.

Key Success Factors

Since moving away from a waterfall model several years ago, the Hotmail team has found that the above-mentioned set of principles have had a very positive impact on the quality of the code, and the team's overall agility. These principles collectively have helped the team to continuously innovate on its services, while still achieving a high level of quality and reliability. However, the team cites its move to iterative development and, in particular, specific practices that move quality upstream as the most impactful improvement in its software development processes. More specifically, the team feels that the practices that have had the most positive effect on the quality of its work during iterative development include:

Delivering testable units   This practice ensures that the development of features proceeds only as fast as features can be verified and tested. Once a feature is coded and ready to test and has passed the required developer-written unit test, it is handed off for a more thorough test pass prior to being checked into the working branch of the source tree. This process ensures that the feature being developed is of high enough quality to be integrated into the working branch of the source code and is not likely to break a full build of the application.

Running daily builds   As development of features progresses and testable units are being integrated into the working branch of the source code, full application builds are automatically run each day. Daily builds are accompanied by a set of automated tests, called build verification tests (BVTs), which help ensure that none of the previous day's source check-ins introduced any new bugs into the core features of the application. This process helps the team manage the overall quality of the application on a daily basis. Build breaks are treated very seriously, and, in the event of a BVT breaking bug, all work on features ceases until the issue is addressed and the suite of tests pass.

Running automated BVTs with daily builds   This suite of automated tests ensures that basic functionality of the application is of high quality and that the build can be released for more formal end-to-end testing. Automation ensures that tests are repeatable and can be executed rapidly to determine build quality. Executing and passing these tests daily ensures a consistent quality bar throughout the development cycle. At least once per week, the team releases one of these daily builds to an internal "dogfood" environment to allow internal Microsoft early adopters to use the most recent product build and provide feedback to the team.

Ship to a "dogfood" environment early and often   "Dogfood" is a Microsoft colloquialism for "eating your own dogfood," or conveying confidence in your own products at an early stage of development. The Hotmail team believes in shipping early and often to its users and, as previously mentioned, provides a weekly prerelease version of the product to a small set of Microsoft employees who are eager to evaluate and test a new version of the product. The team believes that adhering to an iterative rhythm of coding, building, testing, and releasing to dogfood helps the team to keep the end-to-end quality of the product as high as possible throughout the development cycle.

During the development of Windows Live Hotmail, which released in 2007, the team moved to a more iterative software development model as it spent time building the entire application in managed code. By leveraging the practices mentioned above, such as building testable units, running daily builds, and releasing to the dogfood environment early and often, the team found that the quality of its work improved dramatically as compared with what it experienced when using a waterfall model. Particularly, the team noted that its bug counts using an iterative development method grew more slowly and peaked at much lower numbers as compared with the waterfall method, which had often left the team with high bug counts at the end of the development cycle. The slower growth rate and lower overall bug counts allowed the team to resolve bugs faster and maintain control over code changes, which ensured the continued stability of the product. The comparison of the bug counts when using a waterfall development model versus an iterative development model are illustrated in Figure 1-4.

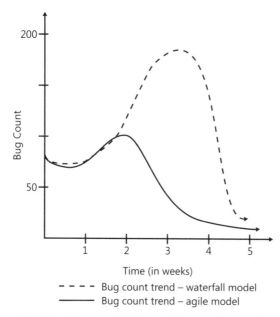

Time (in weeks)

- - - - Bug count trend – waterfall model
———— Bug count trend – agile model

FIGURE 1-4 Windows Live Hotmail bug trend comparison.

The team attributes its success in releasing a high-quality product to the repetitive processes it established to govern its application quality at early stages of the development life cycle. The Hotmail team has proved through experience that implementing quality-focused practices—such as delivering testable units, running daily builds, and using automated test suites—upstream in the development cycle ensures a greater level of quality in the application as well as a more predictable outcome of the development life cycle. In February 2007, this was validated when Hotmail was awarded *PC Magazine*'s Editor's Choice award for Web-based e-mail products. This award is clearly a testament to the team's focus on delivering high-quality, reliable, and scalable application code and infrastructure.

Tactics for Writing Solid Code

The principle of moving quality upstream illustrates the importance of integrating quality-focused engineering practices into daily development and integration rigor. By not applying quality practices such as testing earlier in the development cycle, teams are likely to accumulate a great deal of test work for each additional feature added, subsequently increasing the risk of delivering the software late and with a low degree of quality. For many organizations, this will be a significant cultural change in addition to a tactical one, but embracing this culture and these practices will ultimately lead to better engineering and delivery of solid code. As we progress through this book, we'll explore both tactical and cultural recommendations for improving the overall quality of the software you and your team deliver. The rest of this chapter briefly describes these recommendations, presenting them thematically ("Focus on Design," for example), with the thematic sections' subsections ("Class design and prototyping," for example) corresponding to the book's remaining chapters.

Focus on Design

Design is perhaps the first line of defense against introducing poor quality into your software application. Traditional and agile methods agree that design is a critical step in the process of shipping high-quality software. There are numerous great design principles for which there are volumes of text written by incredibly smart people. As you might imagine, choosing a small set of design principles on which to focus this book was quite difficult. Fortunately, I have spent the past several years of my career working on software applications of various sizes, many of which were developed in managed code. The obvious choice was to focus on the design principles that have proven most useful in my experience.

Class design and prototyping   When developing an application, object-oriented programming begins with class design and prototyping. Generally, this starts with identifying participants, or "types," in the application and how they relate and interact with one another. The interaction and relationship model is translated into design documents, using Unified Modeling Language (UML). From there, a prototype is built, and the concepts, relationships, and interactions are tested for correctness and completeness. It is during this stage that it is most important to analyze the risk associated with the proposed design, prior to implementation.

Metaprogramming   Reducing complexity and improving the maintainability of software directly contributes to increasing its quality. By abstracting behaviors out of the code and into application metadata, the application design becomes inherently more robust, flexible, and adaptable. As a result, application and test code can be much more simplified. In managed code applications, the use of XML as a metaprogramming language is encouraged as a means to modify application behavior at run time. It is this design practice that ultimately provides lower-cost application maintenance and flexibility, especially in post-release, live production circumstances.

Performance   Designing well-performing applications could be considered a competitive feature of an application. Quality in software extends beyond just visible bugs to the overall end-user experience in using the application. This is especially true when building live services over the Web or smart clients that rely on Internet-based endpoints to function properly. Network latency, payload size, and even certain protocols can have negative impacts on online end-user experiences. As a core engineering tenet, performance considerations should be part of every design. Deferring these considerations until late in the development cycle can create significant code churn after performance bugs are discovered.

Scalability   As software evolves beyond the desktop to a server-based delivery model, scalability has become a critical element to high-quality software designs. Due to the nature of server-based applications, managing resources in your application has direct influence on both the way your application performs and the cost associated with scaling your application to meet user demands. Scale factors should always be considered as part of software design and in many instances will even force certain feature trade-offs. In addition to driving high operational costs, delaying scalability considerations beyond the design and coding phases of the development cycle could force design changes and subsequently increase code churn when bugs and general application health issues are discovered under increased load.

Security   Perhaps the most important of the core engineering tenets, and often the root of many quality problems, is security, and it should be a key design focus for all application developers. As software and users have become more connected, the threats against software have significantly increased in frequency and severity. Software designs need to give careful consideration to application threats and their appropriate countermeasures, through the use of threat modeling. Incorporating security into the entire development life cycle, and especially design, will ultimately lead to a safer and more secure experience for the users of your software.

Defend and Debug

Inasmuch as design is a critical element to developing solid code, knowing the pitfalls that hinder the ability to deliver bug-free code is equally important. Understanding typical programming mistakes can greatly reduce or eliminate a known set of potential issues. Beyond that, developers must employ defensive tactics when writing code that will help to reduce another, less obvious class of logic bugs. When proactively defending code is not enough, actively testing code will prove effective in eradicating these issues. Finally, any remaining bugs should be pursued by aggressively debugging. These principles are germane to all managed code developers who wish to proactively address quality issues in their code.

Memory management   Memory management in managed code is substantially different than native code. However, the difference is not just technical. It is also philosophical. For the most part, developers had ownership of memory management in native code. The state of memory was their responsibility. That changes in managed code. The developer must share responsibility with the Common Language Runtime—particularly the Garbage Collector. This requires the developer to delegate to the Garbage Collector is some circumstances, such as garbage collection.

Defensive programming techniques   Applying defensive techniques to software development helps to proactively limit the number of bugs being introduced into the application. These techniques can be as simple as conducting frequent code reviews and setting compiler options or as advanced as using pattern-based programming to leverage reliable and tested algorithms. Applying these practices in your software development process can greatly reduce the potential for logic bugs.

Debugging   Just as elements of the software development life cycle are iterative, so is the process of debugging. Most developers associate debugging with post-release bugs or runtime issues. However, proactively debugging code to ensure that it behaves as expected under all circumstances will greatly improve the release quality of the code. When bugs do creep into post-build or post-release code, though, a software developer with knowledge of a debugging tool set like Visual Studio 2008 should be well equipped to solve the problems.

Analyze and Test

Beyond implementing thoughtful designs and the application of development best practices, code must be exercised. This is fundamental to understanding how an application will perform when users begin interacting with it. While manual testing is a great method for discovering usability-centric issues with applications, programmatic unit testing and code coverage testing almost always find bugs early and help improve overall code quality. These processes should be incorporated during the development cycle so that code quality can be managed in real time during feature development, not after development is completed.

Code analysis, coverage, and testing   When code analysis, unit testing, and code coverage testing are applied within software development teams, the result is generally higher code quality, fewer regression bugs, and more stable application builds. Tools such as code analysis and unit test frameworks in Visual Studio 2008 provide software development teams the automated support to ensure the process is repeatable and predictable. Applying this level of automated rigor in the development process accrues value with every feature that gets added to the application. As software complexity increases, automated test execution and coverage keeps pace and helps maintain the quality of the application.

Improve Processes and Attitudes

Design, coding, debugging, and testing best practices are invaluable tools for improving software quality. Assembling these various practices may prove effective for some software development teams. In most cases, however, it is the processes and attitudes of the team that ultimately fuses with best practices to enable a culture of quality, where every team member shares the responsibility of releasing high-quality software.

Improving engineering processes   It is through testing and debugging that bugs are found and eradicated. Software developers learn from these mistakes and hopefully never repeat them, as they get immortalized and documented in great detail within bug-tracking systems. This process is relevant for software development methodologies as well. Successful teams often self-evaluate and make adjustments to their future processes in hopes of never repeating the mistakes of their past. Implementing changes that improve efficiencies in the engineering process ultimately improve the quality of the work being delivered. Practices like establishing milestone, check-in, and release criteria to improve quality are just some examples of how processes can be combined with practices to close the loop on how solid code can be achieved without heavyweight development processes.

Attitude is everything   Writing bug-free code is more than just adhering to a prescribed list of best practices and policies. It is also about the dynamics of software development teams, the interactions with customers and partners, and the moxie software developers bring to work every day to accomplish the incredibly difficult job they have. There are important human factors that affect us all every day as we develop software, and it is important to understand how to work well in these highly dynamic environments.

Summary

Improvements in programming languages and rapid development tooling, like .NET and Visual Studio, continue to fuel the industry to deliver better quality software faster, cheaper, and with more frequent upgrades or refreshes. Despite this continued demand for more software and the evolution in our tools and processes, building and releasing quality software remains the responsibility of the developer and a challenging one at that. We, as software developers, constantly seek improvements to our methodologies and practices as we struggle to meet the demands of our managers, organizations, and customers to release high-quality software.

There are many great project management frameworks, tools, and engineering practices that can be very effective in improving quality and software delivery when successfully applied. But the combination of quality and agility are best achieved when great engineering practices are combined with the project delivery rigor and rhythm that best fits your team's needs. While the definition of agility in software delivery will differ across organizations, teams, and software markets, there is a core set of engineering practices for writing managed code that will universally improve the quality of the software your organization delivers. We will explore each of these practices in depth in subsequent chapters of this book.

Key Points

- There are many software development methods out there today. Many of them, both waterfall and agile, provide great frameworks and value to the software development process. Both deliver the same outcome: high-quality software produced quickly for customers. Choose one that best fits your organization's culture and needs.

- Agile methodologies focus a great deal on improving quality in the software development process. Individually and collectively, many of them recommend practices that should be applied early in the development process.

- Quality practices should be applied early (moved upstream) in the development process to ensure that:

  - Issues with designs or code are discovered early.

  - Developers have time to respond accordingly with code and design changes.

  - Testers can adequately ensure complete test coverage.

  - Schedule commitments are not compromised.

- Apply the following practices during the development of your software applications:

  - Incorporate class designing and prototyping.

  - Add flexibility, add maintainability, and reduce complexity with metaprogramming.

  - Design for performance, scalability, and security.

  - Learn how to manage memory effectively.

  - Practice defensive programming.

  - Proactively debug routines.

  - Incorporate automated unit testing and invest in a repeatable testing process.

  - Implement code coverage testing.

Chapter 2
Class Design and Prototyping

In art the hand can never execute anything higher than the heart can inspire.

—Ralph Waldo Emerson

Programming is a creative process. The heart of that process is the requirements analysis and design phase of the software development life cycle. There are several different versions or renditions of the software development life cycle. Figure 2-1 is one depiction. The result of this creativity, your program, cannot exceed the quality of the design. For many, comparing a developer to van Gogh might be considered heresy, but parallels do exist. Programming is as much creative as it is analytical. An artist does not start with a paintbrush and a canvas. There is considerable preparation before painting can begin. For example, Michelangelo devoted many years in preparation, including drawing several sketches that are now famous, before painting the Sistine Chapel. Similarly, developers do not simply start writing code. The requirements analysis must be undertaken, a design drafted, the prototyping of class operations, and only then, finally, the implementation.

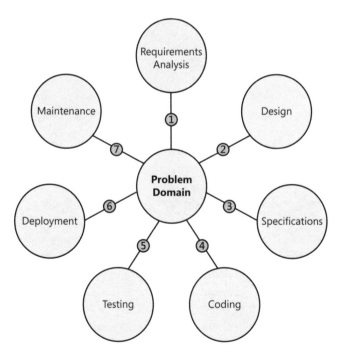

FIGURE 2-1 The software development life cycle.

This chapter presents techniques and best practices for software modeling, which is integral to the software development life cycle. Software modeling documents various phases of the software development life cycle. This is particularly relevant to the design phase. Most important, software modeling provides a tangible representation of the various phases of the software development life cycle. This provides an ability to validate the correctness of the analysis, design, specification, and so on. This validation is essential to developing and deploying high-quality software. A modeling language can be used to paint various perspectives of a software system. Together, this combined perspective provides a complete picture of the software system. As mentioned, software modeling has the greatest relevance to the design phase, which is the emphasis of this chapter. However, while this chapter provides some best practices for designing the application, subsequent chapters will continue the focus on overall application design and address other key aspects of application design, such as metaprogramming, performance, and security.

Later in the chapter, prototyping is discussed with recommended best practices and policies. Prototyping should occur before the code phase of the software development cycle or when implementation of the application begins. Prototyping is a natural extension of software modeling that allows you to validate many of the assumptions made in modeling the software development life cycle.

Visual Studio is the primary tool in this chapter for both software modeling and prototyping. Visual Studio is a collaborative tool, where software architects can build class diagrams and developers can implement solutions.

Collaboration in Visual Studio

Microsoft has expanded the role of Visual Studio. It is no longer a developer-centric tool. Visual Studio has features that benefit everyone who participates in the software development life cycle. Microsoft, some time ago, realized that developers are not islands unto themselves. They work together with other professionals, such as program managers and testers, in a collaborative environment to create stable and robust products. Previously these various roles in the software life cycle, such as software architect or designer, were segregated by technology. No single tool encompassed most of the features needed by everyone. Learning and maintaining separate tools hurt productivity and inherently resulted in brittle solutions. Microsoft realized this and started moving Visual Studio in a more collaborative direction— particularly with the advent of Visual Studio Team System (VSTS). With successive iterations of the product, Visual Studio has expanded upon the repertoire of collaborative features. For example, the class diagram capability is a relatively new feature that is beneficial for developers but also software architects. Unit testing and code analysis were recently introduced and they further integrate testers and quality assurance professionals into Visual Studio. Here are some of the benefits of this integration:

- Visual Studio is the apex of all things related to the software development life cycle, which is convenient and efficient.

- As such, Visual Studio becomes a permanent record of each aspect of the software development life cycle.

- It provides a single location to maintain and version design documents, class diagrams, unit tests, code, and other documents pertaining to the project.

Integration of various roles into Visual Studio is demonstrated and highlighted in this chapter. The benefits are clearly shown.

Think First, Code Later

Everyone in the software development life cycle needs to recognize the importance of the design phase and other work leading up to coding. Object-oriented programming is more than implementing classes and creating objects. You must embrace the design phase as the precursor to writing code. Some developers mistakenly allow implementation to drive design. When this occurs, the resulting solution is compromised. If the design models the implementation, there is a detachment between the problem domain and implementation, which diminishes the effectiveness of the solution. It is difficult, but not impossible, to write procedural code in the .NET environment. This is especially true of solutions ported from the native environment into .NET. When this happens, you lose most of the benefits of object-oriented programming. Unlike procedural programming, it is estimated that the average developer should spend 40 to 50 percent of his or her time in design and not writing code. If you plan to spend so much time on anything, you should do it well. That is what this chapter is about.

Sometimes culture prevents developers from a "design-first-and-code-later" approach. The reality persists in many organizations that programmers are evaluated by quantity—lines of code generated. This is a false barometer. Managers in particular must understand this and provide an opportunity and even encourage an investment in other aspects of the software development life cycle. Deadlines often amplify this behavior. When deadlines are approaching, management should not encourage an abandonment of the process and a direct-to-programming mindset. Shortcutting or omitting portions of the software development life cycle—particularly requirements analysis, design, and testing—compromises quality. Implementing a well-documented and automated development process that requires the team to go through each of the process steps for every project is a defense against deadline-induced process shortcuts. A quote from Benjamin Disraeli is relevant here: "The secret of success is constancy to purpose." This is especially important because, in most methodologies, design is an iterative phase, which requires follow through. Not updating the design as needed throughout the software development life cycle negates most of the benefit of the original work. This is primarily the responsibility of developers and testers who validate the design through implementation and testing. Therefore, your help is required to keep the design documents relevant.

In Chapter 1, "Code Quality in an Agile World," we established that finding flaws within our applications early in the development life cycle significantly contributes to the overall quality and stability of the final output. Table 2-1 compares the amount of effort required to fix bugs found early versus late in the software development life cycle. For example, uncovering a bug during design would be *early*, while finding a bug during maintenance would be considered *late*. This table comes from "The Economic Impacts of Inadequate Infrastructure for Software Testing," a report by Gregory Tassey, PhD, and published by National Institute of Standards and Technology. It shows that it takes about four times longer to correct a problem in testing than to correct one in the design phase. This is another confirmation of the importance of investing the appropriate time in the design and other early phases of the software development life cycle.

TABLE 2-1 A comparison of time to resolve bugs in the software development life cycle

Location	Hours to fix	Percent of defects found
Requirements/Design/ Architecture	1.2	7%
Coding/Unit testing	4.9	4.9%
Integration	9.5	28%
Beta testing	12.1	13%
Post-product release	15.3	10%

Keeping a design current and available is imperative. Similar to comments and just as important, the design documents a program. When new resources are added to a project, such as a quality assurance engineer or additional developer, the design provides critical information. This helps someone without prior knowledge of the software system to navigate the intricacies of a product. As mentioned already, the design phase is iterative. Design documents should be updated to consistently mirror changes to the implementation. Stale design documents are more detrimental than no design documents because stale design documents represent disinformation. Finally, design documents should remain available even after product development is completed. For this reason, checking versioned design documents into source control is strongly encouraged. You should have a version of the design document checked into source control for every public version of the product. That preserves them while maintaining appropriate versioning. Unfortunately, most companies I have consulted with have outdated or entirely misplaced design documents. In the *Hitchhiker's Guide to the Galaxy*, Douglas Adams wrote, "It was on display in the bottom of a locked filing cabinet stuck in a disused lavatory with a sign on the door saying 'Beware of the Leopard.'" Make sure your design documents are not in that filing cabinet.

Modeling the solution is part of the design phase and integral to documenting the software system. It should be done in a known syntax, such as Unified Modeling Language (UML). UML is the de facto standard for software modeling. UML is a general purpose modeling syntax and was created from the combined effort of the three amigos: Grady Booch, James

Rumbaugh, and Ivar Jacobson. These three are the pillars of object-oriented programming and originally had competing syntaxes for domain modeling. All three now work for IBM at Rational Software. For domain-specific modeling, Domain-Specific Modeling (DSM) is an alternative to UML. Either approach provides a representation of the software application or system that can then be implemented.

Software Modeling

Software applications should simulate (model) the real world with close affinity to the problem domain. When the real world changes, which inevitably will occur, your application should be sufficiently malleable or extensible to adapt to the new reality. C# is a direct descendant of C++. Further, C++ is indirectly derived from Simula (short for *simula*tion). Simula, Simula 1, and then Simula 67 were created in the 1960s at the Norwegian Computing Center in Oslo, Norway, and were considered the first object-oriented programming languages. Simula was developed to create simulations of real-world problems. Bjarne Stroustup merged C and Simula to create C++. Of course, C# is heavily influenced by C++.

The example used in this chapter is a software application for customer banking at a bank branch. The problem domain is customers entering a bank and using one of the available services, such as bank withdrawal, deposits, or wiring money. The application is used by bank management to simulate the retail banking environment. This is used for planning purposes to assure the correct balance of resources at a branch. One of the first steps is to create scenarios that in aggregate model the various dimensions of the problem domain. From those scenarios, you can identify potential objects, behaviors, and attributes. For example, select the nouns from the problem domain as possible future objects. See Table 2-2 for some of the nouns found in the retail banking scenarios. The complete scenarios are available at the Web site for this book, which is *http://www.microsoft.com/learning/en/us/books/12792.aspx*.

TABLE 2-2 Nouns in the retail banking scenarios

Account holder	Social Security number	Street address	City
State	Zip code	Phone number	Checking account
Savings account	Teller	Bank branch office	Transaction

The next logical step is to identify the verbs and verb phrases in the problem domain. These are the potential behaviors. Table 2-3 is a list of the possible behaviors found in the retail banking scenarios.

TABLE 2-3 Verbs and verb phrases in the retail banking scenarios

Open checking	Open savings	Close checking	Close savings
Get teller	Deposit checking	Withdraw checking	Deposit savings
Withdraw savings	Transfer money	Wire money	Charge fee

Finally, from the scenarios, identify the adjectives or other descriptive phrases that are potential attributes. Table 2-4 is a list of some of the adjectives from the retail banking scenarios.

TABLE 2-4 The adjectives in the retail banking scenarios

Balance	Age	Gender	Open date
Close date	Last transaction	Branch	Routing number
Account number	Opening teller	Interest	Security alert

Tables 2-2, 2-3, and 2-4 represent a short list of items found in the problem domain for retail banking. The actual list of valid items would be considerably longer. At this phase of the design, include everything. Do not prejudge the usefulness of a particular item in the problem domain. For example, *bank branch office* is a noun found in the problem domain. Even though it is likely to be removed in a later phase, include *bank branch office* in the list of potential objects. While in the design phase, it is imperative that implementation decisions be deferred to later. Considering implementation details prematurely detracts from the purity of the design process. Let the design dictate the implementation and not vice versa. For example, in a later phase, objects that do not communicate with other objects will be identified. If an object does not communicate or associate with another object in your problem domain, that entity is probably not useful from the perspective of your application and can be removed. Based on the scenarios for our application, *bank branch office* does not collaborate with any other objects. At that time, and not earlier, the design would dictate that the *bank branch office* be removed from the list of objects. In this circumstance, design analysis drove the decision to remove the object.

There should be a way to clearly model various phases of the software development life cycle, including the design analysis. A single syntax that everyone, regardless of his or her role in the software development life cycle, will understand. That is the goal of UML. It provides a consistent and standardized syntax for modeling aspects of the software development life cycle.

Unified Modeling Language

UML is a formal language for modeling software system design and architecture. UML documents the objects, behaviors, attributes, collaboration, and associations through a variety of diagrams. These diagrams provide different perspectives on a software system. For example, the class diagram documents the classes found in a software system and their interaction. While class diagrams are static, sequence diagrams are dynamic and document the sequence of interactions between elements of the software system. Diagrams, such as the class and sequence diagrams, are essential. UML 2.0 defines 13 diagrams:

- **Activity diagram**   The activity diagram can be at either a conceptual or functional level. This diagram models a complex use case or application logic.

- **Class diagram**   The class diagram lists the classes of the software system. For each class, the behaviors, attributes, and relationships are detailed.

- **Communication diagram**   The communication diagram depicts the dynamic aspect of a software system. It documents the messages (communication) between classes collaborating on a single task.

- **Component diagram**   The component diagram depicts the relationship between subsystems or groups of components. This provides an overview of the software system.

- **Composite structure diagram**   The composite structure diagram highlights the internal architecture of a classifier. This diagram consists of several elements, such as parts, collaborations, and ports. Parts represent the composition of a classifier. Collaborations define behaviors that intersect parts and the surrounding classifier. Ports represent dependencies that are exposed from a part or imported from the external environment.

- **Deployment diagram**   The deployment diagram shows the hardware configuration necessary to deploy a software system, which includes defining the relationship between the hardware infrastructure and the software system.

- **Interaction overview diagram**   The interaction overview diagram is a derivative of the activity diagram but shows an overview of the flow from various interactions. In the diagram, nodes often represent interaction overview diagrams.

- **Object diagram**   The object diagram describes the relationship between object instances with a software system at a particular point in time. You can also display a snapshot of the state of each of the instances.

- **Package diagram**   The package diagram provides an overview of the software system by grouping related classifiers. Any relationships or dependencies between the groups are then depicted in the diagram.

- **Sequence diagram**   The sequence diagram is a dynamic graph and shows the logical flow of messages within a software system or subsystem. This is probably one of the most important and commonly used diagrams.

- **State machine diagram**   The state machine diagram is a dynamic diagram and depicts the confluence of state and behavior. This diagram shows the behavior of a software system based on the state of certain object instances at a point in time.

- **Timing diagram**   The timing diagram graphs the behavior and resulting change of state of one or more object instances against a timeline.

- **Use case diagram**   The use case diagram highlights the relationships between actors and use cases.

You can create UML diagrams with Microsoft Office Visio 2007. Currently, you are not able to create UML diagrams directly in Visual Studio. Microsoft Office Visio 2007 allows you to visualize complex concepts and transform single dimensional textual representations into dazzling reports with depth. This means you can convert stale columnar reports to images that instantly convey a concept. Visio allows individuals who are not artistically inclined—like me—to create compelling graphics without hiring a professional. Visio has a variety of tools and shapes useful for creating a variety of technical documents. Visio documents can then be exported as a Web page, PDF file, or other formats. To save a file in PDF format, you must first install the Microsoft Save As PDF add-in for the 2007 Microsoft Office system. In Microsoft Office Visio 2007, you can create several UML diagrams to model a software system.

- Use Case diagram
- Collaboration diagram
- Sequence diagram
- Component diagram
- Deployment diagram
- Activity diagram
- A variety of Static Structure diagrams, such as the Class or Object diagram

Microsoft Office Visio 2007 does not natively support UML 2.0 diagrams. There are a variety of sources for UML 2.0 stencils for Visio. Here are some resources:

Visio Café: http://www.visiocafe.com/

Software Stencils: http://softwarestencils.com/uml

The following diagrams were created using Microsoft Office Visio 2007. Figure 2-2 is a Use Case diagram. Figure 2-3 is a Class diagram, while Figure 2-4 is a Sequence diagram. The three diagrams are only partially completed for the retail banking software application and available for demonstrative purposes only.

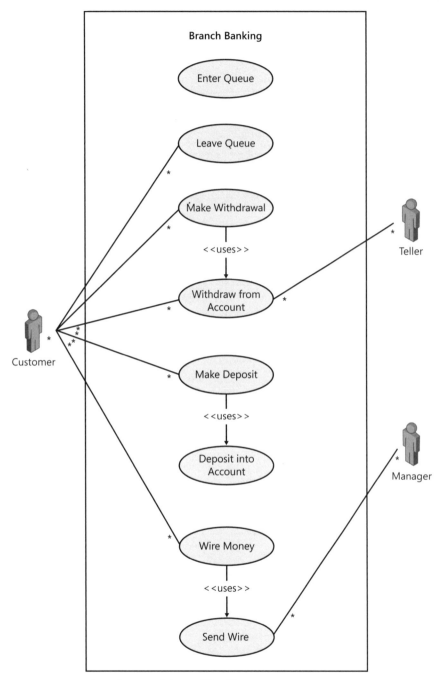

FIGURE 2-2 Use Case diagram of the retail banking system.

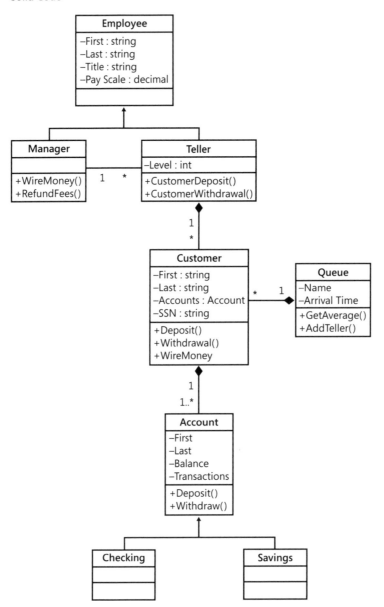

FIGURE 2-3 Partial State diagram of the retail banking system.

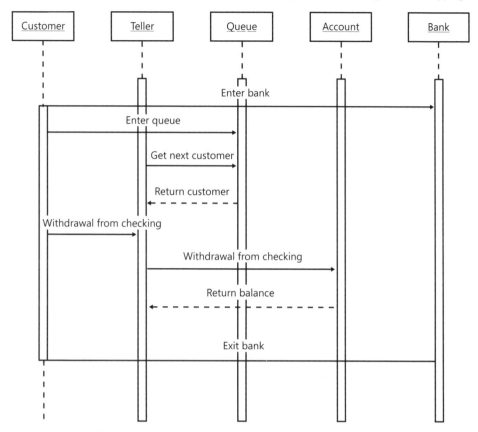

FIGURE 2-4 Partial Sequence diagram for the retail banking system.

Microsoft Office Visio 2007 provides templates to make diagramming a bit easier. These templates provide a core set of shapes for creating illustrations and diagrams. Templates consist of stencils and sometimes toolbars and menus that are added to the Microsoft Office Visio 2007 environment. Stencils have shapes that target a specific objective, such as creating a class diagram. A stencil has shapes and styles. You can drag shapes from the stencil onto a Visio document as part of creating an illustration. The Visio document can contain shapes from more than one stencil. For example, the UML Model Diagram includes several stencils: UML Collaboration, UML Component, UML Sequence, and others, which contain shapes for drawing Collaboration, Component, and Sequence diagrams correspondingly. The UML Sequence stencil has the common shapes used in a Sequence diagram, as shown in Figure 2-5.

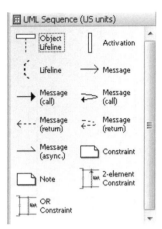

FIGURE 2-5 The UML Sequence stencil is used to create UML Sequence diagrams.

Currently, one of the new features planned for Visual Studio 2010 is UML Modeling. Rosario is the next revision of Visual Studio after Visual Studio 2008. UML Modeling will be available in the Architecture Edition and will support UML 2.0 diagrams. You can forward or reverse engineer the diagrams, depending on whether the code base is already established. Community Technology Previews (CTPs) for Rosario are available at the Microsoft Web site. The release date for Rosario is probably sometime in 2009. However, Microsoft has not published a firm release date, and until the software reaches Beta 1, features are subject to change.

Visio Example

Figure 2-3 is a State diagram that was created with Microsoft Office Visio 2007. This section is a tutorial for creating a portion of that State diagram and a general overview of Microsoft Office Visio 2007. For a comprehensive book on Microsoft Office Visio 2007, I would recommend *Microsoft Office Visio 2007 Inside Out*, authored by Mark Walker and published by Microsoft Press.

Creating a UML diagram begins with selecting the appropriate template in Microsoft Office Visio 2007. Start Microsoft Office Visio 2007. From the menu, choose File, and then choose New. From the New submenu, select Software and Database. A list of diagrams should appear on the drop-down menu. Choose UML Model Diagram (Metric) or UML Model Diagram (US Units) from this list, depending on your preference. After selecting the template, an empty environment, including a new Visio document, is presented. Conversely, an existing document can be opened from the menu with File and then Open or simply by selecting the relevant document from the most recently used (MRU) list.

The Microsoft Office Visio 2007 environment includes a Visio document, Shapes pane, Model Explorer, default toolbars, and menu. Figure 2-6 shows the standard environment for a UML diagram.

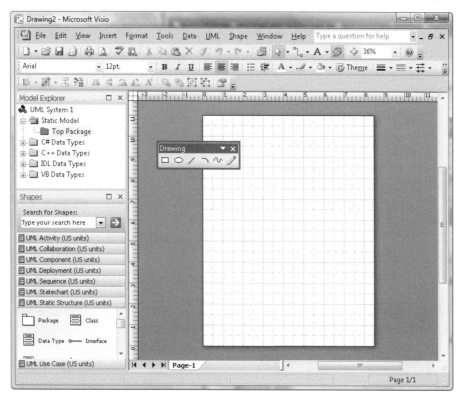

FIGURE 2-6 Visio environment for a new template.

The UML Model Diagram stencil, as expected, has several stencils for creating an assortment of UML diagrams:

- UML Activity stencil contains shapes for creating Activity and Interaction overview diagrams.

- UML Collaboration stencil contains shapes for creating Collaboration (UML 1.2) and Communication diagrams (UML 2.0).

- UML Component stencil contains shapes for creating Component diagrams.

- UML Deployment stencil contains shapes for creating Deployment diagrams.

- UML Sequence stencil contains shapes for creating Sequence diagrams.

- UML Statechart stencil contains shapes for creating State machine diagrams.

- UML Static Structure contains shapes for creating Class and Object diagrams.

- UML Use Case contains shapes for creating Use Case diagrams.

You can drag shapes from a stencil onto the Visio document. The drawing document is similar to most graphics windows, where graphical elements can be selected (handles will appear), dragged, resized, deleted, edited, and so on. Some shapes can be connected to other shapes. For example, an Interface shape can be connected to a Class shape. Both of these shapes are found in the UML Static Structure stencil. When connecting, the intersection of the two shapes is highlighted. This is the same behavior observed when connecting any two shapes.

The Model Explorer contains all of the models for a software system, which could include several diagrams. It is organized into models and packages that provide a hierarchal structure to the Model Explorer. Each model represents a model of a software system, while packages offer different views of a software system. Figure 2-7 shows the default Model Explorer of Microsoft Office Visio 2007. The Static Model is the root folder for any new UML Model diagram. You can customize this folder as desired. Each model has one top package, appropriately called Top Package, which is the root package for the model. There is only one root package in the model—all other packages are organized within this package. Packages can contain other packages. In addition, a package can contain diagrams. Collectively, the diagrams in a package represent a particular view of a model.

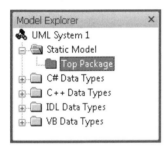

FIGURE 2-7 Model Explorer of the Visio environment.

Here are steps to create the correct model and related packages for the retail banking system. The top model will be renamed *YourName* Bank to represent your banking company. We will create a package called Retail Banking for branch banking. There will be a second package called Private Banking to model a software system for high–net worth clients.

1. Rename the Static Model to *Your Bank*. Open the context menu (right-click) for the Static Model folder, and choose Properties. Enter the new name in the Name field.

2. Rename the Top Page package similarly using the Properties window. Rename the top package to Bank.

3. Add two packages to the Bank package. Open the context menu for the Bank package and choose New. Select Package from the list of choices. In the UML Package Properties, name the package **Retail Banking**. Repeat the same steps to create a second package, which should be named **Private Banking**.

4. Next, let us add the appropriate diagrams to the Retail Banking package. Choose New from the context menu of the Retail Banking package. The list of UML diagrams

appears in the bottom half of the list. After adding the new diagram, a Visio document will appear for drawing that diagram. You can then drag shapes onto the document to complete the diagram. For our example, we will create a Class diagram. You can practice separately from the book and create the Use Case and Sequence diagrams as shown in Figures 2-2 and 2-4 correspondingly.

Here are the steps to create a Class diagram:

1. For the Retail Banking Package, choose New from the context menu, and select Static Structure Diagram. This is the diagram used to create Class and other diagrams.

2. In Model Explorer, select the new Static Structure element. Open the context menu of that item, and choose Rename. Change the name to **Class Diagram**.

3. Open the UML Static Structure stencil. Drag a Class shape from the stencil to the Class diagram document.

4. Open the Properties menu for the class shape. Either double-click on the shape or choose Properties from the context menu. Change the name of the shape to **Employee**. See Figure 2-8.

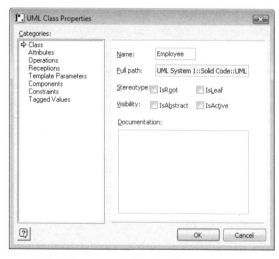

FIGURE 2-8 The properties for the Class shape.

Attributes, operations, constraints, and other information pertaining to the class can be defined in the Properties window. Information is grouped in categories. For example, the Operations category allows the adding, removing, and moving of class methods. You can switch between categories of information in the Categories list box. The Employee class has four attributes and no operations.

Here are the steps to add attributes to the Employee class.

1. If not open, open the Properties for the Employee class shape.

2. Select the Attributes group in the Category list box. The Attributes pane will appear.

3. The first three attributes are First, Last, and Title. The names are entered in the Attribute column. The type for each of these attributes is C#::string.

4. Add Pay Scale as the final attribute. The type is decimal.

The *Manager* and *Teller* classes inherit the *Employee* class. As such, we do not have to replicate in the child classes the attributes inherited from the *Employee* base class. The *Employee* class has no methods to be inherited. Child classes refine the base class and therefore become specialty classes. As such, both the *Manager* and *Teller* classes add members that make them specialty classes. In the Class shape for child classes, only the unique attributes and operations should be added.

Here are the steps to add the *Manager* and *Teller* class shapes to the class diagram.

1. Drag two Class shapes from the UML Static Structure stencil onto the Visio document for the class diagram. Drag the shapes somewhere near the Employee class shape. Place the shapes below left and below right of the Employee class shape.

2. As demonstrated previously, open the Properties of the leftmost Class shape. Name the class Manager. Select the Operations group in the Categories list box. The Operations pane will appear. Enter **WireMoney** and **RefundFees** as the methods. Neither has parameters nor returns an explicit return type.

3. Open the Properties of the rightmost Class shape. Name the class **Teller**. Add the CustomerDeposit and CustomerWithdrawal operations to the class.

Classes can be related through inheritance, association, or composition. There is a shape for each of these relations in the UML Static Structure stencil. Inheritance is defined with the Generalization shape. If a base class is inherited by more than child class, use multiple Generalization shapes. You can create an association between two classes with the Binary Association shape. For composition, use the composition shape. Multiplicity defines the numeric relation between the two classes (class[1] and class[2]) that comprise a composition. For example, a multiplicity of *1 to 1* means that there is exactly one class[1] for each class[2] in the binary association. An example of a 1 to 1 relationship would be a bank and bank president. The bank, which exists, has one—and only one—bank president. Another type of multiplicity is *1..n to **. This means that there is at least one class[1], where for any class[1] there is any number of class[2]. An example of *1..n to ** would be bank branch and customers. There is at least one bank branch. Each bank branch could have any number of customers.

As mentioned previously, both *Manager* and *Teller* classes inherit the *Employee* class. In addition, the relationship between Manager to Teller is *1 to 1..**. Each bank manager can manage one or more tellers. Here are the steps to define the relationships among the *Manager, Teller,* and *Employee* classes.

1. Drag the Generalization shape from the UML Static Structure stencil onto the Visio document. Connect the arrow portion of the Generalization shape to the Employee shape. Connect the opposite end of the arrow shape to the Manager shape. When connected, the location of the connection is highlighted.

2. Drag another Generalization shape from the UML Static Structure stencil onto the Visio document. Connect the arrow portion of the Generalization shape to the same location on the Employee shape as chosen before. Connect the opposite end of the arrow shape to the Teller shape.

3. Drag a Binary Association shape from the UML Static Structure stencil into the drawing. Connect either end of the shape to the Manager and Teller shapes. Open the properties for the Binary Association shape by double-clicking on the Binary Association shape. Alternatively, open the Properties using the context menu for the Binary Association shape. In the Association Properties window, delete the end names, which are in the Association Ends List. See Figure 2-9. Change the multiplicity to *1 to 1..** (many).

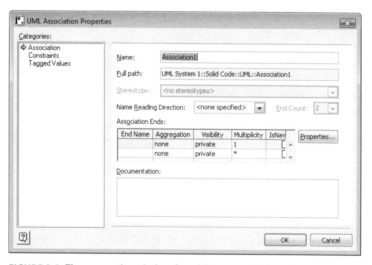

FIGURE 2-9 The properties window for a binary association shape.

Retail banking customers have either a checking or savings account. The checking and savings accounts are related. They are both "is a" kind of bank accounts. In object-oriented programming, "is a" implies inheritance. In this circumstance, *Account* is a base class and holds the common members of the *Checking* and *Savings* classes. Both the *Checking* and *Savings* classes then inherit from the *Account* base class. For the purpose of this example, only the *Account* class is defined. Customers must have an *Account* class.

Here are the steps to create the *Account* and *Customer* classes.

1. Drag a Class shape from the UML Static Structure stencil onto the Visio document. As shown previously, open the Properties of the new Class shape. Name the class **Account**. Select the Operations group in the Categories list box. The Operations pane will appear. Enter **Deposit** and **Withdrawal** as the methods. The methods have no parameters nor return an explicit return type.

2. Select the Attributes group in the Category list box. The Attributes pane will appear. Enter **First** and **Last** as the names of the first two attributes. Both are C#::string type. Finally, enter an attribute named **Transactions**. For the purposes of this example, the type for this attribute remains undefined.

3. Drag a Class shape from the UML Static Structure stencil onto the Visio document. As shown previously, open the Properties window of the new Class shape. Name the class **Customer**. Select the Operations group in the Categories list box. The Operations pane will appear. Add the *Deposit*, *Withdrawal*, and *WireMoney* methods. The methods have neither parameters nor an explicit return type.

4. Select the Attributes group in the Category list box. The Attributes pane will appear. The first three attributes are First, Last, and SSN, which are entered in the Attribute column. The type for each is C#::string.

Tellers handle a single customer at a time, if any. This is a *1 to 0..1* relationship, where a teller can have zero or one customers. In addition, customers can have one or more accounts, such as checking and savings accounts. This implies composition between the *Customer* and *Account* classes and a *1 to 1..** relationship.

The *Teller*, *Customer*, and *Account* classes were created in the previous steps. Here are the steps to define the relationship among the *Teller*, *Customer*, and *Account* classes.

1. We need to create a relationship between the Teller and Customer classes. Drag a Composition shape from the UML Static Structure stencil onto the Visio document. Connect the arrow portion of the shape to the aggregator, which is the *Teller* class in this circumstance. Connect the other side of the shape to the *Customer* class. Open the properties for the Composition shape. Delete the end names. Define the multiplicity as *1 to 0..1.*

2. Next define the relationship between the *Customer* and *Account* classes. Drag a Composition shape onto the drawing. Connect the arrow portion of the shape to the *Customer* class. Connect the other side of the shape to the *Account* class. Open the Properties for the Composition shape. Double-click the Composition shape to open the Properties window. Alternatively, open the Properties window using the context menu for the Composition association shape. Delete the end names. Define the multiplicity as *1 to 1..*.*

Most of the class diagram, as shown previously in Figure 2-3, has been completed. For practice, you might consider finishing the diagram. Once the modeling is completed, what is the next step? You might say, "at long last, coding!" Not actually. Before coding, there is one more step: prototyping.

Prototyping

Prototyping is an important phase of the software development life cycle and a conduit between product design and implementation. This conduit represents the transition from design to implementation or extensive coding. Prototyping is actually the first level of coding in the actual application but before detailed implementation. After the design work is complete, fight the proclivity to code now! Prototyping is an important validation of the design, a validation that is important before etching your design into concrete—better known as the implementation. Taking this intermediate step can help prevent having to take a jackhammer to your code later.

Prototyping, combined with instrumentation, can provide important conformation of application sequence, which is typically modeled in dynamic UML diagrams. This provides an important roadmap of application execution. Here is a promise: your application will probably not execute properly as long as the flow is invalid. Have you tried going somewhere without proper directions? Without the correct instructions, you will not get there, at least not without some luck. The proper execution of your program should not depend on luck. When possible, prototype the entire application and validate the flow before you begin implementing the first method. At this point, the implementation simply represents noise and can only detract form the ultimate goal. Remember, know where you are going before getting into the car and driving.

Use prototyping to validate the dynamic UML diagrams that you created, such as the sequence diagram. If this validation fails, there are two possibilities. First, the design is incorrect. Second, the prototype does not accurately reflect the modeling. In either circumstance, you are not properly prepared for implementation. Review the design diagrams in relation to the prototype to confirm where changes are necessary. This is an iterative process: design, prototype, validate, revisit design, revisit prototype, validate again, and so on.

Once prototyping is completed and verified, congratulations! You are ready to begin serious coding. In this order, implement a method, the methods of a class, and finally all of the classes of a particular module. This will facilitate orderly testing. If classes have the proper level of isolation, you should be able to implement and test the application one class at a time. Isolation between classes is one of the tenants of object-oriented programming. Testing as each class is implemented helps wring dependencies out of the application design. Chapter 1 mentions correctly that coding should only proceed as fast as it can be tested and verified for accuracy. In addition, frequent testing at this level provides a barometer of the ongoing health of the application.

Here are specific steps to prototype and instrument an application.

1. First, define the class framework in the application code using the UML Class diagram. Make sure to include all the methods, while omitting properties or attributes. In addition, use sparse prototypes for the methods (no parameters or return type). Omitting extraneous information improves clarity and makes detecting the correct sequencing of operations more transparent and instrumentation easier. The details, such as the proper function prototype, can be added before implementation of the related class.

2. Create an external resource, such as a config file, to enable or disable instrumentation.

3. Choose a class to instrument. Instrument the methods minimally with Enter and Exist messages. Further instrumentation can be added based on the level of detail you want.

4. Test classes a class at a time. Afterward, regression test previous classes that were instrumented. This assures that subtle bugs have not been introduced that would affect previously tested code. Repeat the previous steps until the entire system has been instrumented.

Instrumentation is an important aspect of prototyping and is the tangible confirmation of the sequence of events in an application. Instrumentation is sending formatted messages to one or more targets. Each message reports an event or activity, or is informational. An event is a user-defined activity. An activity is a predefined event, such as a start or stop activity. Informational messages are general messages, such as reporting the parameters of a method. In a large software system, with several contributors, the result is often a blizzard of messages. This is where consistency of message format can help. Messages should be standardized to include a minimum set of fields: project name, team member, module, class.function, and source file. Other optional information that might be useful is a time stamp and the build number.

Tracing

In .NET, instrumentation can be orchestrated using tracing. The *Trace* and *TraceSource* classes offer considerable flexibility for this purpose. We have come a long way since the *printf* command. If you are not familiar with *printf*, you are probably under 30 and do not own a C++ book.

Simple tracing is available with the *Trace* class. Most of the methods of the *Trace* class are implemented as static methods, which are called on the class. Alternatively, you can use the *TraceSource* class. The *TraceSource* class has additional functionality for advanced tracing, such as additional tracing levels and filtering. The *Trace* and *TraceSource* classes are discussed fully in Chapter 9, "Debugging." This chapter presents only enough information on tracing to demonstrate prototyping. The *TraceSource* class, not the *Trace* class, is used in this chapter. It is preferred because of added flexibility.

Both the *Trace* and *TraceSource* classes allow remote activation of tracing using a configuration file. You do not have to modify and rebuild the application to change the status of instrumentation. This avoids introducing inadvertently bugs just to enable or disable instru-mentation. This also allows nondevelopers, such as architects and testers, to control instru-mentation. This is particularly important because individuals in this role may not even have access to a compiler.

There are three levels of configuration files: application, public policy, and machine configu-ration file. In this chapter, we focus on the application configuration file. An application con-figuration file will allow you to control instrumentation of a specific application. Application configuration files are placed in the same directory of the assembly. The file name of the con-figuration file is *name.extension*.config. For example, myapp.exe.config is the configuration file for myapp.exe. This is discussed more broadly in Chapter 3, "Metaprogramming."

Here is a sample configuration file that controls tracing.

```
<configuration>
  <system.diagnostics>
    <sources>
      <source name="myTraceSource"
        switchName="mySwitch">
        <listeners>
          <add name="console"
            type="System.Diagnostics.ConsoleTraceListener">
          </add>
            <remove name="Default"/>
        </listeners>
      </source>
    </sources>
    <switches>
      <add name="mySwitch" value="error"/>
    </switches>
  </system.diagnostics>
</configuration>
```

Tracing is defined within the *system.diagnostics* element. The name of a particular trace source is identified in the source element. The source name is used in application code to identify the corresponding trace source, which is provided in the constructor of the *TraceSource* class. Listeners are the target of tracing and defined within the listeners ele-ments. Each listener is added with an *Add* element. You can have multiple simultaneous listeners, such as the console, file, eventlog, and so on. The *Switches* element contains the available switches, which are used to filter message sent to the listeners. Individual switches are added with an *Add* element. The value attribute of the *Add* element identifies the type of switch.

Here is sample code that uses the preceding configuration file.

```
using System;
using System.Collections.Generic;
using System.Linq;
using System.Diagnostics;
```

```
namespace ConsoleApplication {
    class Program {
        private static TraceSource mySource =
            new TraceSource("myTraceSource");

        static void Main(string[] args){
            Activity1();
            mySource.Close();
            return;
        }
        static void Activity1(){
            mySource.TraceEvent(TraceEventType.Error, 1,
                "Error message.");
            mySource.TraceEvent(TraceEventType.Warning, 2,
                "Warning message.");
        }
    }
}
```

In the code, an instance of a *TraceSource* class is created. In the constructor, we associate this trace source with the one in the configuration file (i.e., *myTraceSource*). The new trace source will then inherit the settings from the configuration file, such as displaying to the console window as a listener. The two *TraceSource.TraceEvent* commands trace to this listener. The ultimate status of the messages is controlled by the trace switch settings in the configuration file. An error and warning messages are sent. However, only the error message is displayed. The warning message is filtered per the switch in the configuration file. Change the value of the switch in the configuration file from error to warning. Now both the warning and error messages are displayed. This change can be made without having to recompile the application, which is one of the benefits of using the *TraceSource* class and configuration file.

Visual Studio Class Designer

A picture is worth a thousand words. For the Visual Studio Class Designer, instead of words, we are referring to lines of code. The Class Designer is a depiction of a UML class diagram. You can quickly and easily convey some of the concepts of a class diagram, such as class relationships and membership. Complex concepts, such as composition, can be easily rendered in a visual chart. Like a UML diagram, the primary components of the Class Designer are classifiers, such as classes, structures, interfaces, delegates, and enums. You can forward engineer from the Class Designer and convert classifiers from visual representations into code. You can also reverse engineer from code to a Visual Studio class diagram. A class diagram is a Class Designer document.

The Class Designer is excellent for rapid prototyping. There are convenient steps for creating stubs for methods and properties. Beyond creating stubs, the class diagram is automatically synchronized to the project code. Changes to the class diagram are instantly reflected in the code and vice versa. Add a method to a class in the class diagram, and simultaneously a method is added to the same class in the project. Delete an attribute from an interface in the source code, and the associated attribute is removed from the related interface in the class diagram. This synchronization highlights one of the other benefits of the Class Designer, which is refactoring. You can visually and easily refactor an application, including renaming variables, changing accessibility, changing attribute type, updating function prototypes, and more.

After prototyping the software system using the Visual Studio Class Designer, you can easily instrument the resulting code. You can even create a snippet that will automatically insert the appropriate tracing commands for each operation.

There are three important components to the Visual Studio Class Designer: the class diagram, Class Designer toolbox, and Class Details window. As mentioned earlier, a class diagram is an instance of a Class Designer document. The Class Designer toolbox contains shapes that are used to complete the class diagram. Finally, the Class Details window allows you to add, view, and edit members of classes, structs, and interfaces. Figure 2-10 shows the Class Designer environment.

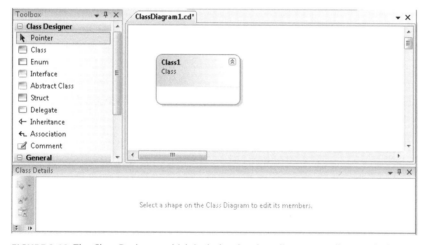

FIGURE 2-10 The Class Designer, which includes the class diagram, toolbox, and Class Details window.

Create a Class Diagram

There are several ways to add a class diagram to a Visual Studio project:

- From the Project menu, choose Add New Item. Select Class Diagram from the list of templates. You can then name the class diagram.

- Alternatively, open the context menu for the project in Solution Explorer. Choose Add and then New Item. Select Class Diagram from the list of templates.

- If this is the first class diagram of the project, you can simply open the context menu for the project in Solution Explorer and choose View Class Diagram.

You can then build the class diagram using drag and drop from the Class Designer toolbox. Drag shapes from the Class Designer toolbox onto the class diagram document. The toolbox includes all the requisite classifiers: class, struct, interface, enum, and delegate.

When you drop a classifier shape on the class diagram, the New dialog box will be presented. In the New dialog box, name the classifier, accessibility, and the file to place the entity. The shape is then added to the class diagram.

After adding a shape, you might also want to edit a particular shape. To modify a shape on the class diagram, first select the shape. A selected shape is highlighted with handles. Edit the shape from the Class Diagram menu. You can also use the context menu to add a member or edit the shape in some other manner. For example, to add a method to a class shape from the Class Diagram menu, select Add and then Method. You can then name the new method. In the Class Details window, define the prototype of the method by entering the return type and parameters. Expand the method row for the class in the Class Details window to view or add parameters. You can also add methods, properties, and attributes directly in the Class Details window instead of using the menu system.

Prototyping with the Class Designer

Prototyping with the Class Designer is easy. Why? It is automatic. Add an operation to a class or struct and the stub is automatically created. You can then instrument the operation with an Enter and Exit message. Even the *Enter* and *Exit* methods can be automated in Visual Studio using code snippets. Code snippets are reusable snippets of code. Snippets can be parameterized to allow customization whenever the snippet is used. This adds considerable flexibility.

Automating Enter and Exit Methods   I have created two snippets that can be used to instrument an operation. The first code snippet creates an instance of the *TraceSource* class to be used for instrumentation. The *TraceSource* is appropriately named Instrumentation. It is a static attribute of a wrapper class called *Instrument*. You insert this snippet once into the application. That will make the *TraceSource* instance available everywhere as *Instrument.ts*. Here is the snippet.

```
<CodeSnippet Format="1.0.0">
  <Header>
    <Title>
      Instrument TraceSource
    </Title>
  </Header>

  <Snippet>
    <Code Language="CSharp">
      <![CDATA[class Instrument
      {
          public static System.Diagnostics.TraceSource ts =
              new System.Diagnostics.TraceSource("Instrumentation");
```

```
      }]]>
    </Code>
  </Snippet>

</CodeSnippet>
```

The second code snippet inserts code that uses the trace source instance defined in the first snippet (*Instrument.ts*) to display Enter and Exit messages for a stubbed method. Insert this snippet in each method to be instrumented. It adds two *TraceEvent* commands to the code. This code snippet has parameters (literals) for assigning the appropriate class and function name. Here is the second snippet.

```
<CodeSnippet Format="1.0.0">
  <Header>
    <Title>
      Instrumentation Enter Exit
    </Title>
  </Header>

  <Snippet>
    <Declarations>
      <Literal>
        <ID>Class</ID>
        <ToolTip>Name of surrounding class</ToolTip>
      </Literal>
      <Literal>
        <ID>Function</ID>
        <ToolTip>Function to instrument</ToolTip>
      </Literal>

    </Declarations>

    <Code Language="CSharp">
      <![CDATA[Instrument.ts.TraceEvent(System.Diagnostics.TraceEventType.Start, 1,
          "Entering $Class$.$Function$");

      // Insert code here

      Instrument.ts.TraceEvent(System.Diagnostics.TraceEventType.Stop, 2,
            "Leaving $Class$.$Function$");]]>
    </Code>
  </Snippet>

</CodeSnippet>
```

The messages from this snippet are sent to listeners defined in an application configuration file. You can send the messages to the console, text file, or any other listener you designate.

Prototyping Example

This walkthrough demonstrates prototyping and the instrumenting of code using Visual Studio. We will convert part of the UML Class Diagram for the retail banking system (see

Figure 2-3, shown previously) to a Visual Studio Class Diagram. Afterward, the class operations will be prototyped and instrumented. Because the intent is to validate the sequence diagram, we will omit attribute and other extraneous information. The aforementioned snippets for instrumentation will be used to instrument the methods of the application. Therefore, you must create and import the snippets before the walkthrough. Steps for importing a snippet can be found online at MSDN. Search for articles on code snippets. The walkthrough uses a console project.

Here are the steps to add a new class diagram to the project. A shape is then added to the diagram.

1. First, review the UML class diagram related to the retail banking system.

2. In Solution Explorer, open a context menu. Choose Add and then New Item. Choose Class Diagram from the list of templates. Name the class diagram **Bank.cd**.

3. From the Class Designer toolbox, drag a class shape onto the class diagram. In the New Class dialog box, name the class **Customer**. Accept the defaults for everything else.

4. Add a method to the class. Open the context menu for the Customer class shape. Choose Add and then Method. Name the method **Deposit**. Repeat these steps, and add the *Withdrawal* and *WireMoney* methods. This will also automatically add stubbed functions for *Deposit*, *Withdrawal*, and *WireMoney* to the source files. Do not add parameters or return types for any of the methods. They are not necessary at this time.

Add the *Employee*, *Manager*, and *Teller* classes to the class diagram. *Employee* is the base class to the *Manager* and *Teller* classes. Here are the steps.

1. Add a class shape to the class diagram. Name the class **Employee**. *Employee* is an abstract type, while *Manager* and *Teller* are concrete. Open the context menu for the Employee shape. Choose Properties. From the Properties window, choose the *Inheritance Modifier* field. Change the field to abstract. Place the *Employee* class in Employee.cs.

2. Add the *Manager* and *Teller* classes to the class diagram. Drag two classes onto the class diagram. Using steps shown previously, name the classes **Manager** and **Teller**. Place both class implementations in Employee.cs. Add the *WireMoney* and *RefundFees* methods to the *Manager* class. For the *Teller* class, add the *CustomerDeposit* and *CustomerWithdrawal* methods.

3. Have the *Manager* class inherit from the *Employee* base class. Select the inheritance shape in the Class Designer toolbox. Drag from the *Manager* to the *Employee* class. An inheritance will appear that connects the two classes. Repeat the previous steps for the *Teller* child class. The *Teller* class also inherits from the *Employee* base class.

4. There is *1 to 1* multiplicity between the *Teller* and *Customer* classes. Click the Association shape in the Class Designer toolbox. Click and drag from the *Teller* class to the *Customer* class. This will draw the association line and connect the two classes.

Figure 2-11 shows the Visual Studio class diagram for the retail banking system.

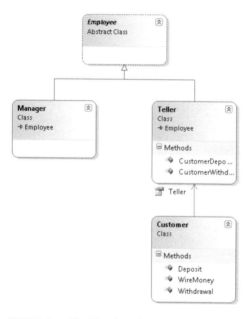

FIGURE 2-11 The Visual Studio class diagram for the retail banking system.

The function prototypes already exist. This occurred when the methods were added to the class diagram. The next step is to instrument the functions. First, we must create the *TraceSource* object to be used. This can be done with the snippet provided earlier. Here are the steps:

1. Insert a new source file: instrument.cs. Delete the sample class that is automatically inserted into the file.

2. Make sure the cursor is within the namespace in the instrument.cs file. Insert the *Instrument TraceSource* snippet. Pressing Ctrl+K and then Ctrl+X will prompt for the snippet. You can then locate and insert the *Instrument TraceSource* snippet. The keystrokes for inserting a snippet can vary depending on your keyboard configuration in Visual Studio.

The trace source is controlled from an application configuration file. In our example, tracing should be sent to a console window. We also want to display all activity tracing, which includes the *Start* and *Stop* events used in the instrumenting of the methods. Here is the application configuration file:

```
<configuration>
  <system.diagnostics>
    <sources>
      <source name="Instrumentation"
        switchName="sourceSwitch">
        <listeners>
          <add name="console"
            type="System.Diagnostics.ConsoleTraceListener">
          </add>
            <remove name="Default"/>
        </listeners>
      </source>
    </sources>
    <switches>
      <add name="sourceSwitch" value="ActivityTracing"/>
    </switches>
  </system.diagnostics>
</configuration>
```

So far, we have created the class diagram, prototyped the methods, defined an instance of the *TraceSource* class, and added an application configuration file. You are ready for the last step. That step is to instrument the methods of each class. A snippet is used to instrument the *Enter* and *Exit* events of a method.

1. Open the Customer.cs file. Review the stubbed methods. Each of the stubbed methods explicitly throws an exception. Select the exception statement in the *Deposit* method and insert the *Instrument Enter Exit* snippet. Pressing Ctrl+K and then Ctrl+X will prompt for the snippet. Locate and insert the snippet. Two literal fields are presented in the snippet. Fill the literal fields with the class and method names respectively. You can tab between the fields.

2. Repeat the previous step to instrument the *Customer.Withdrawal* and *Customer. WireMoney* methods. While in the Customer.cs file, remove the exception from the *Customer* constructor class.

3. Open the employee.cs file. Instrument the *Teller.CustomerWithdrawal* and *Teller. CustomerDeposit* methods as shown previously using the *Instrument Enter Exit* snippet.

According to the class diagram, there is a relationship between the *Customer* and *Teller* classes. For this reason, the *Teller* class is embedded in the *Customer* class. The *Teller* class is exposed as a property of the *Teller* class. In the *Customer* class, you need to update the *Teller* property to use automatic *Get* and *Set* functions, as shown in the following code.

```
public Teller Teller
{
    get; set;

}
```

According to the sequence diagram, the *Customer.Withdrawal* method calls *Teller.CustomerWithdrawal*, while *Customer.Deposit* calls *Teller.CustomerDeposit*. The prototype should confirm this sequence. In Main, the code is written to test this sequence.

```
static void Main(string[] args)
{
    Customer cust = new Customer();
    cust.Teller = new Teller();
    cust.Deposit();
    cust.Withdrawal();
}
```

Run the program, and view results. Congratulations! You have validated the sequence diagram. There were a few steps to accomplish this. Of course, this is a simple example. The more complex the application, the greater the return on investment. You are ready to begin full coding.

Summary

This chapter emphasizes the importance of the design and, in general, the early phase of the software development life cycle. Shortcutting the requirements and analysis, design, or prototyping is counterproductive. Table 2-1 quantifies the benefit. Bugs found early in the software development life cycle are easier to resolve. However, this commitment to the entire life cycle must be embraced by more than the developers; the management also must endorse it. Deadlines should not drive the software development in exclusion of other factors.

You should model the application using UML. Each UML diagram provides a different perspective or insight into the software system. Together all the diagrams present a full picture of the application. You can create UML diagrams using Microsoft Office Visio 2007. After creating the diagram, prototyping with instrumentation can validate some of the dynamic UML diagrams. This confirmation is an important cross check of the object-oriented analysis and design for a software system. You can create class diagrams in Visual Studio that closely represent a UML class diagram. This will automatically create prototypes of each method in the source code. You can then instrument the methods. At the end of this process, you will have a thoughtful, stable, and correct application. Of course, high-quality applications are the collective objective of everyone on the project team.

Key Points

- Around 50 percent of the software development life cycle should be dedicated to phases before coding.

- Do not allow implementation considerations to affect the requirements analysis or design.

- Model the application using UML diagrams. The Use Case, Class, and Sequence diagrams are the most important.

- Do not assume that the software model is correct. Use various best practices and policies to validate the correctness of the model.

- Check UML diagrams into source control for each public version of the product.

- Snippets can further automate prototyping and instrumentation.

- Use configuration files to remotely activate tracing.

Chapter 3
Metaprogramming

We think in generalities, but we live in details.

—*Alfred North Whitehead*

As developers, much of our time is spent designing and writing the algorithms and business logic that drives our application functionality. This logic is highly detailed and critically important to solving the core objectives of the software and, therefore, must be stable, accurate, and efficient in providing business solutions. Software development is a dynamic practice, though, and inevitably the details of our application code will change as business practices evolve or business rules change. These changes can and do occur at any time, and they will present risks to the quality of the application code if the application is improperly designed. It is imperative that, as developers, we embrace this reality and make every effort to write code that is flexible and adaptable to change, thus improving our ability to evolve and maintain the software without compromising quality.

One way to ensure flexibility in your application code is to simply write less code. Software applications tend to be laden with detailed logic rules that govern the behavior of the software. For example, details like installation path, required data sources, and class or method initialization parameters are often tightly coupled with the application business logic. This approach inherently requires more code and does not allow for easy or low-risk changes to the application logic. Applications with more flexible designs decouple this level of detail from their logic and algorithms by storing detailed instructions as metadata. This practice both encourages the development of more generic and reusable algorithms and reduces the amount of code that is needed to meet the objective of the application. Consider the quote from Alfred North Whitehead, a mathematician and philosopher, which describes the way people think versus the way they interact. Similarly, with flexible software application designs, algorithms and business logic are often generalized, while specific logic details are abstracted out of the algorithms and applied at run time. When designing applications, developers should defer the specific logic details, such as run-time configurations, out of the code and into metadata. This will help to increase the overall quality of the application by reducing its complexity and improving maintainability, while increasing the flexibility and adaptability to future changes.

What Is Metadata?

Metadata is often defined as data about data or, alternatively, as information that describes data. It is often used to illustrate attributes and contents of electronic media, such as images or documents. The most common example of metadata, but certainly not the only example,

is that of a database schema, which provides descriptive rules or information about a particular dataset. In the example illustrated in Figure 3-1, metadata is used to describe names or
lengths of fields in the dataset, the data types of each field, or perhaps the relationships between fields across the dataset. Simply stated, metadata is descriptive detail about data that
is abstracted from the data itself.

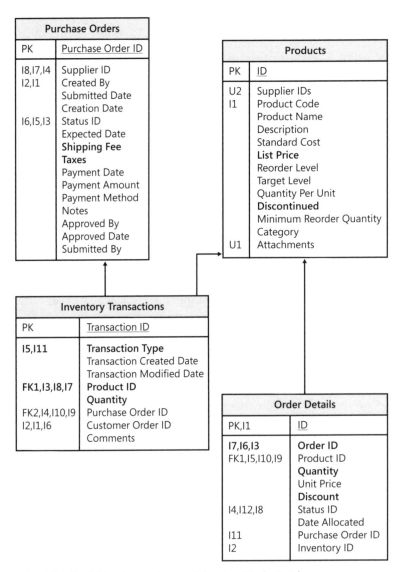

FIGURE 3-1 Partial Database schema—Adventure Works Database.

Metadata is often used in software development as a means to parameterize applications
or to store static detail, like configuration or behavioral information, away from the logic of
the application. It can represent items ranging from a button color or font size to algorithm

selection, regular expression patterns, or security policy. Developers sometimes leverage metadata as a means to modify application behavior during installation or execution. This is often referred to as metaprogramming, and it spans several programming paradigms including, but certainly not limited to:

- **Native code**   Applications developed in native Windows programming languages like Visual C++ or Visual Basic use a combination of initialization (.ini) files or the Windows registry to store application metadata like configuration or initialization parameters in key/value pairs.

- **Java**   Application properties are configuration values stored as key/value pairs in property (.property) files of Java programs. Java provides application developers the ability to store and access application metadata in a structured XML format.

- **Managed code**   Applications developed with the Microsoft .NET Framework can leverage the structure and flexibility of XML to store metadata in the application-level configuration files such as web.config for ASP.NET applications. Developers are provided the ability to store simple key/value pairs or more complex custom structures.

A key attribute of metaprogramming is the use of descriptive data to modify program behavior at run time. Early and less effective uses of metaprogramming, such as storing key/value pairs in .ini files or the Windows registry, did not provide developers with a great deal of flexibility or security. Initialization files lacked structure for storing hierarchical metadata, and the continued use of the Windows registry to store application metadata contributed to an ever-growing, critical, and single point of failure. When the Microsoft .NET Framework emerged, software developers realized greater flexibility for storing application settings and metadata. They were encouraged to leverage XML-based configuration files in the application's root directory and, thus, eliminate the dependency on the Windows registry.

Metadata in Managed Applications

As previously discussed, incorporating the use of metadata within software applications allows developers to decouple specific logic detail from the application code and thus promotes more flexible and maintainable application designs. By storing these details in metadata, our programs become inherently more generic and our algorithms more reusable. Additionally, by simply updating the metadata for an application, we can change the way an application works without recompiling or redeploying it.

The .NET Framework provides software developers with a great deal of flexibility and control for storing and retrieving application metadata. The various serialization interfaces, attributes, and classes in .NET afford developers the ability to manage application metadata in formats ranging from XML to binary. This flexibility is provided globally to all applications at the machine level and, more granularly, to specific programs at an application level. Metadata is most often stored using structured XML, written in configuration files according to specific schemas, and is used to modify application behavior at runtime. This design practice ultimately provides lower-cost application maintenance and flexibility, especially in post-release, live production circumstances. It is important to understand the roles and capabilities of the different configuration and metadata storage options that are offered to managed code developers so that you incorporate their use in the design of your application.

- **Machine configuration settings**   The .NET Framework allows software developers or system administrators to store configuration metadata that is scoped to all applications on a specific machine in the machine configuration file, or machine.config. This file is located in the run-time installation path in a subdirectory called config. This file contains settings that are related to machine-wide policies and should only be augmented with settings that will apply to all applications running on that specific machine.

- **Security configuration settings**   In addition to allowing granular control over machine level settings, the .NET Framework also allows developers or system administrators to modify security configuration files. The security configuration file contains information about the code group hierarchy and permission sets associated with a policy level. Modifying these files manually is not recommended and should be accomplished by using either Caspol.exe or the .NET Framework Configuration Tool (Mscorcfg.msc), which is included in the .NET Framework SDK and can be found in the %windir%\Microsoft.NET\Framework\<Version Number> directory.

- **Application configuration settings**   Unlike the machine configuration file, application configuration files, such as web.config, allow developers to store metadata that is scoped to a particular application. These configuration files are used by both Windows client and ASP.NET applications, and they share a common schema across the application models. While these files do contain settings that are pertinent to the Common Language Runtime (CLR) such as assembly binding policy, they also offer flexibility to add custom metadata sections.

Although the .NET Framework provides these three basic types of configuration files, which all share the same basic schema, each of them clearly has different objectives. Even though both machine and security configuration files are critically important to managed applications, in most cases, customized application-specific metadata will be stored within application-level configuration files. We will explore this in greater detail as we move through this chapter.

Application Configuration Files

As suggested by their name, application configuration files contain metadata that is scoped to a particular application. These files are used by all types of managed applications including but not limited to Windows Forms, Console executable, Web service, ASP.NET, and Windows Presentation Foundation (WPF) applications. The name and location of the application configuration files depend on the particular application model being used, but all application configuration files share the same schema and the same metadata storage and access patterns. Let us examine examples of different managed code application types and their respective configuration files.

- **Executable applications**   For Windows Forms, console-based, and WPF applications, the configuration file resides in the same directory as the application itself and is accessible by the application at run time. The name of the configuration file is the same as the application but with a .config extension. For example, if the application is called AirCargo.exe, then the corresponding configuration file would be called AirCargo.exe.config. This example is further illustrated by Figure 3-2.

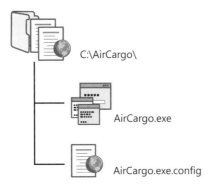

C:\AirCargo\

AirCargo.exe

AirCargo.exe.config

FIGURE 3-2 Executable application and configuration file hierarchy.

- **ASP.NET applications**   For ASP.NET and Web service applications, the configuration files are aptly named web.config and are stored in application's directory hierarchy. Unlike executable applications, ASP.NET configuration files can exist in multiple locations within the ASP.NET application folder hierarchy. When individual pages are requested, the ASP.NET runtime evaluates all available configuration files and chooses the most appropriate configuration setting based on its physical location relative to the resource being requested. This allows settings stored in the application root directory to be overridden by configuration settings stored with resources in subdirectories. Therefore, the requested page will be affected by the settings stored in the nearest web.config, unless an override exists. This is best explained by considering the following scenarios in conjunction with Figure 3-3. For these scenarios, let us assume that the configuration variables are the same across all web.config files but with different values respectively.

  - ❏ **Default.aspx**   Requests for this page would result in the use of configurations from the web.config file stored in the application's virtual root directory of http://localhost/AirCargo.

  - ❏ **Billing.aspx**   Any request for this page would result in the use of metadata from the web.config file stored in the virtual directory http://localhost/AirCargo/Billing.

❑ **CustomerList.aspx** A request for this page would also result in the use of configurations from the web.config file stored in the application's virtual root directory at http://localhost/AirCargo.

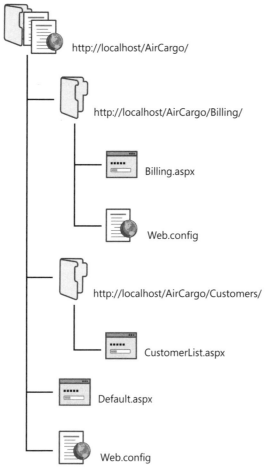

FIGURE 3-3 ASP.NET application and configuration file hierarchy.

These examples clearly illustrate the relationship of configuration files to both Windows executable, like Windows Forms or Console applications, and ASP.NET applications, as well as how they are respectively managed by the .NET runtime environment. While it is important to understand their behavior, it is much more valuable to understand some of the capabilities that are offered by configuration files within managed code applications. In the next few sections, we will explore the range of options that are available to developers for storing simple or more complex metadata within their applications.

Configuration Settings Basics

Before delving into the specifics of storing application metadata in configuration files, it is important to review the basics of application configuration setting storage within .NET applications. As previously mentioned, all configuration file types adhere to a particular XML schema, which defines the entire range of possible configuration settings for machine, security, and application configuration files. This schema is documented in exhaustive detail on MSDN,[1] and since the scope of this chapter is on leveraging the use of metadata in applications, we will focus on reviewing the schema elements that are germane to application configuration storage.

In application configuration files for all types of managed applications, all XML elements are children of the root element called *<configuration>*. The first-level child elements that are important for application setting storage are the *<configSections>*, *<appSettings>*, and *<connectionStrings>* elements. The combined role of these elements is to define and represent the sections of the configuration file that store custom application metadata. More specifically, the *<configSections>* element defines the way in which application settings or metadata will be represented in the configuration file. The *<appSettings>* and *<connectionStrings>* elements represent the detailed storage structure for the metadata defined by their respective *<configSections>* *<section>* element. The following code snippet illustrates the basic XML structure and syntax of these configuration file elements. This is a generic configuration file. The details of a specific configuration file are presented in the next sections.

```
<configuration>
<!-- Defines the configuration sections of the config file -->
  <configSections>
    <section name="appSettings"
      type="System.Configuration.AppSettingsSection,System.Configuration, Version=2.0.0.0,
      Culture=neutral, PublicKeyToken=b03f5f7f11d50a3a" restartOnExternalChanges="false"
      requirePermission="false"/>
    <section name="connectionStrings" type="System.Configuration.ConnectionStringsSection,
      System.Configuration, Version=2.0.0.0, Culture=neutral
      PublicKeyToken=b03f5f7f11d50a3a" requirePermission="false"/>
  </configSections>
<!-- Represents the structure of the metadata defined in the <configSections>
 element for key/value pair storage -->
  <appSettings>
    <add key="…" value="…"/>
    <add key="…" value="…"/>
  </appSettings>
<!-- Represents the structure of the metadata defined in the <configSections>
element for connectionString storage -->
  <connectionStrings>
    <add name="…" providerName="…" connectionString="…"/>
  </connectionStrings>
</configuration>
```

---

[1] *http://msdn2.microsoft.com/en-us/library/1fk1t1t0(VS.85).aspx.*

As we explore options for storing application metadata, it is important to understand the basic structure of application configuration files and the relationship of configuration section types to the storage structures they represent. The .NET Framework provides a core set of metadata storage structures natively, such as *<appSettings>* and *<connectionStrings>*, but also allows developers to add custom structures. Each of these options provides developers with a simple but powerful mechanism to abstract the application metadata away from their code, which allows the application to be much more flexible and adaptable to change. We will examine each of these options in greater depth in the next several sections.

Application Configuration Storage

In the application configuration file, developers can easily store metadata for their applications by simply leveraging the native functionality of .NET. Application settings or other static metadata for the application can be stored in the *<appSettings>* section of the application's configuration file. This is accomplished by simply adding child elements to the *<appSettings>* section that contain key/value pairs representing the application's metadata. The following code snippet demonstrates the addition of three key/value pairs for an air cargo reservations ASP.NET application, which we will discuss throughout the remainder of this chapter.

```
<appSettings>
    <add key="MinimumCargoWeight" value="100"/>
    <add key="MaximumCargoWeight" value="10000"/>
    <add key="DefaultAirportCode" value="SEA"/>
</appSettings>
```

The *<appSettings>* section supports the addition of three element types, which include the *<add>*, *<remove>*, and *<clear>* elements. The *<add>* element adds a new application setting, which is identified by a unique key, to the collection. The *<remove>* element removes a specific setting, based on the unique key, from the collection. The *<clear>* element allows the removal of all elements that have been previously defined in the *<appSettings>* section. The *<remove>* and *<clear>* elements are often used to remove settings from a higher level configuration file when a hierarchy of configuration files is present within the application, as is often the case with ASP.NET applications. Conversely, these settings are not particularly useful in Windows executable applications, which can only leverage the use of a single configuration file.

In many cases, application developers will be able to leverage this simple key/value pair metadata storage within their application configuration files and realize increased flexibility in their applications. There are several scenarios where this feature provides tangible value for application maintainability and extensibility. Consider the snippet of code shown earlier in the context of our air cargo reservation system example and the values that are represented. You may notice that there is metadata in the *<appSettings>* section that represents entities like the minimum cargo weight, maximum cargo weight, and default airport code. Some of the values being represented here are likely to be used throughout the application. By storing them in a key/value pair format in a single location and accessing them using a common pattern within the application code, we not only increase the flexibility of the application but isolate and minimize the scope of required testing. This is illustrated in the example code in the next section, which demonstrates the use of a common metadata access class.

Application Configuration Example

In this code sample, a class is created for managing access to common information and utility methods. This is aptly referred to as the *Utility* class. Inside the *Utility* class, a static method has been created to obtain application-specific information at run time, using the metadata stored in the application configuration file. This information is retrieved by simply using the standard *ConfigurationManager* class, which is a part of the Framework Class Library, for reading from the configuration file. By generalizing this method and centralizing it in a common class, the logic can subsequently be shared across the application and evolved as needed. Additionally, if for some reason we decide to change one of these specific configuration values at run time, we will not need to recompile or redeploy the application, because we chose to abstract these details out of the application code.

```
/// <summary>
/// Class for managing common information and utility methods
/// </summary>

public static class Utility
{
        /// <summary>
        /// Common method for obtaining application metadata
        /// </summary>
        /// <param name="ConfigKey"></param>
        /// <returns>Configuration Value as String</returns>

    public static String GetConfigurationValue(String ConfigKey)
    {
        String value = ConfigurationManager.AppSettings.Get(ConfigKey);
        return value;
    }
}
```

Once the common class and access method are available, each ASP.NET page can simply invoke this method to retrieve the specific value defined in the configuration file. Even though this has only been implemented for one specific user interface element, it could very simply be extended to include an entire set of common user interface properties.

```
lblAircraftMaxWeight.Text = "Minimum cargo weight for this reservation is " +
    Utility.GetConfigurationValue("MinimumWeight") + " lbs.";
```

Note We could have just as easily leveraged the *ConfigurationManager* class directly in our ASP.NET code to access these values. I chose to abstract this from the ASP.NET pages through the *Utility* class to illustrate the point that centralization provides flexibility. This flexibility would allow additional logic or business rules to be incorporated into the *GetConfigurationValue* method, rather than be scattered throughout the application.

As demonstrated, storing metadata as simple key/value pairs in an application configuration file under the *<appSettings>* section is a simple yet effective means of increasing flexibility and reducing complexity of your application. In many cases, this method of storing metadata will provide application developers with the needed flexibility for abstracting the detailed metadata away from the logic of their software applications. However, some applications will be inevitably more complex and require metadata storage mechanisms that will address their needs. Fortunately, managed code applications have additional options for including other types of metadata within the application configuration file like database connection strings or custom XML structures. We will review each of these options in the upcoming sections.

Database Connection String Configurations

It is an accurate assertion to suggest that many managed applications are data driven. After all, data makes applications interesting, useful, and adaptive. Whether those applications are ASP.NET or Windows executable, they may maintain a connection to a database. In fact, in highly distributed environments, applications could maintain connections to multiple databases, perhaps even on multiple platforms. Fortunately, .NET provides application developers with a mechanism for managing the metadata associated with the connections between applications and databases, more commonly known as database connection strings.

As previously discussed, abstracting metadata from application logic increases an application's flexibility and adaptability to change while promoting the development and reuse of more generic algorithms. Managing logic that enables applications to connect to one or more different data sources is a great example of a situation for which we could apply this design principle. Savvy application developers recognize that hard-coding connection strings in application logic is not flexible or maintainable. Inevitably, some aspect of the relationship between the application and the data source will change after the application is deployed, such as the database credentials or perhaps the location of the database. Simply moving from a development environment to a test or production environment is an example of when target database names will change. By storing these relationships in metadata, application logic can be responsive to changes of this nature without requiring a change to the data access code.

In the .NET Framework, configuration files support a section called *<connectionStrings>*, which is specifically designed to store connection string information to supplement application logic. Unlike simple key/value pairs, database connection strings serve a specific purpose and deserve to be treated separately. Not only are they critically important for data-driven applications, but often times they contain information such as user credentials that is more sensitive than information stored in the general-purpose *<appSettings>* section and may be desirable to encrypt. The following code snippet is a good example of the *<connection-Strings>* section of the application configuration file being used to store connection strings for multiple local Microsoft Access databases.

> **Note** Although this book does not discuss protecting metadata using some of the encryption features provided by the .NET Framework, I recommend reviewing Dino Esposito's explanation in his book *Programming Microsoft ASP.NET 2.0 Core Reference* (Microsoft Press, 2005), which covers the subject very well.

```
<connectionStrings>
    <add connectionString="Provider=Microsoft.ACE.OLEDB.12.0;Data
        Source=C:\myFolder\AircraftDB.accdb;Persist Security Info=False;"
        name="CargoAircraftDB"/>
    <add connectionString="Provider=Microsoft.ACE.OLEDB.12.0;Data
        Source=C:\myFolder\CustomerDB.accdb;Persist Security Info=False;"
      name="CargoCustomerDB"/>
</connectionStrings>
```

Similar to the functionality of the *<appSettings>* section mentioned previously, *<add>*, *<remove>*, and *<clear>* can be used to maniplate the contents of the *<connectionStrings>* section. Additionally, each connection string node is identified by a name and can be accessed programmatically using the *ConfigurationManager* class. This is demonstrated in the following code sample, where we extend the aforementioned *Utility* class to include a generic method for returning a database connection object.

```
Using System.Data.Odbc;

public static OdbcConnection GetDatabaseConnection(String datasourcename)

{

  OdbcConnection conn = new
  OdbcConnection(ConfigurationManager.ConnectionStrings[datasourcename].ConnectionString);

  return conn;

}
```

Storing database connection metadata in the *<connectionStrings>* section clearly helps developers abstract the relationship of the application and the database away from the application logic, thus increasing flexibility of the application. The .NET Framework recognizes the uniqueness of this pervasive programming necessity and provides a specific section for managing the information within the application configuration file. While this feature has provided application developers with out-of-the-box convenience, the need to have specific configuration sections goes well beyond database connection strings. As we will review in the next section, the .NET Framework also provides a great deal of flexibility for application developers to define and construct custom metadata storage structures within the application configuration file and strongly typed classes for accessing the information.

Custom Configurations

Thus far, we have explored some basic examples of storing application metadata using the standard configuration options like key/value pairs within the *<appSettings>* section or database connections strings within the *<connectionStrings>* section. Although these methods are in and of themselves quite flexible and valuable, there are other potential solutions that would allow storage of more complex metadata structures within your application. Those solutions include embedding a custom XML structure within the application configuration file and specifying a custom configuration section and associative configuration handler or using an XML file that stores desired data structure. Both options would essentially meet the basic needs, but it's worth examining the benefits of each solution prior to deciding which will work best for your application.

- **Defining a custom configuration section and handler**   As compared with using simple XML files to store application metadata, custom configuration sections provide similar flexibility in terms of metadata storage capabilities. Application developers can define a tailor-made configuration section that represents a custom XML metadata structure. Additionally, they can leverage the native support of the *System.Configuration* classes for optimally accessing the data using custom configuration section handlers. The downside to storing metadata in application configuration files is that they require application restarts for changes to take effect. In most cases, this is not a major concern, which makes this metadata storage option quite appealing.

- **Plain XML file**   Using a simple XML file to define custom metadata structures is certainly a flexible and powerful option. This method provides complete freedom over storage and access patterns and does not force or require application restarts when changes are applied. The downside is that application developers will need to write all of the metadata handling code, and there are obviously no guarantees that this custom code will be as optimized as the more general purpose *System.Configuration* classes.

As a basic rule, leveraging the metadata storage options provided inherently within the .NET Framework should always be the first option to consider. Storing application metadata using simple XML files is certainly more flexible from a programming perspective. However, defining custom configuration sections and handlers provides application developers access to the general-purpose, more optimal *System.Configuation* classes for accessing application metadata. This allows developers to write far less code within their applications and subsequently to reduce the risk of introducing bugs into their metadata access and handling logic.

The following example, building upon the previously discussed air cargo reservation system, explores storing more complex metadata and implementing custom configuration sections and handlers to access that metadata.

Custom Configuration Section Example

In the previous examples, we explored storing simple key/value pair formatted metadata using the standard configuration options available in the *<appSettings>* section of the application configuration file. While this worked well for storing some unstructured bits of metadata, it did not allow us to store much more than a single value for each item. Suppose we wanted to store information about the aircraft that the air cargo company has available in its inventory. Our first inclination might be to store this information in a database. Even though this may be a valid choice in certain application designs, the solution is overkill for this scenario. Let us assume that a custom configuration section is all that is required, so we create a structure that resembles the following XML and its associative *<configSection>* element.

```
<!--Define the configuration section -->
<configSections>
    <section name="Aircraft" type="AircraftConfiguration"/>
</configSections>
<!-- Define the custom metadtata structure -->
<Aircraft>
        <Inventory>
          <add ID="N443BC" type="Lockheed L188C Electra" availability="true"
          inService="true"  category="MEL" year="1977"/>
          <add ID="N122EC" type="Merlin 4A" availability="true" inService="true"
          category="MEL" year="1975"/>
        </Inventory>
</Aircraft>
```

The custom configuration section that has been defined in this example is called "Aircraft" and is established as a section within the *<configSections>* element of the configuration file. This configuration section name must match the subsequent XML metadata structure's root node name in order to function properly. Additionally, the associative configuration handler is named by the type attribute of the *AirCraftConfiguration* section and denotes the class that will handle the processing of the custom section. This markup helps to establish the custom configuration section that stores the metadata within the application configuration file. To be accessible to the application code, though, supporting classes are required.

Once the application's configuration metadata is structurally defined, application developers must subsequently create the appropriate supporting classes to plug into the configuration plumbing provided by the .NET Framework. This begins by defining a class similar to that of the class denoted in the previous markup as *AircraftConfiguration*. This class, which derives from .NET's *ConfigurationSection* class, represents a deserialized object representation of the configuration section *Aircraft*. This class provides one property called *Inventory*, which ultimately provides access to a collection of the items defined in the *Inventory* node of the configuration metadata, and it provides one static method called *GetConfig()*, which encapsulates code for initializing access to the *<Aircraft>* configuration section. This is illustrated with the following code.

```
public class AircraftConfiguration : ConfigurationSection
{
    /// <summary>
    /// Returns an AircraftConfiguration instance - this is provided to optmize access
    /// to the configuration section but is not required.
    /// </summary>
    public static AircraftConfiguration GetConfig()
    { return ConfigurationManager.GetSection("Aircraft") as AircraftConfiguration; }

    // Returns the Aircraft collection object which is a collection of aircraft elements.
    [ConfigurationProperty("Inventory")]
    public AircraftCollection Inventory
    {
        get  { return this["Inventory"] as AircraftCollection; }
    }
}
```

In this class, the *ConfigurationProperty* attribute that is decorating each property indicates that these properties are specified in the custom configuration metadata that was previously defined. The *ConfigurationProperty* attribute accepts the following parameters.

- **Name**   Specifies the name of the property as described by the custom configuration metadata in the configuration file.

- **DefaultValue**   Represents the default value of the property if it is not specified in the configuration metadata.

- **IsRequired**   Illustrates whether the property is required or optional. If this is set to true and the property is not specified in the configuration file, an exception will be thrown.

- **IsKey**   Indicates whether a *ConfigurationProperty* is the key for the containing *ConfigurationElement* object.

- **IsDefaultCollection**   Specifies whether the property is the default collection of an element.

In this example, only name is defined in the *ConfigurationProperty* attribute, which is acceptable since the *Inventory* accessor returns a collection of *Aircraft* objects. These objects are created inside the *AircraftCollection* class, which derives from the *ConfigurationElementCollection* class and manages the deserialization of the elements beneath the *Inventory* node in the configuration file. When extending the *ConfigurationElementCollection* class, application developers must override the *CreateNewElement* and *GetElementKey* methods, which are responsible for creating the new element in the *ConfigurationElementCollection* class and providing an element key respectively. In this case, the XML attribute *ID* from the custom metadata section in the configuration file is mapped as the key for each element in the collection. This is illustrated within the following code.

```
/// <summary>
/// AircraftCollection class represents the collection of elements associated with the
/// <inventory> element of the custom configuration section.
/// </summary>
public class AircraftCollection : ConfigurationElementCollection
{
    public Aircraft this[int index]
    {
        get
        { return base.BaseGet(index) as Aircraft; }
        set
        {
            if (base.BaseGet(index) != null)
            { base.BaseRemoveAt(index); }
            this.BaseAdd(index, value);
        }
    }

    /// <summary>
    /// override the GetElementKey method which maps an xml attribute from the
    /// configuration file to the key of the collection.
    /// </summary>
    protected override object GetElementKey(ConfigurationElement element)
    { return ((Aircraft)element).Id; }

    /// <summary>
    /// override the CreateNewElement method so the new Aircraft class is intialized.
    /// </summary>
    protected override ConfigurationElement CreateNewElement()
    { return new Aircraft(); }
}
```

As previously described, the *AircraftCollection* class returns a collection of *Aircraft* objects, which should represent the deserialized version of the XML elements defined as children of the *<Inventory>* element in the application configuration file. As such, the *Aircraft* class derives from the *ConfigurationElement* class, and each of its properties should appropriately map to the attributes of the XML element in the configuration file. The abridged class definition for the *Aircraft* object is described below and illustrates how the attributes of the XML are exposed as properties of the class.

```
/// <summary>
/// Aircraft class that represents the Aircraft configuration element which is a child to
/// the <inventory> element within the custom configuration section.
/// </summary>
public class Aircraft : ConfigurationElement
{
```

```
// Return the "Id" attribute
[ConfigurationProperty("Id", IsRequired=true)]
public string Id
{ get { return this["Id"] as String; } }

// Return the "Category" attribute
[ConfigurationProperty("Category", IsRequired = false)]
public string Category
{ get { return this["Category"] as String; } }

// Return the "Type" attribute
[ConfigurationProperty("Type", IsRequired = false)]
public string Type
{ get { return this["Type"] as String; } }
...
}
```

Now that the custom application metadata for the air cargo reservations application has been defined in the application configuration file and the supporting *AircraftConfiguration*, *AircraftCollection*, and *Aircraft* classes have been defined, pulling it all together is fairly easy. To illustrate how this configuration metadata can be leveraged within the application's user interface pages, we will wire up a simple dynamic drop-down list box in an ASP.NET page. Once the *DropDownList* object is added to the ASP.NET page, the following code illustrates how to dynamically populate it using the custom configuration metadata, which was previously defined.

```
if (!Page.IsPostBack)
{
    // Retrieve the Aircraft inventory from config and add them to the drop down list
    foreach (Aircraft aircrft in AircraftConfiguration.GetConfig().Inventory)
    {
    this.ddlAircraft.Items.Add(new ListItem(aircrft.type + " - " + aircrft.Id,
    aircrft.Id));
    }
}
```

The result of this example is an ASP.NET application whose user experience is driven by custom-defined application metadata stored in the application's configuration file. By leveraging metadata storage options in the *<appSettings>* configuration section as well as a custom configuration section, the air cargo reservation system's user experience can be changed at any time by simply updating the web.config file that is stored within the application. This flexibility allows future adjustments to the metadata of the application without recompiling or redeploying the application. A sample screen is provided in Figure 3-4, which is the run-time result of the examples defined previously.

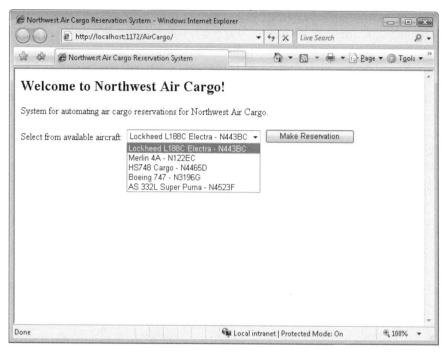

FIGURE 3-4 Northwest Air Cargo Reservations System default screen.

Application Configuration in Practice

In addition to the high degree of flexibility that application configuration files provide developers for storing metadata, the ability to add and update configuration settings in post-release, live production circumstances is equally powerful. With both Windows executable and ASP.NET applications, revising configuration files after an application is compiled and deployed can be accomplished with minimal impact to the running application. In the case of ASP.NET, any change to the web.config files will cause the application domain, which is the virtual address space in which the application is executing, to restart. This will actually result in user sessions being terminated. Once this occurs, the new settings will take effect. Alternatively, with Windows executable applications, changes to the configuration files will take effect when the application restarts. Leveraging this capability within your software applications will clearly help increase the overall quality of the application.

Metadata in Your Applications

Throughout this chapter, we have discussed the use of metadata within managed applications as well as the flexibility provided by the .NET Framework for storing and retrieving metadata from application-specific configuration files. As demonstrated, there are a number of options for how an application developer might choose to leverage metadata within his or her application. In addition to the more tactical options for how best to incorporate and use metadata within your applications, there is a set of design principles enumerated below that should be applied when considering how best to incorporate metadata within your application.

Store application configurations in metadata   Configuration settings are critical to software applications and are very likely to change frequently. Storing configuration settings or any item that resembles configuration data within metadata allows applications to be highly configurable and adaptable to change. Whether storing user preferences, database connection settings, or the enabled/disabled state of a feature, storing metadata in an application's configuration file is incredibly powerful. This practice promotes application extensibility and customization without actually recompiling or redeploying the software.

Store application details in metadata   Software applications contain a lot of details, such as user interface definitions like menu contents, default feature configurations, and other generally descriptive elements of the software. By storing this type of information within the code, the flexibility and maintainability of the application user experience is severely limited. As a rule, user interface definitions similar to the previous examples should be decoupled from the code and stored in metadata. Simple strings should be stored in .RESX files to enable localization, and other user interface metadata should be managed within the application's configuration file or files. Following this guideline will help improve the flexibility and maintainability of the application over time, because user interface changes will be possible without redeploying the application.

Drive application behavior with metadata   Beyond storing metadata for simple preferences and user experience definitions, application developers should endeavor to drive application behavior through the use of metadata. This general principle promotes construction of more generic and reusable algorithms, which rely on metadata at run time to govern their behavior. By promoting code reuse, application developers inherently reduce the risk of introducing bugs into the software as new features are added. Additionally, by creating generic algorithms and abstracting the run-time instructions into metadata, the adaptability of the overall application is increased.

Inside Microsoft: Configuration Management in Windows Live Spaces

Windows Live represents a set of client software products and online services from Microsoft that allows users to connect and share information with friends online. This offering includes Windows Live Spaces, which is a Web-based blogging and media-sharing service that allows users to publish and share blogs, photos, and other types of online media through a highly customizable Web interface. Launched in 2004 under the MSN brand, Windows Live Spaces is delivered today to more than 100 million users[2] worldwide in more than 35 languages. The key features of the service include a personalized blog, photo and file sharing, and other features for publishing content.

Similar to Windows Live Hotmail, Spaces is divided into multiple architectural components, including but not limited to the user-facing front-end Web services, back-end user data storage, and authorization and user management storage. These components are large, extremely complex, and shared across multiple other Windows Live services. Once deployed, the size of the Web front-end subsystems alone is more than 900 MB, almost all of which is developed in managed code.

Suffice it to say that, based on the size and complexity of the service, Windows Live Spaces is an application that requires a high degree of engineering rigor to manage effectively. There are numerous moving parts within the application, variations in business logic by market, complex infrastructure dependencies that change by server environment, and many feature-level dependencies on other products and services. As with any dynamic service on the Web, many of these variables can change—and often do. Certain types of changes, such as enabling a new feature in a specific market, can happen fairly often, while others like infrastructure changes may happen less frequently. In either case, if the application is not designed properly, even minor changes can require a build, deployment, and broad regression testing to ensure quality remains high. It would be unrealistic to expect any team to be able to quickly deploy simple changes to a service of this magnitude when the install footprint is so large and the infrastructure so complex without significant engineering effort.

Gaining Flexibility with Metaprogramming

The team has embraced the challenges of complex business logic, cross-team dependencies, and frequent rate of change, and it has invested in a design that leveraged the use of metadata to enable dynamic control over many aspects of the application. The team believed its objectives for managing dynamic updates to the service should be twofold.

All features are configuration driven whenever possible   This includes ensuring that metadata is completely separated from the code, and features are largely configuration driven. This would allow the team to tweak the logic dynamically when required without recompiling the code or incurring a large regression testing effort. Additionally, this would also allow for increased control over the quality of the application, while subsequently improving the team's ability to be responsive to change.

Configuration updates are managed dynamically   This includes ensuring that getting dynamic updates to the live production site would happen quickly and without a high degree of risk or costly operations work. Building upon the previous objective of making features configuration driven, investing in a system that would allow each configuration file to be

---

2   comScore, March 2008.

managed and deployed reliably across all servers within minutes, would both minimize required operational effort and maximize service management agility.

When reduced to practice, the team was able to accomplish both goals very successfully. For starters, many features are controlled by configuration information using a combination of .NET configuration and simple XML files. This investment has proved to be quite effective in providing very granular levels of control over business logic, features, component dependencies, and deployment logic. This level of control has allowed the team to be more responsive to changes and less burdened by broad regression testing when changes are made to the application via the metadata. Certain classes of feature changes are possible anytime without recompiling the application code. This has increased the overall ability of the application to adapt to dynamic changes in the business, without incurring high cost of engineering.

To address the second goal of enabling dynamic updates to configuration information, the team implemented a system that provides the ability to make site-wide configuration changes. This system would allow the team to execute the changes and deploy them to hundreds of servers, across multiple geographic locations, within minutes. Previously, despite the best engineering efforts, deploying simple configuration changes to the live site would take hours to implement across multiple data centers and hundreds of servers. Even with scripted deployment processes, engineers were prone to making errors, and the risk was high that users could be negatively affected by a change gone awry. This automated system realized almost immediate return on investment as its reliability, speed of deployment, and enforcement of change management rules increased the reliability of configuration deployment while reducing the risk and cost of maintaining the application.

Since implementing the combination of the metaprogramming design practice in conjunction with site-wide configuration management, the Windows Live Spaces team has been able to increase the overall quality and manageability of the various components of the service. This success can be largely attributed to the abstraction of metadata from code and the use of configuration files to drive and govern feature behavior. In and of itself, this practice is a success, but coupling it with the dynamic management system further increased the application's adaptability to change and the team's ability to respond in kind. This implementation of metadata within a managed code application is a true testament to the value of this design best practice, but it also highlights the capabilities of managing configuration data provided within the .NET Framework.

Summary

Reducing complexity and improving maintainability of software directly contributes to increasing its quality. The challenge for developers is that software applications tend to be laden with business logic rules that govern the behavior of the application. By abstracting behaviors out of the code and into application metadata, the application design becomes inherently more robust, flexible, and adaptable. As a result, application and test code can be much more simplified and much easier to maintain or adapt via the application metadata.

Application designs that are more flexible tend to decouple specific details from the logic and algorithms by storing static detail in metadata. In managed code applications, using XML structures to store metadata within application-specific configuration files is encouraged as a means to drive application behavior at run time. It is this design practice that ultimately provides lower-cost application maintenance and flexibility, especially in post-release, live production circumstances.

Key Points

- Increase quality by reducing the complexity and improving maintainability of your application by abstracting program detail out of the code and into application metadata.

- Reduce maintenance and deployment costs and increase flexibility by storing application configurations in metadata.

- Increase the adaptability of your application by driving application behavior with metadata.

- Use XML-based configuration files to store structured metadata for your application. Store simple key/value pairs within the *<appSettings>* element of the application's configuration file.

- If your application is connecting to a data source, store metadata about the connection in the *<connectionStrings>* element of the application's configuration file.

- When your application metadata requires storage of custom XML structures, leverage the extensibility of the .NET Framework configuration classes and build custom configuration handlers with strongly typed objects that represent the data being stored.

Chapter 4
Performance Is a Feature

My speed is my greatest asset.

—Peter Bondra, former professional ice hockey player

Software can possess a broad array of useful features. Certain applications, such as Microsoft Office, include features that can help a user accomplish a near infinite number of tasks, many of which a normal user might never even discover. Other applications, like Notepad, may contain only the features necessary to accomplish a few simple tasks, which might leave certain users desiring more functionality. In either case, the goal of the software is the same: to provide functionality that helps users to accomplish a particular set of tasks. If we also consider how quickly users are able to accomplish that set of tasks, then performance, as suggested by the Peter Bondra quote, should also be considered an important feature of a software application.

As application developers, we spend considerable effort planning and building the key features of our applications. These features are cohesive, enhance the quality of our product, and implicitly improve overall functionality. One of the most important aspects of all features of a software product is performance. Performance is often overlooked or considered late in product design and development. This can lead to inadequate performance results for key features and overall poorer product quality. Performance is critical to the quality of any application but especially to Web applications. By contrast to desktop applications, Web applications depend on the transmission of data and application assets over a worldwide network. This presents architectural and quality challenges for Web application developers that must be mitigated during the design and construction of their applications.

Web application quality extends beyond the visible bugs that end users encounter when using the application. Network latency, payload size, and application architecture can have negative impacts on the performance of online applications. Therefore, performance considerations should be part of every Web application design. Deferring these considerations until late in the development cycle can create significant code churn after performance bugs are discovered. Application developers must understand the impact of the design choices that affect adversely performance and mitigate the risks of releasing a poorly performing Web application by applying many of the best practices discussed in this chapter.

Throughout the remainder of this chapter, we will evaluate some common problems that can negatively affect the performance of Web-based software, and we will discuss several practices that can be applied to proactively address performance bottlenecks. Although this chapter will not focus on techniques that are unique to managed code development, it will discuss several ways to apply performance best practices to your application development life cycle in order to increase the overall quality of your Web-based application, as well as the satisfaction for your application's users.

Common Performance Challenges

Web-based applications that rely on interactions between servers and a user's Web browser inherently require certain design considerations to address the performance challenges present in the application execution environment. These factors are not specific to Web applications developed using ASP.NET; they also affect application developers who utilize Web development programming models like PHP or Java. They include the latency or quality of the connection between the client and server, the payload size of the data being transmitted, as well as poorly optimized application code, to name a few. Let's explore each of these in greater depth.

Network Latency

To understand the impact of network latency and throughput on your Web application, we must first understand the general performance and throughput of the Internet in key regions around the world. This may prove to be an eye-opening experience for many Web application developers. The data in Table 4-1 illustrates how end users are affected by the network topology of the Internet. The data in this table was gathered during daily ping tests conducted between January through September 2008 and provide a breakdown of the average round-trip time (measured in milliseconds [ms]) and average packet loss for users in each specified region. Let us briefly review the definitions of each of these metrics before further evaluating the data in the table.

- **Average round-trip time**   This refers to the average amount of time required for a 100-byte packet of data to complete a network round trip. The value in Table 4-1 is computed by evaluating the round-trip time for daily tests conducted over a period from January through September 2008.

- **Average packet loss**   This metric evaluates the reliability of a connection by measuring the percentage of packets lost during the network round trip of a 100-byte packet of data. In the same way that average round-trip time is determined, the average packet loss is also computed by evaluating the results of daily tests conducted over a period of January through September 2008.

TABLE 4-1 **Internet Network Statistics by Region**

Region	Average Round-Trip Time (ms)	Average Packet Loss (%)
Africa	469	3.70
Australia	204	0.23

Region	Average Round-Trip Time (ms)	Average Packet Loss (%)
Balkans	202	0.74
Central Asia	597	1.24
East Asia	192	0.68
Europe	178	0.48
Latin America	270	1.15
Middle East	279	0.87
North America	59	0.09
Russia	243	2.48
South Asia	424	1.89
South East Asia	254	0.03

Note This data is based upon the results of tests being conducted between Stanford University in Northern California and network end points in 27 countries worldwide. Data obtained from each test is subsequently averaged across all end points within a particular region. The complete data set can be obtained from *http://www-iepm.slac.stanford.edu/.* Data is also available from this site in a summarized, percentile-based format, which shows what users at the 25th, 50th, 75th, 90th, and 95th percentile are likely to experience in terms of average round-trip time and packet loss. At Microsoft, teams generally assume that most of their users will experience connectivity quality at the 75th percentile or better.

There are a few key points to take away from the data presented in this table:

Network reliability is poor in certain regions   The general throughput of data on the Internet varies according to region. This means that even if your Web application is available 100 percent of the time and performing perfectly, an end user in Asia might be affected by suboptimal network conditions such as high latency or packet loss and not be able to access your application easily. Although this seems to be a situation beyond an application developer's control, several mitigation strategies do exist and will be discussed later in this chapter. That said, it is definitely useful to understand the general network behavior across the Internet when you consider what an end user experiences when using your Web application.

Average round-trip time is high   We also notice that the average round-trip time for a piece of data to travel from a point within North America to a point within another region is quite high in certain cases. For example, a single Transmission Control Protocol (TCP) packet of data traveling on the Internet between North America and Central Asia has an average round-trip time of 597 ms. This means that each individual file required by a Web application will incur 597 ms of latency during transfer between the server and the client. Thus, as the number of required requests increases, the performance of the application gets worse. Fortunately, the number of round trips between the client and the server is something every Web application developer can influence.

Packet loss is high   In conjunction with average round-trip time, packet loss also increases significantly for users outside North America. Both of these factors are related to general throughput on the network, so they usually go hand-in-hand. These results demonstrate that, as packet loss increases, additional round trips are required between the browser and the server to obtain the packets of data lost in transmission. Hence, higher packet loss means decreased performance of your Web application. Even though developers cannot control the amount of packet loss a user is likely to experience, you can apply certain tactics to help mitigate the effects, such as decreasing payload size, which will be discussed later in this chapter.

Payload Size and Network Round Trips

The term "payload size" loosely refers to the size of data being transmitted over the network to render the requested page. This could include the dynamic ASPX page content as well as static files such as JavaScript files, images, or cascading style sheets (CSS). The number of TCP requests required to retrieve the data is referred to as the "network round trips." Web application performance is most negatively affected by a combination of the payload size and the required round trips between the browser and the server. Let's take a look at a few examples of how typical Web application designs might contribute to poorly performing Web applications.

Compression is not enabled   Compressing static and dynamic files are not necessarily part of your Web server's default configuration. Compression is strongly recommended for Web applications that use high amounts of bandwidth or when you want to use bandwidth more effectively. Many Web application developers might not be aware of this feature and could be unknowingly sending larger amounts of data to the client browser, thereby increasing the size of the payload. When enabled, compression can significantly reduce the size of the file being transmitted to the client browser. Compression requires additional CPU utilization when compressing dynamic content such as .aspx files. Therefore, if the CPU usage on your Web servers is already high, enabling Internet Information Services (IIS) dynamic compression is not recommended. However, enabling IIS static compression on file types such as JavaScripts, CSS, or HTML files does not increase CPU usage and is, therefore, highly recommended. Hosting static files with a Content Delivery Network service provider generally includes compression with the service offering.

Using multiple small static image files   Most Web application developers naturally use references to individual images or iconography throughout their code. This is how most of us were taught to write our HTML. The reality is that each of these files, no matter how small we make them, results in a separate round trip between the browser and the server. Consider how bad this might be for image-rich Web pages where rendering a single page could generate dozens of round trips to the server!

These are just two simple examples of how typical Web applications could be delivering un-necessarily large payloads as well as initiating numerous round trips. The challenge facing Web application developers is to both reduce the amount of data being transmitted between the server and the client as well as optimize their Web application's architecture to minimize the number of network round trips. Fortunately, a number of tactics can help Web application developers accomplish this, all of which we'll explore later in this chapter. For now, we will continue reviewing some of the more common performance problems facing Web application developers.

Limited TCP Connections

We've discussed how an individual HTTP request is made for each resource (such as JavaScript files, CSS, or images) within a Web page, which can negatively affect the rendering performance of the page. However, it may come as a surprise to you to learn that the HTTP/1.1 specification suggests that browsers should download only two resources at a time in parallel for a given hostname. This implies that, if all content necessary to render a page is originating from the same hostname (e.g., *http://www.live.com*), the browser will retrieve only two resources at a time. Thus, the browser will utilize only two TCP connections between the client and the server. This phenomenon is illustrated in Figure 4-1, and although configurable in some browsers and ignored by newer browsers like Internet Explorer 8, it very likely affects users of your Web application.

> **Note** Even though Internet Explorer allows the number of parallel browser sessions to be con-figured, normal users are unlikely to do this. For more information on how to change this setting in Internet Explorer, see the following Microsoft Knowledge Base article: *http://support.microsoft.com/?kbid=282402.*

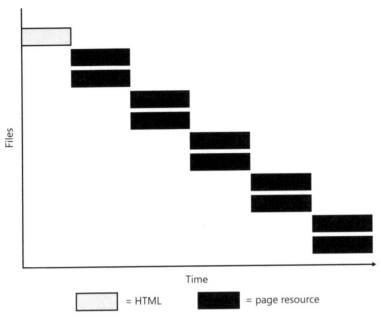

Time

☐ = HTML   ■ = page resource

FIGURE 4-1 Theoretical example of resources downloading in parallel for a single hostname.

Note Several figures in this chapter intend to illustrate how parallel downloading of resources theoretically works in a Web browser. In reality, resources are often of varying sizes and therefore will download in a less structured way than illustrated here. To understand this phenomenon in greater detail, download and run HTTPWatch (*http://www.httpwatch.com*) against your Web application.

As you probably realize, the TCP connection limitation could have profoundly negative effects on performance for Web applications that require a good deal of content to be downloaded. It is critically important for Web application developers to consider this limitation and properly address this phenomenon in the design of their applications. We will evaluate mitigation strategies for this later in this chapter.

Poorly Optimized Code

Performance challenges for Web application developers are not solely related to network topology or data transmission behavior between client browsers and Web servers. It is true that connectivity and data transmission play a big role in the performance of Web applications, but application architecture and application coding play a big role as well. Oftentimes Web application developers will choose a particular implementation within their application architecture or code without fully realizing the impact of the decision on a user of the application. Some examples of common implementations that have a negative impact on Web application performance include the overuse of URL redirects, excessive Domain Name System (DNS) lookups, excessive use of page resources, and poor organization of scripts within a Web page. Let us review each of these in greater detail.

Overuse of redirects   These are typically used by developers to route a user from one URL to another. Common examples include use of the *<meta equiv-http="refresh" content="0; url=http://contoso.com">* directive in HTML and the *Response.Redirect("http://fabrikam.com")* method in ASP.NET. While redirects are often necessary, they obviously delay the start of the page load until the redirect is complete. This could be an acceptable performance degradation in some instances, but, if overused, it could cause undesirable effects on the performance of your Web application's pages.

Excessive DNS lookups   DNS lookups are generally the result of the Web browser being unable to locate the IP address for a given hostname in either its cache or the operating system's cache. If the IP address of a particular hostname is not found in either cache, a lookup against an Internet DNS server will be performed. In the context of a Web page, the number of lookups required will be equal to the number of unique hostnames, such as *http://www. contoso.com* or *http://images.contoso.com*, found in any of the page's JavaScript, CSS, or inline code required to render that page. Therefore, multiple DNS lookups could degrade the performance of your Web application's pages by upwards of n times the number of milliseconds required to resolve the IP address through DNS, where n is equal to the number of unique hostnames found in any of the page's JavaScript, CSS, or inline code requiring a DNS lookup. While there are exceptions to this rule that we will explore when discussing the use of multiple hostnames to increase parallel downloading, it is generally not advisable to include more than a few unique hostnames within your Web applications.

Poorly organized JavaScript and CSS   Web application developers may not have given a lot of thought to how code organization affects performance of Web applications. In many cases, developers choose to separate JavaScript code from CSS for maintainability. While this practice generally makes sense for code organization, it actually hurts performance because it increases the number of HTTP requests required to retrieve the page. In other cases, the location of script and CSS within the structure of the HTML page can have a negative effect on gradual or progressive page rendering and download parallelization.

It is important for Web application developers to understand how these simple choices can affect their Web application's performance, so they can take the appropriate mitigation steps when designing their applications. Let's review an example of how to analyze Web page performance and begin discussing mitigation strategies for the common problems we have been discussing thus far.

Analyzing Application Performance

The key to a fast Web application is to understand the application's behavior from the user's perspective. Naturally, this requires a combination of analysis tools and an investment of time to evaluate the resultant data from the analysis tools. Analyzing Web applications is far from a simple task. Developers must evaluate many facets of the application's behavior, including but not limited to such items as the network traffic, the sequence of events that occurs during a page load, and the different rendering behaviors caused by client-side technologies like JavaScript and CSS. Unfortunately, Microsoft does not offer an end-to-end toolset that works in conjunction with Visual Studio to allow for a holistic analysis of Web application performance. There is, however, a collection of stand-alone tools available, both from Microsoft as well as other vendors, for conducting such an analysis, many of which we will discuss in this chapter.

As we discussed earlier in this chapter, when Web application pages are requested, the browser governs the flow of content from the server to the user and performs rendering based on several different factors. Much of the downloading of content is serial, meaning that, while the browser is retrieving a piece of content, it is delaying the retrieval of other content. To understand this and other interactions between the browser and the server, application developers should familiarize themselves with the diversity of tools that are available for analyzing these interactions. There are several tools that are freely available and very effective at analyzing certain parts of the browser and server interaction, including but not limited to Fiddler, Network Monitor, Visual Round Trip Analyzer, HTTPWatch, Firebug, and Y!Slow. The following information represents an overview of these products. A more detailed review of these tools is beyond the scope of this chapter.

Fiddler This is one of the most widely used tools among Web application developers at Microsoft. Fiddler is a freely available HTTP debugging proxy application that captures all HTTP information between the client browser and the server and allows application developers to inspect and manipulate incoming and outgoing data. This tool was not designed strictly for performance analysis but rather for the broader purpose of enabling detailed inspection of the Web application's HTTP traffic. However, it is quite useful for performance analysis and understanding the detailed HTTP interactions between the browser and the server. This enables developers to gain insight into HTTP transaction details like the number of requests for a given page load, header values, and many other page load characteristics. Most Web application developers would be pleasantly surprised by the power of this tool and are encouraged to spend some time playing with it.

Network Monitor This application has been available from Microsoft for several years and is primarily a protocol analyzer, or packet sniffer. It allows application developers to inspect network traffic at a very low level and analyze application behavior at essentially the packet level. Network Monitor is a great tool for conducting network-level analysis, but it is rather complex to understand and requires knowledge of networking, packet sniffing, and related technologies. It is not the tool you would use all that frequently, but it does provide a depth of information that other tools do not.

Visual Round Trip Analyzer   As a complement to Network Monitor, Microsoft recently released a tool for analyzing page performance and behavior over the network called Visual Round Trip Analyzer (VRTA). Although previously available as an internal Microsoft tool, VRTA is a solid (and free) addition to the commercially available set of performance analysis tools. VRTA works in conjunction with Network Monitor to capture the HTTP traffic between the client and the server, and it renders an informative, graphical representation of the transaction. This analysis includes information about the number, type, and download pattern of all file types in the transaction as well as their respective sizes. It further provides information about how well the page was leveraging the available bandwidth, as well as recommendations for where improvements can be made to the page. Generally speaking, this tool builds on top of the powerful things already being done by Network Monitor but distills the output in a way that presents actionable results for application developers.

HTTPWatch   Similar to Fiddler, HTTPWatch from Simtec Limited captures all HTTP traffic between the client browser and the server and provides a useful interface for analyzing the captured information. Unlike Fiddler, HTTPWatch provides a more powerful graphical representation of the page rendering behavior. This allows an application developer to easily acquire a deep understanding of the interaction between the browser and the server by simply exploring each step of the page rendering process. Figure 4-2 (shown later in this chapter) illustrates an analysis of Microsoft's Live Search home page.

In addition to those just described, there are other tools that are also helpful for developers when analyzing Web page performance. Those include the freely available Firebug, which is an add-on for the Firefox Web browser; the developer toolbar for Internet Explorer, which helps with page troubleshooting and debugging; and Y!Slow, which is a tool built by the performance team at Yahoo!. Each of these tools shares functionality similar to the tools mentioned above and will likely complement any Web application developer's analysis toolset. Application developers are encouraged to investigate each of the tools discussed and to choose the tool or tools that best help to augment their analysis efforts. A list of these tools and their respective Web sites has been provided in Appendix B of this book.

Analyzing the Performance of Live Search

To further illustrate how developers can analyze their Web applications using the tools mentioned previously, we will review Microsoft's Live Search application. Using HTTPWatch, which runs as an Internet Explorer add on, we clear the browsers cache and use the recording functionality to capture the results of a main page load from *http://www.live.com*. HTTPWatch generates the analysis shown in Figure 4-2.

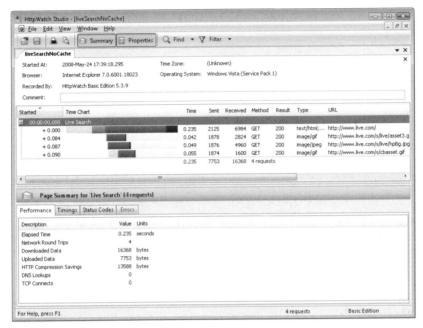

FIGURE 4-2 HTTPWatch analysis of *http://www.live.com* without browser caching.

In the lower window, under the performance tab, HTTPWatch generates some statistics about the page load. Metrics such as the elapsed time, number of network round trips, size of the downloaded data, and the HTTP compression efficiency provide some indication about how this page is performing. Note that some of the features in this window may not be available in the Basic Edition of HTTPWatch, which is available for free. Specifically, we note the following to be true.

- The elapsed page load time is 0.235 seconds.

- The total number of network round trips was four.

- The amount of data downloaded was 16.3 kilobytes (KB), which includes all relevant content, JavaScript, CSS, and image assets.

- The amount of data uploaded was 7.7 KB, which includes the transmission of cookies and request header values.

- HTTP compression saved 13.5 KB from being transferred to the client, which is an approximate 45 percent reduction.

- DNS was served from a local machine cache, which saved remote DNS lookups.

- TCP connects indicate that Keep-Alives are enabled on the Web servers.

This data helps us to understand what is happening between the browser and the server quite well. However, to better understand what the user is experiencing, we need to observe the interaction between the server and the browser through the illustration in the upper window. This Gantt chart–style illustration depicts the behavior of the application from the initial server request to the end of the page load, where each bar represents an instance of an HTTP request for a particular application asset or assets, like HTML, images, or JavaScript. Notice that the first bar shows how much time elapsed before the main content of the page was retrieved, and the subsequent bars show the point at which certain image assets are being rendered. In this case, the end point of the first bar indicates when the user actually sees the content get rendered, which is 0.235 seconds after the request was issued. As previously noted, the total page content was delivered to the browser in 0.235 seconds, which consisted of four total network round trips.

Based on the brief analysis of this data, we can conclude that this is an example of a page that is well optimized for performance. This is evident from the low number of HTTP requests, the size of the data being downloaded, and the use of several other best practices, all of which we will discuss later in this chapter. As an experiment, download a free copy of HTTPWatch and use it yourself against a few of your favorite pages. You may be surprised by what you find. Although the capabilities of the free version of HTTPWatch will be limited, you will quickly obtain a visual representation of your page performance.

Although this was a simple example, it does provide interesting data points that help depict the page load characteristics of the Live Search Web application. Tools like HTTPWatch and Fiddler provide developers the ability to evaluate the detailed HTTP information being transferred between the server and the browser, so each page load behavior can be better understood, and performance problems can be prevented. When combined with packet sniffing tools like Network Monitor, developers can quickly gain insight into the end-to-end page load characteristics from the network layer to the Web browser. In general, this toolset will allow Web application developers to get a better understanding for what their users are experiencing, so that performance issues or bottlenecks can be avoided before the application is released.

Tactics for Improving Web Application Performance

Earlier in this chapter, we discussed several of the architectural challenges that face developers when building high-performance Web applications. Many of these challenges stem from the basic interaction model between Web browsers and Web servers. They include such issues as network latency and the quality of the connection, payload size and round trips between client and server, as well as the way code is written and organized. These issues generally transcend multiple development platforms and affect every Web application developer, whether they are developing ASP.NET and managed code Web applications or using an alternative technology like PHP or Java. It is important for developers to understand these issues and incorporate performance considerations in their application designs. Performance bugs that are discovered late in the release cycle can create significant code churn and add risk to delivering a stable and high-quality application.

There are several best practices for improving the performance of a Web application, which have been categorized into four basic principles below. These principles are intended to help organize very specific, tactical best practices into simple, high-level concepts. They include the following:

- **Reduce payload size**   Application developers should optimize Web applications to ensure the smallest possible data transfer footprint on the network.

- **Cache effectively**   Performance can be improved when application developers reduce the number of HTTP requests required for the application to function by caching content effectively.

- **Optimize network traffic**   Application developers should ensure that their application uses the bandwidth as efficiently as possible by optimizing the interactions between the Web browser and the server.

- **Organize and write code for better performance**   It is important to organize Web application code in a way that improves gradual or progressive page rendering and ensures reductions in HTTP requests.

Let us review each of these principles thematically and discuss more specific, tactical examples for applying performance best practices to several facets of your Web application.

Reduce Payload Size

As reviewed earlier in this chapter, one of the primary challenges to delivering high-performance Web applications is the bandwidth and network latency between the client and the server. Both will vary between users and most certainly vary by locale. To ensure that users of your Web application have an optimal browsing experience, application developers should optimize each page to create the smallest possible footprint on the network between the Web server and the user's browser. There are a number of best practices that developers can leverage to accomplish this. Let us review each of these in greater detail.

Reduce total bytes by using HTTP compression   Web servers like IIS, Apache, and others offer the ability to compress both static and dynamic content using standard compression methods like gzip and deflate. This practice ensures that static content (JavaScript files, CSS, and HTML files) and dynamic content (ASP and ASPX files) are compressed by the Web server prior to being delivered to the client browser. Once delivered to the client, the browser will decompress the files and leverage their contents from the local cache. This ensures that the size of the data in transit is as small as possible, which contributes to a faster retrieval experience and an improved browsing experience for the user overall. In the example illustrated in

Figure 4-2, compression reduced the payload size by 13.5 KB, or by approximately 45 percent, which is a modest reduction.

Minify JavaScript and CSS   Minification is the practice of evaluating code like JavaScript and CSS and reducing its size by removing unnecessary characters, white space, and comments. This ensures that the size of the code being transferred between the Web server and the client is as small as possible, thus improving the performance of the page load time. There are several minifier utility programs available on the Internet today such as YUI Compressor for CSS or JSMin for JavaScript, and many teams at Microsoft, for instance, share a common minifier utility program for condensing JavaScript and CSS. This practice is very effective at reducing JavaScript and CSS file sizes, but it often renders the JavaScript and CSS unreadable from a debugging perspective. Application developers should not incorporate a minification process into debug builds but rather into application builds that are to be deployed to performance testing environments or live production servers.

Re-palletize images   Another way to reduce the payload size of a Web page is to reduce the size of the images that are being transmitted for use within the page. When coupled with the use of CSS Sprites, which will be discussed later in this chapter, this technique can further optimize the transmission of data between the Web server and the user's computer. Adobe published a whitepaper[1] that provides insight into how reducing the color palette in iconography and static images can have a dramatic savings on the size of an image. By simply reducing the color palette in an image from 32 bit to 16 bit to 8 bit colors, it is possible to reduce the image size by upwards of 40 percent without degrading the quality of the image. This can produce dramatic results when extrapolated out to hundreds of thousands of requests for the same image.

Cache Effectively

As we have seen, Web application performance is improved significantly by incorporating various strategies for reducing the payload size over the network. In addition to shrinking the footprint of the data over the wire, application developers can also leverage page caching strategies that will help reduce the number of HTTP requests sent between the server and the client. Incorporating caching within your application will ensure that the browser does not unnecessarily retrieve data that is locally cached, thereby reducing the amount of data being transferred and the number of required HTTP requests.

Set expiration dates   A Web server uses several HTTP headers to inform the requesting client that it can leverage the copy of the resource it has in its local cache. For example, if certain cache headers are returned for a specific image or script on the page, then the browser will not request the image or script again until that content is deemed stale. There are several examples of these HTTP headers, including *Expires, Cache-Control,* and *ETag.* By

---

[1]   *http://www.adobe.com/uk/education/pdf/cib/ps7_cib/ps7_cib14.pdf*

leveraging these headers effectively, application developers can ensure that HTTP requests sent between the server and the client will be reduced as the resource remains cached. It is important for developers to set this value to a date that is far enough in the future that expiration is unlikely. Let's consider a simple example.

```
Expires: Fri, 14 May 2010 14:00 GMT
```

Note The preceding code is an example of setting an *Expires* header on a specific page resource like a JavaScript file. This header tells the browser that it can use the current copy of the resource until the specified time. Note the specified time is far in the future to ensure that subsequent requests for this resource are avoided for the foreseeable future. Although this is a simple method for reducing the number of HTTP requests through caching, it does require that all page resources, like JavaScript, CSS, or image files, incorporate some form of a versioning scheme to allow for future updates to the site. Without versioning, browsers and proxies will not be able to acquire new versions of the resource until the expiration date passes. To address this, developers can append a version number to the file name of the resource to ensure that resources can be revised in future versions of the application. This is just one example of ways to apply caching to your application's page resources. As mentioned, leveraging *Cache-Control* or *ETag* headers can also help achieve similar results.

Note Each of these HTTP headers requires in-depth knowledge of correct usage patterns. I recommend reading *High Performance Web Sites* (O'Reilly, 2007), by Steve Souders, or *Caching Tutorial for Web Authors and Web Masters*, by Mark Nottingham[2] before incorporating them in your application.

Optimize Network Traffic

The network on which application data is being transferred between the server and the Web browser is one element within the end-to-end Web application pipeline that developers have the least control over, in terms of architecture or implementation. As developers, we must trust that network engineers have done their best to implement the fastest and most efficient networks so that the data we transmit is leveraging the most optimal route between the client and the server. However, the quality of the connection between our Web applications and our users is not always known. Therefore, we need to apply various tactics that both reduce the payload size of the data being transmitted as well as reduce the number of requests being sent and received. Application developers can accomplish this by incorporating the following best practices.

Increase parallel TCP ports If your Web application requires a large number of files to render pages, then increasing the number of parallel TCP ports will allow more page content

---

2 *http://www.mnot.net/cache_docs/*

to be downloaded in parallel. This is a great way to speed up the time it takes to load the pages in your Web application. We discussed earlier how the HTTP/1.1 specification suggests that browsers download only two resources at a time in parallel for a given hostname. Web application developers must utilize additional hostnames within their application to allow the browser to open additional connections for parallel downloading. The simplest way to accomplish this is to organize your static content (e.g., images, videos, etc.) by unique hostname. The following code snippet is a recommendation for how best to accomplish this.

```
<img src="http://images.contoso.com/v1/image1.gif"/>
<embed src="http://video.contoso.com/v1/solidcode.wmv" width="100%"
height="60" align="center"/>
```

By leveraging multiple hostnames, parallel downloading of content by the browser will be encouraged. Figure 4-1, shown previously, illustrated how page content is downloaded when a single hostname is used. Figure 4-3 contrasts that by illustrating how the addition of multiple hostnames affects the downloading of content.

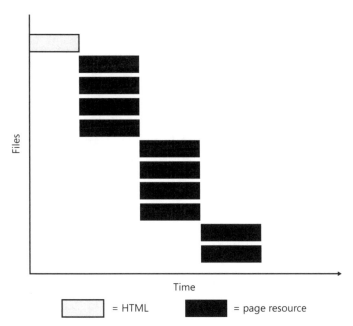

FIGURE 4-3 Theoretical example of resources downloading in parallel for multiple hostnames.

Enable Keep-Alives Keep-Alives is the way in which servers and Web browsers use TCP sockets more efficiently when communicating with one another. This was brought about to address an inefficiency with HTTP/1.0 whereby each HTTP request required a new TCP socket connection. Keep-Alives let Web browsers make multiple HTTP requests over a single connection, which increases the efficiency of the network traffic between the browser and

the server by reducing the number of connections being opened and closed. This is accomplished by leveraging the *Connection* header that is passed between the server and the
browser. The following example is an HTTP response header, which illustrates how Keep-
Alives are enabled for Microsoft's Live Search service.

```
HTTP/1.1 200 OK
Content-Type: text/html; charset=utf-8
X-Powered-By: ASP.NET
P3P: CP="NON UNI COM NAV STA LOC CURa DEVa PSAa PSDa OUR IND",
policyref="http://privacy.msn.com/w3c/p3p.xml"
Vary: Accept-Encoding
Content-Encoding: gzip
Cache-Control: private, max-age=0
Date: Tue, 30 Sep 2008 04:30:19 GMT
Content-Length: 8152
Connection: keep-alive
```

In this example, we notice a set of HTTP headers and their respective values were returned.
This header indicates that an HTTP 200 response was received by the browser from the request to the host Uniform Resource Identifier (URI), which is *www.live.com*. In addition to
other interesting information, such as the content encoding or content length, we also notice
there is an explicit header called *Connection*, which indicates that Keep-Alives are enabled on
the server.

Reduce DNS lookups   Previously, we discussed how DNS lookups are the result of the Web
browser being unable to locate the IP address for a given hostname in either its cache or the
operating system's cache. These lookups require calls to Internet-based DNS servers and can
take up to 120 ms to complete. This can adversely affect the performance of a Web page if
there are a large number of unique hostnames found in any of the JavaScript, CSS, or inline
code required to render that page. Reducing DNS lookups can improve the response time of
a page, but it must be done judiciously as it can also have a negative effect on parallel downloading of content. As a general guideline, it is not recommended to utilize more than four
to six unique hostnames within your Web application. This compromise will maintain a small
number of DNS lookups while still leveraging the benefits of increased parallel downloading. Furthermore, if your application does not contain a large number of assets, it is generally
better to leverage a single hostname.

Avoid redirects   Web page redirects are used to route a user from one URL to another.
While redirects are often necessary, they delay the start of the page load until the redirect
is complete. In some cases, this could be acceptable performance degradation, but overuse could cause undesirable effects on the user experience. Generally, redirects should be
avoided if possible, but understandably they are useful in circumstances where application
developers need to support legacy URLs or certain vanity URLs used to make remembering
a page's location fairly easy. In the sample redirect below, we see how the Live Search team
at Microsoft redirects the URL *http://search.live.com* to *http://www.live.com*. On my computer,

this redirect added an additional 0.210 seconds to the total page load time, as measured with HTTPWatch.

```
HTTP/1.1 302 Moved Temporarily
Content-Length: 0
Location: http://www.live.com/?searchonly=true&mkt=en-US
```

In this example, we notice that the HTTP response code is a 302, which indicates that the requested URI has moved temporarily to another location. The new location is specified in the *Location* header, which informs the browser where to direct the user's request. The browser will then automatically redirect the user to the new location.

Leverage a Content Delivery Network   Earlier in this chapter, we discussed how incorporating caching in Web applications can reduce the number of HTTP requests. In addition to caching, leveraging the services of a Content Delivery Network (CDN) provides a complementary solution that also improves the speed at which static content is delivered to your users. CDNs like those offered by Akamai Technologies or Limelight Networks allow application developers to host static content, such as JavaScript, CSS, or Flash objects on globally distributed servers. Users who request this content required by a particular Web page are dynamically routed to the content that is closest to the originating request. This not only increases the speed of content delivery, but it also offers a level of redundancy for the data being served. Although there can be a high cost associated with implementing a CDN solution, the results are far and away worthwhile for Web applications that typically use a large volume of static content and require global reach.

Incorporate CSS Sprites   CSS Sprites group several smaller images into one composite image and display them using CSS background positioning. This technique is recommended for improving Web application performance, as it promotes a more effective use of bandwidth when compared with downloading several smaller images independently during a page load. This practice is very effective because it leverages the sliding windows algorithms used by TCP. Sliding windows algorithms are used by TCP as a way to control the flow of packets between computers on the Internet. Generally, TCP requires that all transmitted data be acknowledged by the computer that is receiving the data from the initiating computer. Sliding window algorithms are methods that enable multiple packets of data to be acknowledged with a single acknowledgement instead of multiple. Therefore, sliding windows will work better for transmission of fewer, larger files rather than several smaller ones. This means that application developers who build Web applications that require a number of small files like iconography, or other small static artwork, should cluster images together and display those using CSS Sprites. Let us explore an example of how CSS Sprites are utilized.

Consider the following code snippet from Microsoft's Live Search site in conjunction with Figure 4-4. Notice that Figure 4-4 is a collection of four small icon files that have been combined into a single vertical strip of images. The code below loads the single file of three images known as *asset4.gif* and uses CSS positioning to display them as what appears to be singular images. This methodology ensures that only one HTTP request is made for the single image file, instead of four. Although this is a method of rendering images that is very different from what most Web developers have been taught, it promotes a much better performing experience than traditional image rendering. Therefore, this practice is recommended for Web applications that require several small, single images.

```
<style type="text/css">
input.sw_qbtn
{
background-color: #549C00;
background-image: url(/s/live/asset4.gif);
background-position: 0 -64px;
background-repeat: no-repeat;
border: none;
cursor: pointer;
height: 24px;
margin: .14em;
margin-right: .2em;
vertical-align: middle;
width: 24px; padding-top:24px;line-height:500%
}
</style>
```

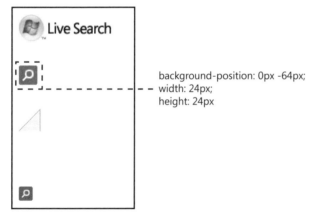

background-position: 0px -64px;
width: 24px;
height: 24px

FIGURE 4-4 Example of a Live Search CSS Sprite.

Organize and Write Code for Better Performance

Thus far, we have discussed some examples of architectural and coding best practices for developing high performance Web applications. Let us review a few additional practices related to the organization and writing of application code that will also help improve the performance of your Web application pages.

Make JavaScript and CSS files external   Application developers have two basic options for incorporating JavaScript and CSS in their Web applications. They can choose to separate the scripts into external files or add the script inline within the page markup. Generally, in terms of pure speed, inserting JavaScript and CSS inline is faster in terms of page load rendering, but there are other factors that make this the incorrect choice. By making JavaScript and CSS external, application users will benefit from the inherent caching of these files within the Web browser, so subsequent requests for the application will be faster. However, the downside to this approach is that the user incurs the additional HTTP requests for fetching the file or files. Clearly there are tradeoffs to making scripts external for initial page loads, but in the long run where users are continuously returning to your application, making scripts external is a much better solution than inserting script inline within the page.

Ensure CSS are in the top of the page   Progressively rendering a Web page is an important visual progress indicator for users of your Web application, especially on slower connections. Ideally, we want the browser to display the page content as quickly as it is received from the server. Unfortunately, some browsers will prohibit progressive rendering of the page if Style Sheets are placed near the bottom of the document. They do this to avoid redrawing elements of the page if their respective styles change. Application developers should always reference the required CSS files within the *HEAD* section of the HTML document so that the browser knows how to properly display the content and can do so gradually. If CSS files are present outside the *HEAD* section of the HTML document, then the browser will block progressive rendering until it finds the necessary styles. This produces a more poorly performing Web browsing experience.

Place JavaScript at the bottom of the page   When Web browsers load JavaScript files, they block additional downloading of other content, including any content being downloaded on parallel TCP ports. The browser behaves in this manner to ensure that the scripts being downloaded execute in the proper order and do not need to alter the page through *document.write* operations. While this makes perfect sense from a page processing perspective, it does little to help the performance of the page load. Therefore, application developers should defer the loading of any JavaScript until the end of the page, which will ensure that the application users get the benefit of progressive page loading.

Note It is worth mentioning that the release of Internet Explorer 8.0 addresses this problem. However, application developers should be cognizant of the browser types that are being utilized to use their application and design accordingly.

Throughout this chapter, we have discussed a variety of common challenges and circumstances that lead to poorly performing Web applications. We have also seen how, with each challenge, there is a corresponding mitigation strategy or technique for ensuring that Web application pages perform well. While these techniques and strategies provide a tactical means to improve the performance of your Web applications, performance best practices must also be incorporated into day-to-day engineering processes and procedures. The key to implementing engineering best practices, such as those associated with performance, is to ensure that they are properly complemented by a sound set of engineering processes that incorporate them into the normal rhythm of software development. Let's review how best to accomplish this.

Incorporating Performance Best Practices

Driving performance best practices within day-to-day engineering processes helps to ensure that overall quality remains a top priority across application development teams within the organization. To do so effectively, organizations should establish a performance excellence program that aligns the goal of releasing high-performance applications with the objectives of the business that is driving the software creation. This practice helps to ensure that application performance goals are properly prioritized and aligned with the goals of the software application from the business perspective.

Establish a Performance Excellence Program

The key goal of any performance excellence program is to drive best practices into engineering processes so that software developers remain focused on building high performance Web applications. This can be accomplished by establishing a simple process that should consider the business drivers of the software application, wrap specific metrics around application performance, and drive results through the implementation of best practices. This process can be broken down into these five steps.

Establish usage scenarios and priorities   This practice will help to prioritize the scenarios that are important to the success of a particular Web application. The goal of this step is to determine the most important usage scenarios for a particular application so that performance improvement efforts are prioritized appropriately. Application developers are likely to rely on program managers or business partners to help identify and prioritize the specific usage scenarios. Customer feedback will also provide valuable insight into scenario prioritization.

Analyze competition   To understand how to set adequate performance goals for the previously established usage scenarios, application developers must also understand the performance of competitive applications for similar scenarios. This not only helps to establish a baseline understanding of what users may expect from your application's performance, but it also helps to learn how your competition measures up. The simplest way to accomplish this is to utilize the tools we discussed earlier in this chapter.

Set performance goals   Once the scenarios and competition are well understood, the next step is to establish goals that will help guide your engineering efforts. These goals can be as simple or as complex as you choose, but it is recommended that goals be aligned with some of the key metrics we have discussed in this chapter, including but not limited to total byte size of the page, time to load, number of files downloaded, and number of HTTP requests.

Implement best practices   To achieve the goals that were previously established, application developers should minimally ensure that the aforementioned best practices have been implemented where applicable. The specific practices applied will very likely vary by application as not all recommendations will be applicable. The application development project team should determine which best practices are likely to provide the greatest benefit to their application and incorporate them. This chapter has provided clear guidance on how to accomplish this.

Measure and test   After goals are established and best practices are implemented, the key is to continuously measure and test your Web applications to ensure that they are both adhering to performance best practices and are meeting the previously established performance goals of the software. This is perhaps one of the most important steps in the process because it focuses on ensuring that the quality of the application performance remains high. Organizations should focus on continuous performance testing in the same vain that they focus on testing other aspects of application quality. While performance bugs may not be as evident as other bugs, they have an equally negative impact on users and should be avoided prior to releasing the application.

Once established, a performance excellence program will ensure that proper focus is always given to this engineering tenet during the application development life cycle. This should be accomplished by establishing a process that considers the business drivers of the software application, incorporates specific metrics around application performance, and drives results through the implementation of best practices and continuous testing. In the next section, we will explore how Microsoft's Live Search team leverages some of the aforementioned processes and practices and ensures continued excellence in the performance of its products.

Inside Microsoft: Tackling Live Search Performance

Live Search is a Web-based search engine launched by Microsoft in September of 2006. The application offers users the ability to search a variety of different types of information, including but not limited to Web sites, news, images, videos, music, and maps. The team recognizes that, to be competitive in the search market, a well-performing product is a necessity to winning with users who have come to expect near immediate results from the competition. This passion and commitment is evident in the way the team approaches the performance of the application; however, this was not always the case.

Shortly after Live Search launched in 2006, the team realized that its performance was suboptimal. Although team members had spent a lot of time testing the application, they did not adequately test the page rendering performance and subsequently released a product that did not perform as well as they would have liked. Fortunately, these issues were quickly recognized, and the team began making changes to improve the performance of the site.

The team realized that several of the application's performance issues were related to user interface and architectural design decisions whose implications were not fully understood. The application's design was promptly re-evaluated, and the team moved to implement many of the best practices mentioned in this chapter, including specific practices like combining scripts and redesigning the page to reduce the size and number of images. The results of the team's efforts included an equally attractive but improved page loading experience for the users, as well as a newly discovered dedication to performance for the team. Eventually, the Live Search team became one of the most performance-focused Web application teams within Microsoft, and its focus is evident in the way it incorporates performance best practices into its end-to-end application development process.

Web Performance Principles

The Live Search engineering team has developed a great deal of experience over the years in the delivery of high performance Web applications to a global audience. As a team, it recognizes the depth and complexity of the engineering challenges it faces and has spent many release cycles perfecting its practices. The team adheres to a set of guiding principles that govern how it considers performance when delivering its software application to market. These principles include:

Set performance budgets for key scenarios   The team believes strongly in setting budgets for certain page load characteristics like the number of get requests, the time to load the page, or the total byte size of the page. These goals help to drive rigorous application design practices or feature tradeoffs to ensure that pages that enable key usage scenarios continue to perform well. Oftentimes these budgets require very creative design tradeoffs that could change the way a specific feature is developed. The team believes, though, that this principle is the first line of defense against developing poorly performing Web application pages.

Continuously analyze and test application performance   In conjunction with setting goals and budgets for page load characteristics, the team also believes strongly in running performance test cases before features are checked into the source library and after features are complete. While this practice does not necessarily prevent features from being checked in that exhaust the budget, it does introduce a certain rigor into the development process that provides early insight into poorly performing code changes. Additionally, this practice also ensures that performance bugs are being logged early and often so that developers have time to address the issues with the code before the application is released.

Experiment and understand user behavior   Experimentation, or A/B testing, is a more advanced approach to understanding user behavior on Web sites. It generally requires a mechanism that allows certain features or application changes to be released to a small subset of users so that behavior can be observed through instrumentation and used to drive feature decisions. The Live Search team has leveraged this methodology to increase its understanding of how performance affects user behavior. The team subsequently incorporates the knowledge gained from these experiments back into the features of the application. The team has used this approach to learn the impact of page size, load times, and even the number of search results displayed to the user. While this requires an investment in a mechanism to enable this type of testing, the results are clearly valuable to product development and improvement.

Understand usage patterns and optimize performance accordingly   The team has learned that, if it can anticipate user behaviors, it can improve the performance of the pages that the user subsequently visits. The team accomplishes this by preemptively downloading scripts asynchronously prior to a user actually visiting the page that requires those scripts. For example, if usage data indicates that a user who wishes to search for images will generally want to preview those images before clicking on them, then the application is built to proactively download the scripts required to render the image preview, before the user even gets to that page. This approach does not interfere with the use of the initial page, and it speeds up the loading of the subsequent page, which is beneficial to the user. Although not listed as a best practice, this approach clearly demonstrates a certain creativity and level of dedication to ensuring application performance is maximized for the user.

Key Success Factors

Since becoming keenly focused on application performance, the Live Search team has found the above-mentioned set of principles to have had a very positive impact on the quality of the code and the overall application performance. These principles collectively have helped the team to incorporate performance excellence into its engineering processes and continuously innovate on its services while still achieving a high level of quality and performance. Although the team continues to learn about the usage of its application and how best to optimize performance for its key usage scenarios, it has found the following lessons and practices have yielded the best results.

Understand end-user perceived performance   The Live Search team has learned that poor end-user perceived performance has little to do with server latency or server health but rather the number of get requests, the number of serialized get requests, and the way in which the user receives the page. Therefore, the team spends a lot of time and energy optimizing the way in which it delivers the pages to the users and less time worrying about how quickly the server is processing the page request.

Incorporating performance test tools   As previously mentioned, the team has incorporated performance analysis and testing into several different places within the engineering process. To enable that testing, the team built a number of custom test tools that leverage applications like Network Monitor, Fiddler, HTTPWatch, Firebug, and others to monitor certain page load characteristics in its development and production environments. These tools continuously evaluate the application and ensure that bugs get logged when issues are discovered and appropriately assigned to developers to address.

Learn and live the best practices   The team strongly believes that application developers should learn and incorporate the performance best practices whenever possible. More specifically, the team believes that the most impactful changes that can be made to any Web application include making fewer requests, consolidating scripts, reducing image sizes, using CSS Sprites, enabling HTTP compression, and incorporating edge caching using a CDN.

The Live Search team clearly believes strongly in the importance of incorporating performance excellence and best practices into its engineering processes. This is evident from both the way the team governs its engineering processes with respect to performance as well as the way the application performs in the production environment. The team continues to raise the bar with respect to Web application performance best practices among all Web-focused teams within Microsoft.

Summary

As we have discussed in this chapter, performance is a critically important aspect of any application and represents yet another facet of the overall quality of software applications. Developers must understand common Web performance problems, their respective mitigation strategies, and the importance of establishing and maintaining a performance excellence program within their day-to-day software engineering processes. Incorporating these processes and best practices into the application development life cycle will definitely yield higher quality, better performing user experiences for any Web-based software application.

Key Points

- Understand common Web performance challenges.

- Analyze and evaluate your application's performance.

- Apply the key Web performance best practices.

- Establish a performance excellence program within your organization.

    - Analyze the performance of your competition.

    - Set performance goals.

    - Implement performance best practices during application or feature design.

    - Continuously analyze, test, and improve performance.

Chapter 5
Designing for Scale

A rock pile ceases to be a rock pile the moment a single man contemplates it,
bearing within him the image of a cathedral.

—*Antoine de Saint-Exupery*

As application developers, we hope that the software we painstakingly design, code, test, and deploy will be used and loved by many people. As the quote suggests, it is our vision and desire for great software that drives us to build successful applications from mere ones and zeros. We often measure the success of these applications with criteria such as user satisfaction or bug count. Part of our software's success criteria can also be measured by the number of people who use it. When we design these applications, we must ensure that our end-to-end architecture will always support the needs of our users, even as the adoption and usage of the application grows. This is especially true for Web applications, which require specific design considerations to scale properly.

Designing Web applications for small audiences can be quite easy to accomplish, given the plethora of great tools and resources available to application developers. However, designing applications that scale to meet the needs of large numbers of users is quite challenging. Certain techniques that work well for applications that support small audiences can become problematic as the application's usage begins to grow. For example, a Web application that performs very well for 10,000 concurrent users may produce a reasonably good user experience when growth doubles to 20,000 users. However, the same application may become unusable when growth again doubles, thus requiring additional hardware resources or code changes to ensure a consistent user experience as growth continues to trend upward. Quality and design issues that are the result of an application's inability to scale properly are extremely costly to find and fix, and they may actually encourage users to switch to a competitor whose application properly scales.

As software has evolved beyond the desktop to a server-based delivery model, application scalability has become a critical element to high-quality software designs. Due to the nature of server-based applications, scale factors such as hardware infrastructure design, load balancing, deployment, and application manageability have a direct influence on both the application design and the cost associated with scaling to meet user demands. Scale factors should always be considered as part of the application design in order to prevent quality issues in real-world production scenarios.

Understanding Application Scalability

Scaling and scalability are terms used to describe a Web application's ability to handle increased usage or load from a growing demand for application resources. An application is considered "scalable" when it has the capability to increase total throughput under an increased load after additional hardware is added to the application's hardware infrastructure. By contrast, applications whose designs fail as usage demand increases, despite the availability or addition of hardware resources, are not considered scalable. While this is a sufficient and general definition of scalability, it does not completely represent the characteristics of an application that is truly scalable. Let us examine some more specific characteristics of a scalable Web application.

- **Scalable applications can handle increased usage or data**   As user demand for Web application features increase, the application should be able to expand to accommodate the additional user load in a linear way. This means that additional hardware infrastructure in the form of servers, data storage, or networking equipment could be added to handle the potential application usage overload. This also implies that users of the application should experience a consistency in the overall performance and behavior of the application regardless of load.

- **Scalable applications are always available and fault tolerant**   Application scalability goes beyond just being able to apply hardware to address growth and consumption. Applications must always be available to their users to remain successful. Hardware and software problems will arise, application maintenance will be required, and users should not be affected by either scenario. Designing redundancy and fault tolerance into Web applications and deployment topologies ensures that both applications and infrastructure are resilient to everyday occurrences like disk failures or subsystem dependency outages.

- **Scalable applications are manageable and maintainable**   As applications scale to meet user demand, hardware must be added to accommodate demand. An expanded hardware and software deployment footprint adds maintenance and manageability complexity that can lead to quality of service issues with the application. It is critically important that application developers design software that can be easily configured, deployed, and monitored once released.

An application that is designed to be scalable should possess the characteristics described above. When applied, they ensure that application growth can be a linear progression that is not encumbered by application design or operational issues. These characteristics should not be confused with other features of the application such as the overall performance or the choice of technology. The performance of an application is measured in terms of raw speed and does not indicate the application's ability to accommodate additional demand. In fact, as previously mentioned, application performance should be consistent under a broad spectrum of usage load. Additionally, application scalability is not a problem that can be solved by a particular technology like .NET, PHP, or Java, but rather through development best practices. Web applications built in any language can be designed to scale provided they possess the characteristics described above.

Now that we have discussed a few characteristics of a scalable application, let us consider an example that illustrates the importance of ensuring that application designs meet scale requirements. Consider a Web application that is positioned to deliver social networking features to high school and college students (not an uncommon product these days). If this application's usage is projected to be around 20 million page views per day, then the application architecture needs to support an average of about 230 page requests per second. (For simplicity, let's assume an even distribution of load. In reality, application development teams need to plan for traffic peaks and even spikes depending on the scenario.) Additionally, suppose this application is going to store user data in a relational or structured data store. If each page reads the database two times, then the application data store needs to scale to accommodate approximately 460 queries per second. Let's assume that an average Web or database server would individually not be able to accommodate these usage projections. Therefore, the application design must account for a strategy to support these projections and potentially scale beyond them as the demand requires. Let us explore the basic options for approaching scalability of applications.

Approaches to Scalability

Designing Web applications requires developers to consider all aspects of the end-to-end system design, including the hardware requirements of the application. Scalable application designs allow hardware to be added to the application infrastructure to meet the demand of increased user load. Therefore, application developers should be familiar with the appropriate tactics for scaling applications and incorporate them within their designs. Let us review the most common strategies for scaling applications properly.

There are two basic strategies for scaling an application to expand its hardware capacity. They are sometimes referred to as vertical and horizontal scaling but are more commonly known as scaling up (vertical) and scaling out (horizontal) strategies. Each of these approaches has certain benefits and drawbacks, which include factors such as cost of ownership and administration. In some cases, scaling up may be a better solution for a particular application than scaling out. It is important to understand the characteristics of each approach in order to best inform the end-to-end application design, so that the correct choice for achieving scale can be made.

Scaling Up

The scaling up strategy for increasing an application's hardware capacity is fairly simple. It involves either adding resources to a single machine or moving the application to a larger machine. Under typical circumstances, this could involve adding additional CPUs, memory, or disk to a single machine that is running the application or moving the application to a more powerful machine. As the applications usage grows, so does the need to purchase more resources for a single machine or, simply, a larger machine. This strategy is illustrated in Figure 5-1.

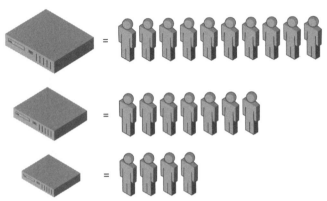

FIGURE 5-1 An example of scaling up by upgrading existing hardware to meet the increased user demand.

The benefit of this approach is that it is perhaps the simplest from a design and implementation perspective. Applications can be designed and deployed to run on a single machine that has the necessary capacity to meet the user demand. As demand increases, the machine will require upgrading to accommodate the increased load. As long as there is hardware available to meet the needs of the application, the model will work effectively. By contrast, however, this model could become very costly as applications require bigger, more expensive hardware to meet their demands. In fact, if the application grows large enough, it may be cost prohibitive to maintain the application as the expense of the "big iron" increases. Additionally, the field of vendors who are building the equipment may also prove to be a limiting factor.

For some applications, scaling up might be the best option if the scope of the applications usage is thought to be small enough to maintain cost effectiveness. However, if application usage is broad and growth is thought to be constant and ever increasing, then scaling out is probably a better strategy in the long run. Let us review the specifics of the scaling out approach.

Scaling Out

The scaling out strategy for increasing an application's hardware capacity is the opposite of the scaling up strategy. Scaling out involves expanding the application's deployment footprint by adding additional machines to help balance the increased user load. Unlike the scale up model that continually requires the addition of more powerful machines, the scale out model requires the addition of one or several servers with identical specifications for components like CPU, memory, and disk. As the application grows, adding capacity to handle the increased demand becomes almost as simple as racking a new server and powering it up. Figure 5-2 illustrates this approach.

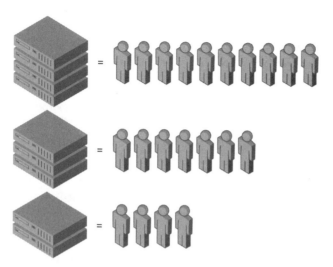

FIGURE 5-2 An example of scaling out with the addition of identical hardware to meet the increased user demand.

There are several benefits to pursuing a scale out strategy over a scale up. Without question, the biggest benefit is the lower cost associated with scaling out versus that of the scale up strategy. This can be achieved by either implementing clusters of high-quality, higher priced, modestly powerful servers or buying larger clusters of less expensive, less powerful, commodity servers. Clusters of commodity servers can be much more cost effective to purchase and operate than a smaller number of more powerful servers. The cost savings for these smaller commodity servers is realized in terms of lower cost of the equipment and the required power consumption. However, choosing commodity hardware over higher quality, higher priced equipment requires an investment in a solid failover solution, because commodity equipment tends to have a higher failure rate. Scaling out with higher priced, higher quality equipment will certainly achieve the core goals of scaling out, while also ensuring better equipment reliability. The best choice will likely vary by application and situation. In comparing the scale up versus scale out models, in certain cases the cost difference between them could be inconsequential. However, for larger-scale application deployments, the scale out model will likely be the more cost-effective choice.

Note Power consumption may sound trivial in this particular explanation, but it should definitely not be underestimated. Companies like Microsoft, Google, and Yahoo! spend considerable time strategizing the expansion of their datacenters into locations that offer the most affordable power. When considering the impact of the power cost to run thousands of machines on the profit margin of a Web service, every kilowatt of power saved contributes to the overall profitability of the service.

In addition to the overall cost effectiveness of the scale out model, there are additional manageability advantages, as well. Given that this model expects our application load to be spread across several servers, it also distributes the risk across those servers. For instance, 1 server out of 20 may fail, and while that represents 5 percent of the traffic, the other 19 servers will balance the load effectively. This provides system administrators the flexibility to investigate a problematic piece of hardware and rebuild or replace it if need be, without affecting the users of the application.

By contrast to the benefits of this model, there are perceived disadvantages to the scale out model, as well. The most common of disadvantages is higher administration costs, or increased resource overhead associated with managing tens, hundreds, or thousands of servers. For large, industry-leading Web applications at Microsoft, these concerns have largely been mitigated by automated administration software that allows the ratio of servers to administrators to be very high. This approach could also be applied to small to mid-sized Web applications, as well, given the availability of application programming interfaces (APIs) for managing all aspects of server administration.

As previously discussed, applications with broad usage and constant, upward growth are good candidates for a scale out approach to addressing capacity needs. In general, the scale out model is much more flexible, cost effective, and lower risk than the scale up strategy. In certain cases, however, application developers may have specific design requirements that will not necessarily scale linearly. An example of this might be an application that needs to aggregate data from all database nodes across all clusters, which would not necessarily scale well using this approach. It is important that these requirements get surfaced early in the design cycle, so that scalability decisions can be addressed long before the application is ready to be deployed.

Database Scalability

Thus far, we have discussed the philosophies of scaling up and scaling out an application's server infrastructure to address increased user load on Web applications. While the afore-mentioned strategies will definitely help to improve the capacity of the servers handling the inbound Web page requests, they do little to help address potential capacity concerns of a database infrastructure. It is a fair assumption that most Web applications today rely heavily on a database management system (DBMS) like Microsoft SQL Server. Therefore, it is criti-cal that application developers, who are designing their applications to scale, consider how to also scale the database infrastructure on which their applications depend. Let us review a common approach to scaling databases.

When considering design options for scaling the database tier of a Web application, the same basic options apply—scale up or scale out. For applications whose scope is fairly lim-ited in terms of the number of users, page views, and database queries or updates, choosing the scale up approach is likely the right choice. However, for applications that expect broad usage, increasing growth, and a large volume of data, then scaling out is the better choice. Scaling databases across several servers is quite a bit more challenging than just buying more powerful equipment and growing the database on a single server or network-connected disk array. Let us review how best to accomplish this.

The most widely accepted method used to scale an application's database infrastructure across multiple servers is data partitioning. This is a process that involves logically and physically dividing the application's data set across multiple servers. Microsoft SQL Server 2008 enables this using a combination of database federation, which transparently integrates several databases into a single federated database, and partitioning. This is accomplished by establishing a group of independent servers that cooperate to process database access requests. The application then interacts with the database through mid-tier routing rules that understand the partitioning scheme and can connect each request with the appropriate member server and partition. Figure 5-3 provides an illustration of how federation, partitioning, and routing are applied to an application that needs to scale its data source.

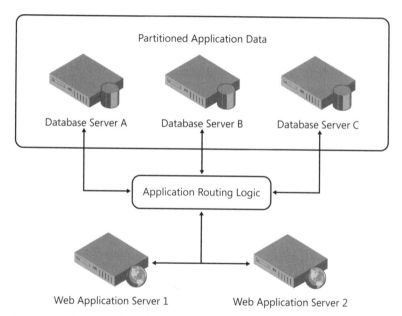

FIGURE 5-3 Conceptual database federation, partitioning, and query routing model.

The strategies previously enumerated are very common approaches to achieving scalable Web application designs, but the detailed requirements for implementation are complex and not to be underestimated. For example, features and capabilities of networking gear can vary by manufacturer, and effectively architecting and configuring hardware infrastructure requires specific expertise in the selected equipment. Scaling services both at the application code tier and data tier can be extremely challenging and requires intense planning and design prior to implementation. The important thing is to address these design considerations up front, rather than after the application is developed. This approach will ensure that your Web application will scale with user demand, and any post-release quality issues related to excessive and unhandled load will be avoided after the application is released. Now that we have reviewed some common scalability strategies that can be applied to your Web application designs, let us review some more specific methods for designing Web applications with scalability in mind.

Tactics for Scaling Web Applications

Earlier in this chapter, we discussed some of the attributes of a Web application that is considered "scalable." Those attributes included the ability to address increased user load or data, the promise of being always available and fault tolerant, and the quality of being operationally manageable and maintainable. These attributes or principles of scalability are serious commitments to a high-quality, robust, and flexible application architecture that users of high availability and broadly used Web applications have come to expect. In this section, we will review specific tactics for ensuring scalable application and infrastructure designs, redundancy, fault tolerance, and operational manageability.

While the recommendations discussed in this chapter do not represent the entire scope of research and development that has gone into this subject, they do provide a good overview of the key areas that developers should consider when designing for scale. There are several best practices for improving the scalability of a Web application, which have been categorized into four basic principles below. These principles are intended to help organize very specific, tactical best practices into simple, high-level concepts. They include choosing scalable application designs, designing application infrastructure to scale effectively, defending against application failure, and ensuring manageability and maintainability of the application. We will review each of these thematically in the following sections.

Note Scalability represents a subject matter that has been explored by many industry leaders. There are a multitude of books, papers, and blog articles about the subject from many seasoned technical people. For a more in-depth perspective on designing scalable Internet applications, I recommend reviewing James Hamilton's paper titled "Designing and Deploying Internet-Scale Services" at *http://mvdirona.com/jrh/talksAndPapers/JamesRH_AmazonDev.pdf*.

Choose Scalable Application Designs

An application's design is perhaps the most critical component to achieving scalability. Without the right design, applications will not scale effectively, and the quality of the application delivery will be poor. Achieving a scalable application design involves making some early decisions about how the application will be constructed, how the application might be deployed from a hardware perspective, and how data will be stored and accessed. Let us review each of these in greater detail.

Design simple application architectures   Application developers should strive to implement simple application architectures. Adding additional complexity within application designs by implementing overly complicated business logic, algorithms, or configurations increases the difficulty of debugging, deploying, and maintaining the application. Developers have a tendency to want to demonstrate their technical prowess with abstract, complex designs that are challenging to manage. Instead, they should consider optimizing their designs to be as simple and scalable as possible, so that the eventual expansion of the application use does not inhibit the application's manageability or maintenance costs.

Design to scale out   As discussed earlier in this chapter, scaling out is a better choice for addressing increased user demand for your application. Compared with scaling up, it is a more cost effective, manageable, flexible, and lower risk solution. This model not only allows us to scale the application easily by simply lighting up additional hardware, it also allows us the flexibility to enable and disable different nodes in the infrastructure to either address problems or perform maintenance without user impact.

Application designs should ensure that the overall structure and architecture of the application will adhere to a scale out strategy. This requires that applications be able to scale linearly across multiple servers. Therefore, application code should be written to accommodate that objective. This can be accomplished by structuring application logic to allow deployment of the application to a single server or multiple servers respectively, without depending on complex interactions between servers of the same role. For example, an application that is running on all Web servers within a cluster or pod should not depend on other servers in that cluster for a particular component or service. This ensures that all servers are equal participants in handling the work load, and any server can be removed or added to the cluster at any time without affecting users of the application.

Ideally, application developers will always be able to build applications that scale linearly. This is, however, not always practical. In some cases, our application designs may require portions of our application to perform tasks, such as aggregating information from multiple application server nodes, which do not scale well linearly. It is important to structure as much of the application code as possible in a way that allows the application to scale linearly. In cases where portions of the application will not scale linearly, it may make sense to isolate that functionality and pursue a scale up model for that portion of the application. For example, if an application has a requirement to aggregate data across multiple database partitions into a data warehouse for reporting, it might make sense to separate the aggregation portion of the application onto a larger, single machine.

Partition data effectively   Scaling out the database tier of an application is perhaps the most complex portion of the application design. As previously mentioned, this requires a combination of federating member databases across multiple servers and partitioning the data in a way that is most effective for the application being developed. Inevitably, most of the effort expended to achieve these goals will be spent designing the partitioning scheme.

This is clearly the most important aspect of successfully scaling application data across machines.

When partitioning databases, application developers should take great care to ensure that partitions are adjustable, granular, and not bound to any specific entity such as the letter of a person's last name or a company name. Inevitably, this will lead to an uneven distribution of data across multiple servers and, therefore, not scale effectively. It is widely recommended to pursue a partitioning scheme that uses a mid-tier lookup service that maps data to an available partition. An example of such a design was illustrated in Figure 5-3. A mid-tier lookup service allows a finer granularity of control over partitioning and the distribution of data, which leads to better management and data scalability control.

Design Application Infrastructure to Scale

We have discussed some specific recommendations for how best to write application code to be scalable, but the key to achieving scalable application architecture is to actually design the hardware infrastructure to support the application. As mentioned, the most common approaches to scaling applications are scaling up and scaling out. Because scaling up involves continuing to add more powerful hardware as demand increases, the hardware infrastructure requirements are much simpler. However, scaling out involves adding servers as load increases, which requires a more complex hardware infrastructure to keep up with the continuous addition of machines. Earlier, we recommended choosing a scale out approach to expand the capacity of your Web application. Hence, the following specific infrastructure recommendations will largely be biased toward that recommendation. Let us review each of these infrastructure recommendations in more detail.

Load balance with hardware   Scaling out a Web application requires a solution for balancing the incoming HTTP traffic across the multiple servers that are managing the load. Typically, requests for a Web application communicate with the primary Uniform Resource Identifier (URI) of the application, such as Contoso.com. Because Contoso.com ultimately translates into an IP address, a solution is required that spreads the incoming requests to Contoso.com across multiple machines that each have a unique IP address. There are several options for accomplishing this. There is software available that could accomplish this requirement, or application developers could use DNS to load balance requests, as well. However, the best possible solution for balancing traffic across multiple servers is to implement a hardware appliance that specializes in distributing HTTP requests across an available pool of servers.

Hardware load balancing is a relatively simple concept to explain but can be tedious to implement. Essentially, load balancing with hardware requires the implementation of a specific network appliance that functions as the gatekeeper for all requests. The appliance is represented by the primary IP address of Contoso.com on the network and returns virtual IP (VIP) addresses of individual servers that it is managing through a routing table whenever

Contoso.com is requested. The pool of servers available to handle traffic is managed through configuration of the load balancer, which is usually equipped with configuration software. Figure 5-4 illustrates how load balancing with hardware is accomplished.

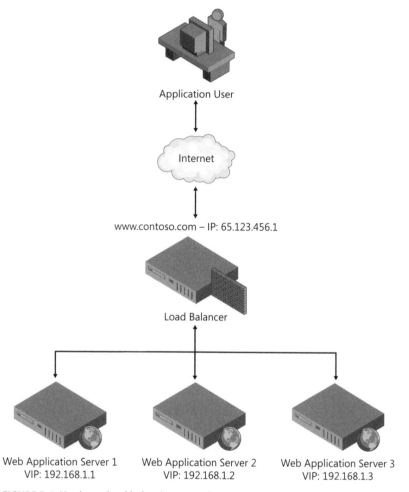

FIGURE 5-4 Hardware load balancing example.

The benefit to load balancing a Web application with a hardware device is primarily manage-ability. Once configured, the device allows management of the server pool dynamically so that servers can be added or removed on the fly. Additionally, when servers fail, traffic is auto-matically routed to a healthy server in the pool, which provides a high degree of resiliency in the application. These are quite obviously important benefits to the overall application archi-tecture and manageability. The downside of load balancing with hardware, however, is the cost associated with the purchase of the device. The equipment tends to be 5 to 10 times the cost of an actual server and, for redundancy, is generally purchased in pairs. While this can be prohibitive from a financial perspective, the benefits far outweigh the drawbacks.

> **Note** There are a variety of load balancers available in the market today, and most ship with additional capabilities like caching, HTTP compression, HTTPS acceleration, and denial of service protection. It is definitely worth doing some homework before purchasing one of these devices. A clear understanding of present and future application architecture requirements will help to identify the appropriate device for your application.

Choose the appropriate hardware   Choosing the right hardware for your Web application can be driven by many factors. If your hardware purchase is in the range of dozens to a few hundred servers, then your decision may largely be driven by the quality of the machine, its useful life, and its ability to be upgraded or repaired. However, if your application (and there are not many) requires hundreds or even thousands of servers, then choosing commodity hardware is probably the way to go.

Some experts in the field of running large-scale Internet facing applications recommend choosing the cheapest, most power conservative servers available. This approach has a positive effect on cost factors like power consumption, but it generally assumes that this type of hardware will fail fairly often, requiring partial or full replacement. While there are some very interesting economics associated with the decision to purchase and run commodity hardware, this often only affects a relatively small number of organizations in the world.

When scaling out a Web application, it is important to choose servers that are small and relatively inexpensive so that adding additional machines is fairly economical. Small servers are generally more cost effective in terms of power consumption, overall price, and maintenance but also perform well enough to handle the needs of most Web applications. Additionally, when clustered together, they individually do not serve a large number of users and therefore will only affect a small number of users if they should fail.

Finally, choosing the right hardware should almost always include choosing the same hardware for all servers of a particular type within the application. Standardizing on equipment not only saves money when bulk purchases are involved, but it also minimizes troubleshooting and maintenance issues.

Use common cluster configurations   When deploying several servers, the more commonality and standardization that exists across the equipment, the more manageable and maintainable the infrastructure becomes. Managing large numbers of servers can be challenging in and of itself without the unnecessary complexities of mismatched software versions and configurations in the infrastructure. It is important that all machines in the infrastructure be properly maintained to minimize the introduction of problems with the application. Ensuring that items like the version of the .NET Framework, machine.config, and security settings are consistent across machines helps to alleviate malfunctioning code or other potential quality issues in the application infrastructure. In many cases, these items can be validated through operational monitoring or probing scripts that periodically profile and validate consistency across machines.

Defend Against Application Failure

In addition to choosing a scalable application design and the appropriate infrastructure, another key principle to developing scalable Web applications is application availability and fault tolerance. All applications will inevitably fail for a variety of different reasons. In some cases, the network may go down, a Web server may crash, an API may not be available, or a database connection may time out. Failures at the component, network, or hardware level are generally unpredictable and even infrequent but never acceptable to users of the applications.

How failures occur within applications is critically important, but even more important is the way by which our applications recover from those failures. Application developers need to make certain that their applications are resilient enough to gracefully handle failures of component-level dependencies or infrastructure and smart enough to catalog the details of the issues for future analysis and understanding. This level of fault tolerance and resiliency ensures that end users only experience what appears to be a healthy and functioning application, rather than obnoxious exception messages or application time-outs. Let us review a few ways that application developers can insulate application functionality from failures.

Ensure that the application is fault tolerant   Adding fault tolerance to your application enables the continued function of the service even when a key component has failed. Generally, this implies that, during a failure of a critical component, the application is able to continue to operate in a degraded mode. A typical example of an application feature that is fault tolerant is that of an order-processing application. In the event that one area of the order processing workflow, which is normally real-time, is unavailable, the application may utilize a work queue for processing additional incoming requests. This allows the application to continue to service user requests, queue the work, and preserve the inbound orders—but with less throughput or responsiveness. Examples such as this demonstrate how fault tolerance is important to business-critical components of an application.

Implementing fault tolerance into components of an application can be a costly endeavor and should be applied to the more mission-critical features of the application. While the value of fault tolerance is obvious, the hidden downside to any implementation is the additional effort required to develop, test, and maintain the code as well as any additional hardware requirements to support fault tolerance for the feature. Clearly, under the right circumstances, these are not insurmountable issues, but they are worth noting as potential scope and economic drivers for the development of the application.

Build redundancy into the application   Application failures can have a broad range of impacts on the end users of the software. These failures could range from component-level issues or network-level failures that result in simple error messages to complete datacenter outages, which would render the service unavailable. Hardening applications against such failures requires specific mitigation strategies that should be incorporated into the overall application design. Typically, these mitigation strategies are applied toward significant failure cases such as hardware- or network-level failures, rather than component issues.

The biggest problem addressed by a redundancy strategy is hardware failure. This can occur with various types of hardware, including but not limited to disk storage, Web servers, network switches, or even hardware load balancers. In some cases, minimal hardware failures like disk storage could be mitigated by the appropriate disk striping implementation, which is pretty common with server hardware. Failures of complete Web servers may result in the load balancing of traffic to additional servers in the pool that have capacity to handle the increased load. To ensure that resources are available to accommodate complete failover, it is recommended that capacity planning efforts account for having additional hardware resources standing by. In many cases, this level of redundancy is fairly easy to attain, given many of the previously discussed practices for scaling applications effectively. However, addressing catastrophic failures such as complete cluster or even total datacenter outages are a much more challenging problem to solve, and they require a more significant investment in strategy, process, and equipment. An example of a catastrophic failure could be as simple as a long-term power loss due to a significant weather event or something as devastating as an earthquake that might destroy the datacenter or render it offline. Failures of this caliber are very rare, but they can and do occur. Most organizations that are technically mature understand this and will apply the most applicable level of redundancy to their infrastructure.

For application developers, choosing the right level of redundancy is something generally left up to the individuals who manage risk for your organization. After all, the appropriate level of redundancy is an expenditure that is often decided by analyzing the risk associated with the loss and determining the cost benefit to the business as a whole. However, it is important for developers to not only design applications with redundancy in mind but also to help inform those decision makers about the importance of having redundant application infrastructure and the various options available for implementation.

Insulate against dependency failures   Oftentimes the applications that we build are being implemented on top of a platform, shared set of code, third-party components, or common services. Architecturally speaking, it makes perfect sense to build application-specific business logic on top of generic components or services that other applications share. This is inarguably a good practice for many reasons. However, it does present challenges for user-facing applications that experience failures from the various platform assets that the application is built on.

It is critically important for application developers to design their applications with mitigation strategies for dependency failures. This principle is very similar to that of being fault tolerant, but it is more specifically targeting shared application code or services. For example, if an application was depending on a shared subsystem to perform an access control list check every time a user wanted to access a piece of data, then the application should ensure that the access control list data is always available to its respective method invocations. Applying a simple caching strategy on a separate machine, or set of machines, for access control data might be one way to insulate against a failure of the access control subsystem. This ensures that users do not experience any issues with their experience when a critical subsystem is unavailable. Application users inherently do not understand the complexities and depth of the applications they are using. As application developers, it is our job to ensure that the software always appears to be healthy and functional, regardless of what may be going on behind the scenes. In some cases, this may require temporary degradation to the application in terms of functionality, but this is often better than displaying a failure message to the user.

Ensure Manageability and Maintainability

Thus far we have discussed tactics to address two of the three principles outlined in the previous section. Those tactics enumerated specific and actionable recommendations for how to design applications to address scalability and availability in your applications. While both of those goals and their respective tactics for achieving them are critically important, they are complemented by the third and equally important principle that applications be manageable and maintainable from an operational perspective.

As applications begin to scale out to accommodate more users, the complexity of the application infrastructure, live site issues, and management overhead can increase, as well. This can lead to potential quality problems with the delivery of the application, which will negatively affect users while simultaneously driving up the cost of maintenance. Live site bugs, capacity issues, and general server reliability problems are just a few examples of issues that may arise unexpectedly and require diagnosis and supportive action. It is important that application developers consider the necessary features that enable their applications to be supported and managed by individuals who may not have actually written the executing application code. Adding instrumentation, interfaces for connecting monitoring tools, and application health reporting are just a few examples of features that help to paint a clear picture of how the application is working in the live production environment. This will inevitably lead to an improvement in managing the application, as well as diagnosing and addressing issues on the live site even as the application scales to accommodate additional users.

Unfortunately, addressing manageability and maintainability within application designs is often not the first priority for development teams. As application developers, we tend to gravitate toward the set of "problems" that are most interesting for us to solve from an architectural and business perspective. This generally means that the set of work required to ensure that the application can be operationally managed and maintained is prioritized lower than design work for other parts of the application. Therefore, the correct level of development investment in areas of manageability and maintainability is not always made during the design of the application. For small applications, it may make sense to shrink the investment in these areas, but for applications that intend to scale to large user communities, early investment in the right features and processes can make all the difference in the quality of service in the long run. Let us review a few tactics for addressing any potential manageability or maintenance issues with your application.

Instrument the application code   Operational management of Web applications can be challenging work. This is especially true when the first tier of incident support is the systems engineers who generally have limited knowledge of the running application code. In the event of an incident in the live production environment, it is critically important to be able to detect, identify, understand, and solve the problem as quickly as possible. To do this effectively, the application code needs to provide diagnostic information about its execution state at all times. This can be accomplished in a variety of different ways, including but not limited to simple logging, writing to the system event logs, or building a custom service that aggregates instrumentation data from the running application. Once diagnostic information is available from the application code, real-time monitoring and alerting systems can then be integrated with the application.

Run-time instrumentation data from an application is quite powerful information for many reasons. As suggested, it can be used for real-time monitoring and alerting, but it can also be used for other analysis purposes such as issue tracking or trending, or just understanding overall system health metrics. The most important thing is that application developers instrument the code to enable this type of data collection and provide documentation to the service engineers that illustrates recovery steps for the instrumented error detection. This not only requires a commitment to write the instrumentation code but also the upfront analysis to determine what needs to be monitored, tracked, and reported downstream. Ideally, application developers should instrument and capture as much data as possible and choose which data points should be monitored in real time versus getting archived directly. A typical example of an approach such as this might result in instrumentation data flowing into two different endpoints, where one endpoint is a real-time monitoring system and the other a data warehouse of instrumentation data. This approach is illustrated in Figure 5-5.

During design, application developers should ensure that their designs account for an approach to instrumentation and monitoring that will provide operational data that can be used for diagnostics, troubleshooting, or just understanding the run-time behavior of the application. As previously mentioned, this can be accomplished in a variety of ways, including simple logging to a file, adding performance counters, or writing to the event viewer. The selection of an instrumentation methodology is going to vary from application to application, but the important thing is to choose a mechanism that will scale well with the application. For example, as the scope of features increases, adding and maintaining a large number of performance counters might be too challenging, and simple logs might be a better choice. Regardless of the chosen implementation, the main goal should be to instrument as much of the application as possible so that run-time behavior can be better understood and diagnosed. These investments in instrumentation also allow operational tools and infrastructure to be integrated with the application to further enable real-time monitoring and historical reporting.

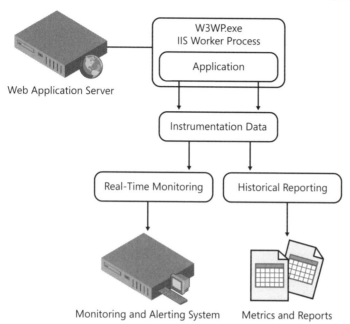

W3WP.exe
IIS Worker Process

Application

Web Application Server

Instrumentation Data

Real-Time Monitoring

Historical Reporting

Monitoring and Alerting System

Metrics and Reports

FIGURE 5-5 Dual-purpose approach to using instrumentation data.

Actively monitor the application   Once the application is properly instrumented, the obvious next step is to apply the appropriate level of health monitoring to the live application.
There are various ways to accomplish this with both Microsoft and third-party tooling, but
the most important thing is that application development teams invest in getting the appropriate tools in place prior to releasing the application. This work goes hand in hand with the
instrumentation effort discussed in the previous section, and it is important to understanding
the end-to-end run-time health of the application. Leveraging the tools and infrastructure
available from Microsoft is a great way to pursue a health monitoring strategy. Management
applications such as Microsoft System Center Operations Manager (SCOM) are available out
of the box with a variety of ways to hook into an application's instrumentation solution and
conduct real-time monitoring. There will inevitably be effort expended on tuning the overall monitoring solution, but generally this is something that can be fine tuned over time. As
mentioned, the key is to ensure that a solution is prioritized and implemented prior to the
application being launched.

Establish key live site metrics and goals   As the application gets designed to scale out to
the projected user load, it is important that application developers work with their Program
Management, Operations, and Test counterparts to establish the metrics and goals for the
health of the running product. Establishing metrics and goals adds a level of accountability
for the quality of the product that helps to ensure that the application always performs and
operates as expected. Oftentimes these metrics are drivers for much of the data getting
collected through the instrumentation mechanism that was previously discussed. Typically,
metrics such as site availability and reliability are used to indicate what percentage of time

the users of the application experience problems. This is generally expressed in terms of a percentage of transactions that result in a positive outcome, with most major services on the Internet setting their goals above 99.9 percent.

Plan for growth and failures   A big part of managing a live Web application is knowing when to expand the infrastructure to accommodate user load, as well as what to do when everything comes crashing down in failure. While this description represents a dichotomy of run-time circumstances, it does represent the reality of Web application manageability. Application developers and their stakeholder counterparts in Program Management, Operations, and Test should work together to establish the process for addressing both scenarios.

Under the best possible circumstances, applications will remain healthy and user load will increase steadily. Success for your application will be assured, provided that it can keep up with the demand your users place upon it. Conversely, if your application infrastructure cannot keep up with user demand, users of the application are not likely to be satisfied with their experience and will take their business elsewhere. It is important to understand when your application needs more capacity so that infrastructure can be made available to accommodate it. Typically, this type of planning can be accomplished by analyzing the application run-time data that is collected using the instrumented code within the application. This data allows certain variables like ASP.NET requests per second, CPU consumption, or available memory to be analyzed and used to understand the resources being utilized by the application. With this information, application developers can predict when additional hardware might be required to meet the needs of the growing application.

In the event application health reaches a suboptimal state and users experience major failures across the service, a proper recovery plan must be executed to ensure a rapid and successful restoration of the application to a completely healthy state. Problems of this nature could range from minor to catastrophic, as we discussed earlier in this chapter. Minor failures might require a server reboot, while catastrophic failures may induce full failover to a separate data center. Failures are certainly unpredictable but can be planned for. Live site outages require very specific, tactical processes for achieving a smooth recovery. Without those processes, recovery could be chaotic and subsequently result in additional downtime. Typically, operational teams and their application development counterparts establish procedures for dealing with outages of a predefined severity level so that the recovery time can be minimized. These processes generally ensure a more coordinated and calculated recovery effort and ensure that roles, procedures, and responsibilities are very clearly defined. While it is not necessary that processes of this nature be established during the application design cycle, it is important that they get established prior to the application being deployed.

Inside Microsoft: Managing the Windows Live Messenger Service Infrastructure

Windows Live Messenger is a Win32-based communication product offered by Microsoft within the Windows Live suite of clients and services. Windows Live Messenger is perhaps one of the most well known of all instant messaging services on the Internet, and it remains a dominant player against AOL, Google, and others. For many years, Windows Live Messenger was provided under the MSN brand of services until being updated and relaunched under the Windows Live brand in 2007. At present, Windows Live Messenger is the most used free instant messaging service in the world and is delivered to more than 320 million active users worldwide. The key components of the application vary by version, but the latest client includes online and offline instant messaging to address book contacts, peer-to-peer file sharing, video chat, and SMS messaging features.

Windows Live Messenger is more than just a simple instant messaging client application. The end-to-end client and supporting service is a complex combination of a peer-to-peer and client/server architecture that supports billions of instant messages per day, which represents the daily communications of millions of people worldwide. The client is supported by one of the most scalable, heavily used Internet-based communication platforms in the world. This service infrastructure delivers all the necessary plumbing to enable the various communication scenarios supported by the Messenger client application, including integration with several mobile phone platforms via SMS and instant messaging, as well as peer-to-peer file sharing and interoperability with other services like Yahoo! Messenger.

Engineering Principles

The Windows Live Messenger service infrastructure team has developed a great deal of experience over the years in the delivery of a high-quality and reliable communication platform to a global audience. The team members recognize the complexity of the engineering challenges they face and have spent years perfecting their practices. They adhere to a set of guiding principles that govern how they address scalability and manageability issues in the delivery of their service to market. These principles are outlined below.

Design to scale out   As you might imagine, the Windows Live Messenger service infrastructure components participate in various types of communication scenarios. These scenarios, such as instant messaging or SMS, are represented as separate functions within the Windows Live Messenger application and generally operate independently. This separation of functionality allows the service to be designed to scale by "service role," which means that specific areas of functionality are designed to scale linearly on their own rather than as one application. The team believes that, as applications achieve massive scale, there are no benefits to running the entire service on a single machine and scaling out the number of machines performing all tasks. Separating functionality into "roles" allows those individual roles to scale more granularly if necessary. The key to success, the team indicates, is to balance simplicity with scale. It is important to separate basic functionality of the application for scalability purposes but not to trend toward an approach that is too granular.

Design every aspect of the application to fail gracefully   A critically important philosophy for the Windows Live Messenger team is that each aspect of the application be designed to fail gracefully. Application developers assume that key dependencies could be unavailable or that infrastructure may go offline during critical processing. The team believes in keeping the application interaction model as stateless as possible so that, when failures do occur, clean failover can happen and users may continue uninterrupted. To accomplish this, the team has applied strategies for caching data for certain features to insulate against failures in dependency services. In other cases, the team has moved to more asynchronous calls during application startup, where the team can dynamically choose which features to make available when certain service roles are experiencing problems. These practices allow the end-to-end service to appear completely healthy and available, instead of abruptly showing exceptions to the user when a small feature area is experiencing issues.

Automate key manageability tasks   Managing a service that is the size of Messenger creates challenges for executing simple manageability tasks. Actions such as deploying a service upgrade or monitoring the health of the live site when there are thousands of servers to manage can be extremely challenging and expensive from an operational perspective. To address these challenges, the Windows Live Messenger team incorporated an application,[1] which manages a number of live site management tasks. This application monitors and manages each server in the Windows Live Messenger service. It automates the health monitoring, deployment, and maintenance of the servers so that only a few operations engineers are required to manage the service.

The infrastructure management application works by continuously monitoring each machine's health until it detects a failure. When the failure is detected, the software runs through a series of diagnostic steps, beginning with a simple reboot, and gradually tries to bring the server back online to receive traffic. In the most severe of circumstances, it will even re-image the machine with a new operating system and application install. If it is unsuccessful at trying to get the Windows Live Messenger application up and running again, it ultimately assumes that a hardware failure has occurred and removes the machine from service. Because the management application is in complete control at all times, application developers are forced to write their code to be responsive to application or complete server failures, thus ensuring a fully automated operational approach to handling service issues.

In addition to health monitoring, this management software also handles the deployment of new versions of the Windows Live Messenger service in a fully automated fashion. Because the software has the necessary control and information about the server topology, it also

---

1   *http://research.microsoft.com/users/misard/papers/osr2007.pdf.*

bears the responsibility of deploying and configuring the application across the server infra-structure. Given the amount of hardware servicing the users of the Windows Live Messenger service, an automated deployment that eliminates both human intervention and error greatly improves both the cost of managing the service as well as the quality and predictability of the deployment.

Continuously evaluate and plan infrastructure capacity   Understanding the usage and resource consumption patterns of your application is extremely beneficial to being able to adequately forecast and plan for hardware needs. The Windows Live Messenger team believes in having a strong and repeatable process for evaluating the capacity and resource consumption of all aspects of its service, so it can plan in advance to acquire and deploy new hardware to meet the user load. The team accomplishes this by first establishing the key resource measurement for each component of the service. This is generally accomplished by mapping specific server performance counters to application components and profiling each component's resource consumption. Each component is then evaluated on a monthly basis, or after a major service upgrade, to understand growth trends. The end-to-end appli-cation infrastructure is then examined holistically on a quarterly basis, and the team makes the determination whether to scale out the service with additional machines. This continuous evaluation and planning cycle allows the team to stay ahead of the growth curve, thus ensur-ing that the service never reaches a critical threshold that negatively affects users.

Plan to recover from outages   Despite the valiant efforts of the Windows Live Messenger service infrastructure team, service outages can occur from time to time. For all the effort that goes into preventing issues with the health, availability, and reliability of the live site, nearly all services will eventually go down. Ironically, most teams spend countless amounts of effort trying to prevent an outage but spend little effort in planning how to recover from one. The Windows Live Messenger team has experienced circumstances that it believes require both technology- and process-based solutions to recover from an outage effectively. By applying this combined implementation, the team is able to maximize its ability to return 100 percent of its users back to full service. These experiences have shown the team that oftentimes the flood of users returning to the service after a critical outage causes the service to become unresponsive and subsequently go down again. The team recommends having a process and a technical solution that allows for an incremental restoration of usage or traffic back to the service after any significant downtime. This solution will ensure that additional service downtime is avoidable as components of the service are adequately ramped back up to full capacity.

As illustrated above, the Windows Live Messenger service infrastructure team has devel-oped a great deal of experience in the delivery of a high-quality and reliable Internet-based communication platform. The principles highlighted above represent just a few of the best practices acquired by the team over the many years that this service has been available. Even though some of these practices are most effective when the scale of the infrastruc-ture is really large, there are still several that universally apply to services of all sizes. It is important for application developers to learn from the experiences of mega-scale Internet services like Windows Live Messenger and apply the knowledge gained to other applications of varying sizes.

Summary

Scalability has often been a term used to describe a Web-based application's ability to handle increased load after additional hardware has been added to the infrastructure. Web-based applications are considered "scalable" when they have the ability to increase total throughput under an increased user load after additional hardware has been added. As software has evolved beyond the desktop to a server-based delivery model, application scalability has become a key element to high-quality software designs. For Web-based server applications, scalability considerations such as hardware infrastructure design, load balancing, deployment, and application manageability have a direct influence on both the application design and the cost associated with scaling to meet user demands. To ensure that Web-based applications can scale effectively to accommodate increased user load, scale factors should always be considered as part of the application design. By doing so, application developers can help to mitigate post-release quality or application health issues discovered under heavy load.

Key Points

- Scalable applications can handle increased usage or data
    - Choose scalable application designs
        - Design simple application architectures
        - Design to scale out
        - Partition data effectively
    - Design application infrastructure to scale
        - Load balance with hardware
        - Choose the appropriate hardware
        - Use common cluster configurations

- Scalable applications are always available and fault tolerant
  - Defend against application failure
    - Ensure that the application is fault tolerant
    - Build redundancy into the application
  - Insulate against dependency failures
- Scalable applications are manageable and maintainable
  - Ensure manageability and maintainability
    - Instrument the application code
    - Establish key live site metrics and goals
    - Plan for disasters
    - Invest in change management

Chapter 6
Security Design and Implementation

There is no security on this earth, only opportunity.

—*General Douglas MacArthur*

Ensuring that software applications are secure is one of the most challenging aspects to software development—and perhaps the most important issue for application developers to contend with today. With the evolution of software beyond the desktop to more integrated, globally connected, Web-based experiences, users are now faced with broader exposure to malicious acts being perpetrated through software. Security is extremely important to our users, and, although the quote from General MacArthur is blunt, it is unfortunately accurate. Security can only be realized when malicious attacks are thwarted by defensive countermeasures. Therefore, application security depends on the breadth and depth of the preventative measures established by the application developer.

Implementing secure designs is not an offensive tactic but rather a defensive one. The attacker who is interested in exploiting vulnerabilities in your application is not likely to provide warnings about the specifics or timing of the attack. Software designs must carefully consider the application's potential threats, the scope of the attack surface, and the available mitigation strategies to defend against a variety of potential attacks. Application developers must embrace security principles and practices during design and implementation to avoid introducing a class of security bugs that could be very difficult and time consuming to address late in the development cycle. In this chapter, we will evaluate the common application security threats facing application developers, discuss the principles of designing secure applications, as well as enumerate tactics for achieving greater levels of security within your products. Incorporating security-focused principles and practices into the development life cycle, especially during design and implementation, will ultimately lead to a safer and more secure experience for the users of the software. Let's begin by reviewing some common security threats that your products are likely to encounter.

Common Application Security Threats

There are a number of security threats facing application developers today. These threats attempt to abuse all facets of the application architecture, including but not limited to the network the application utilizes, protocols, the operating system the application is running on, and the application code itself. Many of these threats, such as remote code execution, have existed for decades, but as the Internet has become a communication hub for people and software, new threats have evolved. These include attacks like cross-site scripting, cross-site request forgery, Trojan horse viruses, and phishing, to name a few. An exhaustive list of categorized security threats has been provided in Table 6-1. This list is an adaptation of the information provided in the MSDN Patterns and Practices article, "Improving Web Application Security: Threats and Countermeasures," which can be found at *http://msdn .microsoft.com/en=us/library/ms994921.aspx*. For now, let's consider a few examples that are common challenges for .NET application developers today.

- **SQL Injection**   This type of attack affects any application, both Web and Win32 client, that accepts user input and subsequently executes database queries. SQL injection attacks can inject database commands into the user input stream as a means to maliciously modify the SQL commands that are being sent to the back-end database. This attack can be perpetrated using the application's database login credentials and potentially wreak havoc on user data or the database itself.

- **Cross-site scripting (XSS)**   Perhaps the most common form of online security exploit, this vulnerability is found in Web-based applications, which allow Hypertext Markup Language (HTML) and client-side script inputs into the application's pages. A classic example of this attack is that of a malicious hyperlink stored in an online forum, blog, or other site that accepts HTML and script input. For the attacker, the goal is to present the malicious script on the Web page as content that appears to belong to the page. The attacker may craft the hyperlink in a way that executes a malicious script, downloads a file, or even obtains access to sensitive data on the local machine when the link is invoked by any user who visits the site. This type of vulnerability has been reported on many of today's popular Web sites.

- **Cross-site request forgery**   This attack (also known as the one-click attack, or session riding) attempts to exploit a Web site's trust of a particular user. Cross-site request forgery affects Web applications that accept user input. The attack works by using a hyperlink that attempts to run unauthorized commands against a particular Web site on behalf of a user who the Web site trusts, specifically the user who was clicked the hyperlink. Typically, these attacks are perpetrated against Web applications that perform actions based on inputs from authenticated users, without requiring the user to authorize the action. The canonical example of this attack is that of a Web-based mail application that accepts HTTP request-based method invocations. If an attacker were to craft a URL that performs a malicious action, such as deleting the inbox, and successfully get a user who uses that application to click on that URL, then based on the site's trust of that user, the method would be executed. Applications that allow user authentication to be persisted in a local cookie are particularly at risk.

TABLE 6-1 **Categories of Common Security Threats**

Category	Examples of Specific Threats
Authentication	Credential theft, eavesdropping, dictionary and brute force attacks, cookie replay.
Authorization	Elevation of privilege, data tampering, disclosure of confidential data.
Application configuration	Process and service accounts with elevated privileges, retrieval of clear text configuration data.
Auditing and logging	An attacker exploits an application or user without leaving traceable evidence of the attack.
Cryptography	Weak encryption, lack of robust key generation or key management.
Exception management	Denial of service, disclosure of sensitive information.
Input validation	Buffer overflow, cross-site scripting, SQL injection, cross-site request forgery.
Machine threats	Viruses, Trojans, worms, password cracks, arbitrary code execution, unauthorized access to machine.
Parameter manipulation	Query string, cookie, HTTP header manipulation.
Privacy and data compromise	Access to sensitive data in storage or on the wire, data tampering.
Session management	Session hijacking or replay, man in the middle.

Upon reviewing the breadth of these security threats, application developers should have a healthy fear about protecting their applications, infrastructure, and users from would-be predators online or within the corporate network. These threats are much more pervasive than you may realize. The *Symantec Government Internet Security Threat Report*, which was published in April 2008 by Symantec, reported that in the second half of 2007, 499,811 new malicious code threats were reported to Symantec. This figure represented a 136 percent increase over the first half of 2007. Clearly, application security threats represent a formidable foe to all application developers. Being able to effectively mitigate these threats is paramount for all application developers. Let us consider how to design our applications to be more secure and effectively mitigate the aforementioned risks.

Principles for Designing Secure Applications

We have already established the irrefutable importance of security in application design and development. It should be quite clear that security is a primary engineering tenet within application development. Microsoft embraced this belief as part of the larger Trustworthy Computing (TWC) initiative, which began in 2002, and has subsequently created a security-focused culture within the company. Although the TWC initiative is broader than just security, several great security processes and practices have emerged from TWC and are incorporated across the company today. Let's review the security principles outlined by the TWC initiative that developers should incorporate within the application development life cycle to avoid introducing security bugs into their software.

Security Design Principles

Embracing a culture of security within your company is an important first step in designing and building secure applications. This requires that all disciplines, including program management, development, and test, incorporate security-focused principles into their respective work streams. From application feature conception to design and testing, security should always be top of mind when building software. Let's review the specific tactics that application development teams should incorporate into their existing processes to help foster a security-focused culture.

Establish a Security Process

Most application development organizations already have a well-defined process established for building applications. Augmenting that process to include security-related objectives and tasks will ensure that application development teams spend less time fixing security bugs toward the end of the release cycle and ultimately release a more secure product. Simply stated, the applications that your team builds can only be secure if there is a security process interwoven into the application development process. At Microsoft, the security process that is incorporated into product release cycles is called the Microsoft Security Development Lifecycle (SDL). The SDL represents a holistic approach to application security and privacy that includes milestone-based goals and objectives ranging from individual team member security training to specific design, implementation, and testing tactics. It is important that application development teams incorporate a process that will ensure repeatable and reliable delivery of secure applications. The SDL is an example of such a process. A visual representation of the SDL and its milestone-based goals has been provided in Figure 6-1.

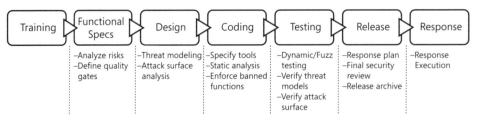

FIGURE 6-1 The Microsoft Security Development Lifecycle (SDL).

Note Implementing an SDL within your company is a commitment that may seem like a large amount of work. However, the benefit to your application's users in terms of increasing security quality is undeniable. For more information on each step of the Microsoft Security Development Lifecycle, I recommend reading more at *http://msdn.microsoft.com/en-us/library/84aed186-1d75-4366-8e61-8d258746bopq.aspx*.

Application development teams should augment their existing software development processes to include a holistic focus on security. This will ensure that a culture of security is encouraged across the company, which will ultimately lead to the construction and delivery of more secure software. Despite the criticism from Microsoft's rivals about the company's historical approach to security, the SDL outlined by the TWC initiative is an example that other software development organizations should definitely learn from. Microsoft now finds itself with a much better reputation since the TWC initiative began.

Incorporate Defense-in-Depth

In addition to establishing a security process within your organization, it is also important to apply specific strategies to ensure secure application designs. Defense-in-depth is a technique that has been proven to reduce the exposure of vulnerabilities in application designs. Defense-in-depth is actually a military strategy that intends to delay the advances of an attacker rather than actually prevent it. It is based on the idea that an attacker loses momentum over a period of time, or as the attacker is required to cover a broader attack surface. In software development, this technique is used to apply multiple layers of security around the application, so that if the outer layer were to be penetrated, the inner layers would continue to secure the application, thus preventing the application from immediate compromise. By applying defense-in-depth, even a series of imperfect attack mitigations can stop a potential exploit. Developers should apply this strategy when designing application architectures to ensure that critical infrastructure and applications are protected by multiple layers of security.

Apply the SD3+C Strategy for Secure Applications

As a means to help developers apply the defense-in-depth technique, Microsoft created a strategy that is referred to as the SD3+C. This acronym stands for secure by design, secure by default, and secure in deployment and communication. This strategy establishes four major security tenets, each of which contains a set of best practices for securing applications. It is recommended that application developers adhere to these tenets during the design and implementation of their application code to ensure that security best practices are properly incorporated. Let's review these tenets and best practices in greater detail.

SD3+C Strategy and Practices for Secure Applications

The SD3+C strategy and practices was born out of the previously mentioned TWC initiative and the subsequent creation of the SDL. As previously mentioned, the primary goal of the SDL was to augment a software development organization's processes by integrating principles and practices that lead to improved software security. The SD3+C represents a framework that organizes key security best practices into a set of simple principles. In the next several pages, we will review each of these principles in greater detail and enumerate a number of their associated best practices.

Secure by Design

The strategy of securing by design encourages application developers to focus on applying security-focused principles during the application design phase. This includes analyzing the security risks posed by the application's features, modeling the various threats to the application, and applying security best practices to the application design and code. Security practices applied during the application design are perhaps the most effective to the overall quality and security of the application. Decisions and actions taken during the application design will ultimately have the greatest impact downstream during application testing. These decisions, as you will see, begin with threat modeling and risk analysis.

Implement Threat Modeling and Risk Mitigation Tactics

Threat modeling is based on the idea that the application possesses assets that are desirable to protect. Therefore, it is important that threat analysis be conducted to identify potential vulnerabilities or attack vectors. The goal of threat modeling not only includes identifying the potential threats but also surfacing mitigation tactics that can be applied to the application. When threat modeling, application development teams wear the hat of the attacker and attempt to identify weaknesses in their design or implementation. Threat modeling is one of the most important security practices a team can apply. The process requires an investment of time, but it is not complicated, and the results yield fewer security bugs in the long run. As we have been discussing throughout this book, finding issues early in the development cycle are significantly less costly and risky to address. Threat modeling is a great methodology for finding security design flaws early. The overall process involves several steps, including the following:

- Identifying the assets of the application and the entry points.

- Analyzing the data flow of the application.

- Analyzing or brainstorming the known threats to the application.

- Evaluating and ranking the threats by decreasing risk level and identifying threats that are exploitable vulnerabilities in the application.

- Identifying mitigation strategies and tactics for reducing or eliminating the threats.

- Choosing the appropriate technologies for applying the mitigation strategies.

Developing threat models and analyzing vulnerabilities involves building data flow diagrams of the application features and determining how specific threats map to particular application components. The Microsoft methodology for completing this exercise is to apply what is known as the STRIDE threat model. STRIDE is an acronym for a set of categorized security threats. The letters represent the following principles:

- **Spoofing**   Defined as an attempt to obtain access to an application by using a false identity.

- **Tampering**   Involves the unauthorized usage or modification of application data.

- **Repudiation**   Represents the ability of either known or unknown users to deny that they performed a particular action within the application.

- **Information disclosure**   The unauthorized or unwanted disclosure of sensitive data within the application.

- **Denial of service**   The act of rendering all or parts of an application unavailable to its users.

- **Elevation of privilege**   When the identity of a user with elevated privileges is assumed by a user with limited privileges and gains access to data or functionality that is not intended for them.

> **Note** For additional, more detailed information about threat modeling and the practices associated with threat modeling, I recommend reading *Writing Secure Code*, Second Edition, by Michael Howard and David LeBlanc (Microsoft Press, 2002). This book is the definitive security reference at Microsoft. In addition to this title, *Threat Modeling*, by Frank Swiderski and Window Snyder (Microsoft Press, 2004), presents an insightful deep dive on the specific practice of threat modeling.

As mentioned, developing a threat model can require an investment of time on the part of the development team. Fortunately, Microsoft has released the SDL Threat Modeling tool, which can help guide application development teams through the threat modeling process. It can be found at *http://msdn.microsoft.com/en-us/security/dd206731.aspx*.

Once the team has identified and categorized the threats, which are likely to be similar to the threats defined in Table 6-1, the next steps involve stack ranking the threats in order of risk level and developing mitigation strategies and plans for addressing the threats. Let's review the design best practices that .NET developers can apply to mitigate application security threats discovered during the threat modeling process.

Apply Best Practices to Application Design

Thus far in this chapter, we have discussed the importance of applications being designed to withstand potentially hostile conditions. Additionally, we reviewed the importance of analyzing the potential threats to your application and applying a layered approach to defending your application against predators. Incorporating security considerations into your application from the early stages of the design will not only ensure that your application and its users are protected from attackers, but it will also decrease the risk of finding high-impact security bugs late in the development cycle. The following represent specific design tactics that will help you avoid introducing security vulnerabilities into your application.

Apply .NET authentication and authorization mechanisms   Many applications require users to be authenticated to the application and subsequently authorized to access specific features within the application. Authentication mechanisms like Windows Security or ASP.NET forms-based security in the .NET Framework support the process of identifying a user, while authorization mechanisms like role-based security provide access control.

Application developers who wish to leverage Windows security for authentication should implement the *WindowsIdentity* and *WindowsPrinciple* classes to interrogate the current user's Windows authentication credentials. If Windows security is not the desired implementation choice, application developers should create custom authentication infrastructure by leveraging the *GenericIdentity* and *GenericPrinciple* classes, respectively. Each of these methods offers ample functionality for developers who need to implement user authentication.

Applications requiring user authentication are very likely to require user authorization as well. Role-based security demands are a great technique for restricting access to specific methods or functionality within your application code. These techniques allow specific user roles to be defined either using Windows authentication or custom authentication mechanisms and subsequently get verified or demanded prior to execution of a specific method or block of code. Unauthorized access results in a security exception, which can be caught, logged, and messaged appropriately to the user.

Encrypt sensitive data   Protecting user data is perhaps one of the most important responsibilities of an application development team. Many applications today, especially those found on the Web, request personal information from users to facilitate use of the software. This data is incredibly risky to transmit and store. Personally identifiable information, or PII as it is commonly known, is any piece of information that can be used to uniquely identify, contact, or locate an individual person. It is critically important to take the necessary precautions to ensure that data of this classification does not get exposed to unauthorized users or, worse, a malicious hacker. Application designs should ensure transmission and storage of sensitive data leverages strong encryption and access to the machines and data stores is limited to personnel who have been properly authorized. In some cases, certain types of data may require specific handling as defined by certain governing bodies. We will explore this later when we discuss the secure in deployment and communication strategy.

Assume external applications and code is insecure   If your application relies on an external application or API, it is best to assume that the external dependency is not secure. Because the external system or API is out of your immediate control, it cannot be assumed that the person or persons responsible for that system have implemented a robust security model. Application developers who find themselves in this situation should take the necessary precautions, especially when accepting user-inserted data, to defend against possible attack. This could involve any number of mitigation tactics such as sanitizing data, using encrypted communications, or enabling IP range filtering.

Design to fail, and fail securely   Application failures will happen, whether they are the result of attacks or normal operating calamities like hardware failures or system bugs. The practical approach to this problem is for application developers to plan for failure and implement designs that will ensure failures happen both gracefully and securely. As discussed in Chapter 5, "Designing for Scale," redundancy in design can help overcome unanticipated failures. However, ensuring that your application code is prepared for failure and does not accidently offer elevated permissions or disclose sensitive data during a failure scenario requires implementation by application developers.

Handle errors and exceptions securely   Imagine making an online purchase and, upon entering your credit card information and proceeding to the next step, you encounter an application error. In the error message, you note a sufficiently cryptic error message accompanied by an error code and your credit card number in plain text. How confident would you feel about the data-handling practices of the online merchant? If all confidential information were handled effectively, there would be a lot less fraud in the world. Application developers need to handle all transaction failures with the same security and privacy practices that are used in handling successful application transactions. Therefore, developers should make sure that precautions are taken to protect sensitive data in exception messages, event logs, and in debug sessions.

Implement least privilege   If you have ever run Microsoft SQL server using the "sa" account, raise your hand. Many of us are guilty of not adhering to the principle of least privilege. Arguably, it is the simplest way to get our applications to work properly. However, it is also the most insecure. Applications should be designed to execute with the least possible privileges required to meet the requirements. This will ensure that, if the application identity were to be exploited, the potential scope of damage could be minimized. It is best to incorporate this early in the development process to ensure that developers can build and test their code using the permission set that will be applied in a production setting.

Implement privilege separation   Similar to the principle of least privilege, the principle of separation of privilege recommends the separation of application functionality into parts that require minimal privileges, such as normal-use features, from those that require elevated privileges, such as administrative or management features. This ensures that, if the primary application identity were to be compromised, minimal damage could be inflicted by the attacker.

Sanitize input   With cross-site scripting and SQL injection being two of the most widely perpetrated exploits of applications, it is critically important for application developers to focus a great deal of energy on sanitizing user input in their applications. User-created input should be considered evil until proven otherwise. Application developers should incorporate the appropriate countermeasures to ensure that all input data is interrogated and sanitized as a means to prevent script or SQL injection. The simplest way to accomplish this is to remove potentially offending markup from the input. In the case of cross-site scripting, Microsoft has released an encoding library called the Anti-Cross Site Scripting Library, which helps developers protect their Web-based applications from cross-site scripting attacks. The library can be downloaded from *http://www.microsoft.com/downloads/details.aspx?FamilyId=EFB9C819-53FF-4F82-BFAF-E11625130C25&displaylang=en*.

Validate security coding best practices with FxCop   In addition to applying security design best practices to your application, it is also important to ensure that your code adheres to the .NET Framework design guidelines for security. Validating your application code against these best practices is quite simple using FxCop or the code analysis features within Visual Studio 2008. For example, FxCop has approximately 25 code analysis rules available out of the box that inspect application code for potential vulnerabilities. These rules include recommendations for sealing methods that satisfy private interfaces as well as making static constructors private. As we will review in Chapter 10, "Code Analysis," code analysis rules can be extremely useful in raising the quality (or security, in this case) of your code during the feature development period.

Incorporate security-focused code reviews   In the spirit of applying security best practices to application code, it is also helpful to incorporate security-focused code reviews. Typically, organizations assign an individual to be the Chief Security Officer or Security Architect. This person is responsible for security overall and will likely conduct security code reviews in addition to the threat modeling and threat assessments that have already been done. This is an important additional step in ensuring that vulnerabilities are not introduced into the application code.

Secure by Default

The second tenet of the SD3+C strategy is secure by default. The strategy of securing by default encourages developers to implement security-focused default settings for their applications. It is a widely held belief that most application users accept the application default settings during installation. By applying that rationale, we can assume that the default settings will be the configurations most commonly used in a production setting. Therefore, your users are likely to realize the most benefit when the default configurations provide the most security. The challenge to providing secure default configurations, you might imagine, is to ensure that the default configuration settings are both secure and user friendly. It is not appropriate to place the burden of securing the application on the user by asking him or her to alter configurations after installation. Therefore, application developers should ensure that default application configurations provide the most security for their users. Let's consider a few specific approaches to ensuring secure defaults.

Install only necessary components by default   As we have discussed earlier in this chapter, it is important to reduce the overall attack surface of the application. Therefore, installing more components of the application than are required only increases the potential set of vulnerabilities. It is important that application developers be vigilant about reducing the number of components that are installed by default while also ensuring that the customer's expectations for the desired feature set are met. To strike the right balance with the application user community, it is recommended that application development teams solicit feedback from average and power users and use that feedback to achieve the appropriate set of defaults.

Configure restrictive permissions by default   Securing by default is a principle that puts authorization in the control of the application user. Many commonly used applications, such as Windows Defender, employ this principle to ensure that the application does not take any liberties not afforded to it by the actual user. For example, Windows Defender builds a white list, or "allow list," of applications that are allowed to access the Internet by simply asking the user to grant access initially. This same practice is also visible in Windows Vista, where actions that require elevated permissions or affect system-level resources require an additional affirmation from the user. Although some may see this tactic as a suboptimal user experience, there are certainly more clever ways to implement it and achieve the same result. Regardless of implementation specifics, this practice does, in fact, create a much more secure runtime environment for users.

Secure in Deployment and Communication

The strategy of securing in deployment and communication primarily focuses on applying security processes and practices to the management of your application during run time, or rather, after it has been deployed. Despite any best effort made during the application development process to avert security bugs, inevitably there will be vulnerabilities discovered after the software releases. Therefore, the secure in deployment and communication tenet reminds application developers to ensure that processes and practices are in place to find and mitigate security issues after the application is in the hands of our users. Further, it recommends that development teams provide timely communication and remediation for any issues discovered post release. These practices not only provide ongoing support and security improvements for users of the software, but they also directly engage customers in the dialog about the importance of security. Let's review the recommended best practices for implementing the secure in deployment and communication strategy for your applications.

Establish a support and bug remediation process   Every application development team requires a plan for supporting the application once it has been released to a production environment. This also includes establishing a process for addressing issues with the application as the issues get discovered or reported. Certain classes of application bugs, such as functional issues, may afford developers the luxury of patching the application on a pre-defined schedule. Security bugs often are the exception, however. Security vulnerabilities discovered after release require a rapid response from application development teams, but they also require a response that is effective. To accomplish this, teams should consider defining and publishing the processes and procedures they will follow to expedite security bug fixes as they are discovered.

Provide setup and configuration guidance to users   When discussing the secure by default tenet, we highlighted the importance of providing users with the most secure set of default configurations in the first run experience of your application. This obviously benefits the larger percentage of application users since most are likely to desire only defaults. However, for the remaining and arguably the savviest set of users, it is important to provide guidance about the security implications of enabling the additional feature set. This can be accomplished by simply providing the appropriate level of documentation through readme files, white papers, or integrated help applications.

Adhere to compliance requirements   Security compliance requirements are becoming more and more prevalent in certain industries. For example, in the health-care industry, the Health Insurance Portability and Accountability Act (HIPAA) of 1996 established specific security requirements for health insurance data handling and storage practices. While HIPAA standards and practices are defined at the governmental level, other private organizations have also established data security and handling guidelines. For instance, the Payment Card Industry Data Security Standard (PCI DSS) provides recommended security guidelines for processing card payments online. In each of these scenarios, there are clear guidelines and either requirements or recommendations for security compliance. Application developers should be aware of these requirements, work with their corporate attorneys to understand the implications from a business perspective, and ensure that the application is designed from the outset to handle specific needs. These requirements can and often do vary by industry, but it is imperative to understand the implications they can have on the security of the application or the application data.

Involve users in the security dialog   Although it may seem trivial, it is nonetheless important to have an open dialog about security with the users of your application. Proactively engaging users, discussing vulnerabilities, and educating them on the importance and relevance of security are critical to ensuring the best experience possible for your users. This type of engagement can also improve the perception of your application's security. For example, despite the large investment in security in Windows Vista, it could be argued that it has been at times perceived by the user community as not being very secure. We know that all software has security flaws, but perhaps the perception of Windows Vista may have been different had users been more knowledgeable about the value that the software provides them. By contrast, though, if we all knew how much crime there is in the world, we might appreciate the value of law enforcement but never go outside. Therefore, it is important to engage users in the security dialog but not to create panic.

Establish a security response and communication plan   As we just mentioned, communication with the user community is important in establishing a relationship of trust with your users. If security vulnerabilities are discovered, it is best to respond to those vulnerabilities with communication and a remediation plan. For example, Microsoft has established the Microsoft Security Response Center (MSRC) as a means to identify, monitor, resolve, and respond to security vulnerabilities. One of its key responsibilities is to communicate in a timely manner with the user community, which in this case includes enterprise customers and highly skilled technical users. It enables this communication through its blog and other Web-centric communication mechanisms like e-mail and Really Simple Syndication (RSS) feeds. Additionally, Microsoft combines this communication with updates to its software via the Windows Update service. This allows Microsoft to provide software updates to the user community quickly, which ensures that vulnerabilities are mitigated as soon as possible. While this scenario may not apply to all application developers, it nevertheless illustrates the importance of response and communication around security vulnerabilities, especially in an environment as fluid as the Internet, where new security issues are being discovered every day.

As you have read, the SD3+C provides a great framework of security principles that helps to distill a broad set of best practices into a simple, organized model. Although a number of the principles and practices we discussed earlier in this chapter are applicable to a broad range of software development technologies, this is a book focused predominantly on managed code. Therefore, it is important that we review the key security principles of the .NET Framework and the flexibility it provides to application developers to secure their applications.

Understanding .NET Framework Security Principles

The .NET Framework was introduced at a time when software applications were becoming increasingly more distributed, interconnected, and subsequently more vulnerable to attack. Application development was evolving from the desktop to "smart," or connected, client software and intranet- or Internet-based delivery models. This evolution brought about the need for a new paradigm in application security that would provide developers a greater level of security control to defend their applications and users against malicious attacks that could be perpetrated from external entities. Up to this point, Windows security was the norm for enforcing application access control and had traditionally been role-based. Many developers were accustomed to allowing applications to have unfettered access to local machine resources, as long as the user or user context of the running application was authorized. When .NET emerged, it was accompanied by a more integrated security model that allowed resources to be secured in a much more granular way than traditional Windows security would allow. This security model gives application developers the ability to enforce security policy within the code itself by leveraging the infrastructure that the .NET Framework provides. Let's review some of the .NET Framework security basics.

> **Note** It is worth noting that this chapter will not cover .NET Framework security at the level that is necessary to fully understand its features and capabilities. We will review core concepts and make recommendations, but to be truly effective with your application security policy, I recommend application developers seek a resource that provides more depth. Of course, I am a fan of the book .*NET Security Programming*, by Donis Marshall (Wiley, 2003).

Runtime Security Policy

The essence of Runtime Security Policy in the .NET Framework asserts that all assemblies are considered security principals and are therefore granted permissions to securable resources or particular operations. Unlike traditional Windows security, where users are the primary security principals, Runtime Security Policy in the .NET Framework challenges assemblies to authenticate themselves and be assigned execution permissions at run time. This allows application developers to govern access control within the application and subsequently provide an extra layer of security to the application users. To understand how the .NET Framework accomplishes this, let's review the following elements of Runtime Security Policy.

- **Evidence**   This is best described as the identity and origin of the executing assembly. For Runtime Security Policy to understand who the assembly is and where it is originating from, evidence must be supplied. The identity for the assembly, such as a strong name, comes from the assembly's metadata, which gets extracted by the Common Language Runtime (CLR). Evidence of origination is submitted by the host that launches the assembly, such as the ASP.NET runtime.

- **Permissions and permission sets**   These elements define specific access rights granted to a particular resource or operation. Permissions represent a grant of access rights to a singular entity, while permission sets are groupings of individual permissions that reflect a collective trust level. The .NET Framework provides several standard permissions, such as *EventLogPermission*, *FileIOPermission*, and *FileDialogPermission*, and several named permission sets, which include examples like *FullTrust*, *Execution*, and *LocalIntranet*. At run time, permission sets, not individual permissions, are what get assigned to assemblies. The .NET Framework supports custom permissions and permission sets to allow application developers to customize their needs.

- **Code groups**   Simply stated, a code group is represented by an association of evidence with a permission set. Assemblies are then granted the permissions of the code group when the specific membership condition, such as having a strong name, of the code group is met. Examples of default code groups within the .NET Framework include *My_Computer_Zone* and *Internet_Zone*, to name a couple.

- **Policy levels**   Policy levels reflect boundaries for the .NET Framework to calculate permission grants. There are four policy levels in .NET: Enterprise, Machine, User, and Application Domain, which are hierarchical. Additionally, each level maintains its own hierarchy of code groups and permission sets. At run time, permissions are determined based on the intersection of permission sets granted to the assembly at each policy level. Therefore, the final permission grant is represented by the sum of permissions allowed by all participating policy levels.

When granting permissions to an executing assembly, the runtime must consider the assembly's requested permissions, the evidence provided by the host, and the security policies defined across all policy levels before rendering a decision to allow or deny access to the requested resource. Figure 6-2 illustrates how this is accomplished through the cooperative efforts of the various elements of the Runtime Security Policy.

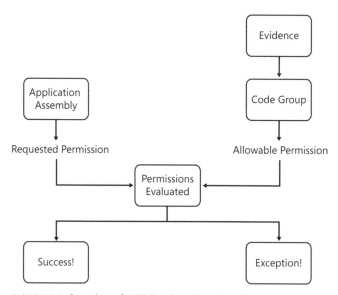

FIGURE 6-2 Overview of .NET Runtime Security Policy.

Now that we have reviewed the basics of Runtime Security Policy, let's discuss how application developers can leverage the abilities of Runtime Security Policy using Code Access Security to enforce security requirements.

Code Access Security

In the .NET Framework, Code Access Security (CAS) is used to prevent code that is not trusted from accessing information or performing actions that are considered privileged. This is accomplished through collaboration with the Runtime Security Policy, whereby Runtime Security Policy sets the rules by which assemblies must abide, and CAS enforces or refines them. CAS enforces security policy through a set of checks, called demands, which ensure that any callers desiring access to a given resource actually possess permissions to do so and are not depending on the permissions of the called function. These demands initiate a stack walk that subsequently confirms the permissions granted to each method in the call stack and either authorizes access to those specific resources or throws an exception. By contrast, CAS can also be used to refine the level of permissions that an assembly or operation requires as a means to close potential security vulnerabilities. Let's briefly review the list of functions that CAS performs.

- Provides application code the ability to request the permissions it requires in order to run, to request permissions that would be good to have, and further specifies which permissions the code should not be allowed to have.

- Affords administrators the ability to configure security policy by associating sets of permissions with code groups.

- Grants permissions to each assembly that gets loaded, based on the combination of permissions that get requested by the code as well as the operations allowed by security policy.

- Is used to define permissions and permission sets that represent access rights for various protected systems resources.

- Gives application code the ability to demand that its callers have specific permissions.

- Allows application code to demand that its callers possess a digital signature, thus refining access rights to only callers from a particular organization or site to call the protected code.

- Applies restrictions on application code at run time by comparing the granted permissions of every caller on the call stack to the permissions that callers are required to have.

Applying CAS within your application can be accomplished by either using declarative or imperative syntax. Each of these approaches is acceptable, but specific implementation will depend on the security scenario you are trying to address. The following is a brief comparison of the two approaches.

- **Declarative syntax** This method of applying CAS is accomplished by decorating code with custom permission attributes. When decorating a class with declarative security attributes, the command subsequently applies to all methods of that class. By contrast, when declarative security is applied at the method level, the associative command will affect the decorated method and all of its callers.

- **Imperative syntax** This method of applying CAS is accomplished at run time. Instead of decorating classes or methods with custom attributes at design time, using the imperative syntax requires the use of security objects. Unlike the declarative syntax whose applicable granularity is at the method level, the imperative syntax allows application developers the flexibility of wrapping security code around individual lines of code.

As previously mentioned, CAS helps application developers inform the CLR about permissions that are required, not necessary, or specifically not desired. Applications cannot seek more permissions than the runtime provides based on the established policies. However, applications can use specific methods to verify permissions of a caller, refine or reduce permissions that are unnecessary, or vouch for the permissions of a caller. This is accomplished by using specific attributes or methods within your application code. Let's briefly review the role of each type of method.

- **Demanding permissions**   As we discussed at the beginning of this section, application code can demand permissions from its caller to ensure that all callers in the stack have the appropriate permission to access the operation. Once application code issues a demand, the runtime acquires the identity of all previous callers in the stack and checks the access rights of each.

- **Requesting permissions**   This is a method for allowing your application code to inform the .NET runtime about the type of permissions required to execute. This is done by decorating the assembly with the appropriate permission requesting attributes. At run time, the permissions are evaluated and the appropriate security policy is applied. As previously noted, an assembly cannot request permissions beyond what the runtime assigns from the local policy. However, by applying permission request attributes to the assembly, the Runtime Security Policy will be refined further to ensure that the code is only granted the permissions that are necessary.

- **Asserting permissions**   Contrary to the way demanding permissions ensures that callers higher in the stack have access to the protected resource, asserting permissions performs the opposite of demands. Asserting permissions provides application developers the ability to grant access to a protected resource even when calling code does not have permission to the resource. As you might imagine, with this power comes great responsibility. If not used correctly, permission asserts can lead to security vulnerabilities. Therefore, consider their use carefully before implementation.

Using CAS within your application designs is an important step in securing resources as well as protecting application users from potential vulnerabilities. However, all good things often come at a price. For CAS, this price is paid in application performance. This is primarily due to the stack walk performed when executing demands. When compared with the alternative of less application security, it is an acceptable design tradeoff. The important point to remember is that application performance is often easier to mitigate than a lack of security.

Applying Runtime Security Policy

Thus far, we have reviewed the basics of how Runtime Security Policy is applied by the .NET Framework through the use of evidence, permission sets, code groups, and policies. Additionally, we explored how application developers can refine or fine-tune security policies using Code Access Security. It is important for application developers and security experts within your organization to work together to establish a holistic approach to applying security across the various policy boundaries and within application code. Application security policy can be applied as a means to ensure that specific applications, Web sites, or publishers have less permission than default policy provides them. This is accomplished by using the .NET Framework Configuration Tool (Mscorcfg.msc), the Code Access Security Tool (Caspol.exe), or the Permissions View Tool (Permview.exe), which are provided with the .NET Framework software development kit (SDK), to administer security across policy levels. After reviewing the tools that are available for configuring and managing application security policy, I recommend investing some time understanding the security policy best practices outlined by Microsoft at *http://msdn.microsoft.com/en-us/library/sa4se9bc.aspx*.

- **The .NET Framework configuration tool**   This is a Microsoft Management Console (MMC) snap-in that allows developers or system administrators to configure security policy. This tool also has the ability to manage assemblies in the global assembly cache (GAC) and configure remoting services or individual applications. From a Runtime Security Policy perspective, though, this tool provides features for increasing assembly trust, adjusting zone security, and resetting all policy levels. Mscorcfg.msc was originally released as part of the .NET redistributable package with version 1.1 of the .NET Framework. For versions 2.0 and later, Mscorcfg.msc was released with the .NET Framework SDK. To alter configuration settings on a workstation that has multiple versions of the .NET Framework, you must make the changes in the associative versions of the configuration tool.

- **Code Access Security Policy tool**   This is a command-line tool that enables users and administrators to modify security policy for the machine, user, and enterprise security policy levels.

- **Permissions View tool**   This is a command-line tool used to view minimal, optional, or refused permission sets requested by a particular assembly. Additionally, it is possible to use Permview.exe to view all declarative security used by an assembly.

Upon reviewing the Runtime Security Policy and Code Access Security capabilities of the .NET Framework, it should be apparent to application developers how these features could be leveraged to improve the overall security of their applications. These capabilities, in conjunction with the principles and tactics discussed earlier in this chapter, provide application developers with a framework or foundation for increasing application security and thus improving the quality of their applications. These tactics are intended to be applied during design and implementation. However, there are other practices that application development teams can apply during other stages of development as well.

Additional Security Best Practices

In the previous sections of this chapter, we discussed a number of principles and practices for incorporating security into the design and implementation of software products. These principles and practices intend to foster a culture of security within the application development life cycle and ultimately improve the security of the software being produced. This chapter has covered a lot of ground. In reality, though, we have only scratched the surface in terms of the breadth of possible threats and the technical depth of security mitigation tactics. There are many great books and online resources on this subject matter that provide much more detail. The primary purpose of this chapter is to provoke critical thinking about security and emphasize the importance of focusing on security design and implementation early in the product life cycle and to avoid introducing security bugs that could be costly to address, require invasive fixes, or both.

The security principles and practices that were outlined previously are critically important to improving application security during the early phases of development. Security best practices go well beyond the design and implementation phase of the product life cycle. There are other tactics that can be applied during the application testing phase, or perhaps to the application infrastructure instead of the code. We would be remiss if we did not at least mention a few of these tactics. Let's briefly review a few of these practices in greater detail.

Conduct security-focused testing   Application testing consists of several different types of testing, which ranges from unit testing and Build Verification Testing (BVT) to functional and integration testing. These types of testing are often conducted with a goal of finding functional or stability bugs in the application code. Chapter 10 explores different forms of code analysis and testing methods in greater depth. Security testing is not specifically covered in Chapter 10, but it is critically important to the overall testing process. Security testing should be driven by the details of the threat model, which is completed before coding. Because threat models describe the likely attacks on the application as well as the mitigation strategies, a security-focused test plan can be easily scoped to the identified attack surface. Clearly, the value of security testing should not be underestimated. A well-defined and focused security-testing strategy helps to close the loop on much of the security-focused design and implementation work recommended in this chapter. Application development teams should ensure that their respective test strategies include a specific focus on security.

Incorporate penetration testing   In addition to investing in a repeatable security-testing process within your organization, it is also quite valuable to conduct periodic penetration tests against your application. Penetration testing is a method of evaluating your application, infrastructure, or both to determine weaknesses or vulnerabilities. This is often performed by third-party vendors who conduct testing from the perspective of the malicious user. The scope of testing can be targeted toward a specific application or broadened to include social engineering to attempt to gain access to software applications or protected resources. As you might imagine, the intent of penetration testing is to determine the feasibility of an attack and the business impact that could result from a successful exploit. Results of a penetration test are usually presented in the form of a security risk analysis, a set of discovered vulnerabilities, and recommendations for mitigation strategies. It is recommended that organizations invest in penetration testing periodically to not only ensure the security of their application or infrastructure but to get a third-party perspective as well.

Review application security before release   Within the Microsoft SDL, the final step in the process is the Final Security Review, or FSR. This process is initiated a few weeks before the final release date of the product, at which time the end-to-end security plan, threat models, risk mitigation strategies, and bug reports are reviewed. The goal of this process is to ensure that the security team within the company has a chance to conduct a final evaluation of the application security prior to release. The results of this process can range from pure acceptance and approval to release, to FSR escalation, which has the potential to delay release. Escalations are often the result of the team failing to meet some portion of the SDL criteria. This process is very beneficial to both the product team and the company as a whole. It ensures that a standard quality bar for security is set and enforced across the products, which ultimately benefits the users from a security perspective and the company from the perspective of reputation and risk management. For additional detail on implementing an FSR process within your company, I recommend reviewing the documentation at *http://msdn. microsoft.com/en-us/library/cc307409.aspx*.

Add protective infrastructure components   We spent a great deal of time in this chapter discussing process and software-based security best practices. It is also important to this subject to mention best practices for protecting your application infrastructure with hardware devices. The most common examples of hardware-based infrastructure components that are designed to improve security include firewalls, Intrusion Detection Systems (IDS), and denial of service appliances. These components are often used as a first line of defense against certain forms of attacks. For instance, firewalls are network appliances that are installed between user computers and protected resources on a network. They are used to inspect network traffic that is passing through and either permit or deny access to the resource based on the predefined rules. In contrast, an IDS works in conjunction with a firewall to interrogate network traffic and attempts to detect certain malicious behaviors that are attempting to exploit the resources that it protects. Unlike firewalls, an IDS can detect specific types of attacks such as brute force data-driven application attacks or elevation of privilege attacks. When combined, a firewall and an IDS can offer a solid layer of protection for your application infrastructure. If your applications are Internet facing, you may also find it necessary to add a denial of service appliance. Like firewalls and the IDS, these appliances also monitor network traffic and attempt to detect anomalies in the traffic such as quick ramp-ups or traffic spikes, which could indicate an impending denial of service attack. If these devices detect such anomalies, they can rapidly begin blocking specific IP addresses or perhaps even IP address ranges.

Summary

Security is perhaps one of the most important engineering focus areas for application development teams. Unlike functional bugs, security bugs can potentially produce disastrous results for applications, application infrastructure, or users. It is incredibly important for application development teams to invest in a holistic approach to software security. This begins with an investment in a security process that will help focus the team on understanding application vulnerabilities and addressing them through a series of best practices for design and implementation. These processes and practices are outlined in the SD3+C framework for securing applications by design, by default, and in deployment and communications.

Application development teams need to integrate security-focused processes and practices into the earliest phases of the application development life cycle to ensure that any vulnerabilities or security bugs are found and addressed as early as possible. Security bugs can be quite challenging to find and are often risky to fix once the application code reaches a certain state of completion. Therefore, discovering and addressing security bugs early in the release process reduces potential code churn later in the development cycle and thus increases application quality and reduces risk of delayed delivery to market.

Key Points

- Learn and understand common application security threats.

- Apply security design principles within your application development team.

  - ❑ Establish a security process.

  - ❑ Incorporate defense-in-depth.

  - ❑ Apply the SD3+C strategy for secure applications.

- Apply best practices for securing by design.

  - ❑ Apply .NET authentication and authorization mechanisms.

  - ❑ Encrypt sensitive data.

  - ❑ Assume external applications and code is insecure.

  - ❑ Design to fail, and fail securely.

  - ❑ Implement least privilege.

  - ❑ Implement privilege separation.

  - ❑ Sanitize input.

  - ❑ Validate security coding best practices with FxCop.

  - ❑ Incorporate security-focused code reviews.

- Apply best practices for securing by default.

    - Install only necessary components by default.

    - Configure restrictive permissions by default.

- Apply best practices for securing in deployment and communication.

    - Handle failures and errors securely.

    - Establish a support and bug remediation process.

    - Provide setup and configuration guidance to users.

    - Adhere to compliance requirements.

    - Involve users in the security dialog.

    - Establish a security response communication plan.

- Understand and apply .NET Runtime Security Policies and Code Access Security.

- Apply security-focused best practices in application testing processes.

- Invest in protective infrastructure components.

Chapter 7
Managed Memory Model

The first rule of management is delegation. Don't try and do everything yourself, because you can't.

—Anthea Turner

In managed code, garbage collection is delegated to the Common Language Runtime (CLR). The Garbage Collector (GC) is a component of the CLR and responsible for managing managed memory. This chapter is a practical discussion of the Garbage Collector and the memory mode of the .NET Framework. In managed code, memory is allocated on demand for dynamic objects with the new operator. However, the Garbage Collector is responsible for freeing the memory for that object when necessary. There is no *delete* operator as in the C++ language.

In C++, the developer was responsible for managing dynamic memory. Dynamic memory is allocated at run time. The *new* and *delete* operators exist for this reason. The *new* operator allocates memory, while the *delete* operator frees memory. There are also advanced techniques for allocating dynamic memory in native code. *HeapCreate*, *HeapAlloc*, *HeapFree*, *HeapDestroy*, and related functions are used to create and obtain memory from a native heap. To access virtual memory directly, there is *VirtualAllocEx* and *VirtualFreeEx*. For memory mapped files, the application programming interfaces (APIs) *CreateFile*, *CreateFileMapping*, and *MapViewOfFileEx* are available. Pointers are the common thread through the various options to allocate memory at run time. Historically, mismanagement of pointers has been the reason for untold problems, such as memory leaks and memory corruption. The C++ dynamic memory model overly involved the developer. The primary goal of the developer is to create a solution to a problem, not to manage pointers. Managed code allows developers to focus on solving problems rather than on the intricacies of memory management.

Memory management for managed code is the responsibility of the developer and the Garbage Collector. The developer is responsible for allocating objects, while the Garbage Collector is responsible for freeing objects. When objects are created at run time, they reside on the managed heap. You refer to an object with a reference, which is an abstraction of a pointer. The reference abstracts the developer writing managed code from managing pointers, which prevents pointer-related problems. In this way, the developer delegates to the CLR and the Garbage Collector to manage the managed heap and pointers. This delegation is an important shift in responsibility in the managed environment from the native environment.

Two basic assumptions dominate the memory management model of .NET. Large objects are long-lived objects. Similarly sized objects are more likely to communicate with each other.

For these reasons, the Garbage Collector uses a concept called generations to group objects by size and age. As a practice, architect your program to match these assumptions. This will adversely affect the performance of garbage collection and, consequently, your application.

Memory utilization in .NET revolves around the managed heap. When you allocate a new object, it is placed on the managed heap. When unreachable, the Garbage Collector will free that object. That will reclaim the memory for that object on the managed heap.

Managed Heap

The managed heap is partitioned into generations and the Large Object Heap. Generations 0, 1, and 2 are used to group objects by size and age. The ephemeral generations exclude the oldest generation. At the moment, the ephemeral generations include Generations 0 and 1. The reason for the distinction is that the ephemeral generations and the oldest generation sometimes can behave differently. Generation 0 is the smallest generation, Generation 1 is medium sized, while Generation 2 is the largest. For this reason, it is more likely that larger objects will appear in Generations 1 and 2. Generation 0 is simply not large enough to hold many larger objects.

The managed heap is partitioned into large objects and everything else. Large objects are greater than 85,000 bytes (85 KB) and reside on the Large Object Heap. This is not documented and is subject to change. Everything else resides on Generation 0, 1, or 2.

The Garbage Collector is responsible for freeing memory during a garbage collection. There are three events that initiate garbage collection. First is an allocation that, if successful, would exceed the memory threshold of Generation 0. Objects are always allocated to Generation 0. You cannot directly place an object on Generation 1 or 2. Because objects always start their life at Generation 0, it holds the youngest objects. Second is allocating a large object when there is insufficient memory available on the large object heap. The third event is calling the *GC.Collect* method. This will force garbage collection on demand.

The Garbage Collector collects the generations in order: Generation 0, 1, and then 2. Whenever a generation is collected, the younger generations of that generation are also collected. If Generation 1 is collected, then Generation 0 is also collected. Collecting Generation 2, which is considered a full collection, will also collect the ephemeral generations. This approach means that younger generations are collected more frequently than the older generations. This is designed for efficiency since the older objects tend to reside on the larger generations. Collecting, reclaiming, and compacting the memory for larger generations is more costly than for smaller generations. Another advantage to this model is the ability to collect a portion of the heap. Partitioning the managed heap generation supports this behavior. You can collect one or more generations and avoid a full collection of the managed heap, which is, naturally, expensive.

Garbage Collection

Natural garbage collection in the managed environment is non-deterministic. It occurs at some point in time and is not entirely predictable. Natural garbage collection is not forced with a call to *GC.Collect*.

When does natural garbage collection occur? Allocations for new objects are added to Generation 0. If that addition exceeds the threshold for Generation 0, garbage collection occurs. The Garbage Collector will attempt to reclaim enough memory from Generation 0 to support the new allocation. If enough memory is not reclaimed, Generation 1 is collected, and then, if necessary, Generation 2. Objects surviving a garbage collection are promoted to the next generation. For example, surviving objects on Generation 0 are then promoted to Generation 1 after garbage collection. This means that older objects tend to migrate to Generation 2. This furthers the policy of grouping objects by age.

The Garbage Collector manages each generation similar to a stack. This makes allocations both quick and efficient. Each generation has an allocation pointer, which delineates the end of the last object and the beginning of the free space. This is where the next object will be allocated. At that time, the new object is stacked upon the previous object, and the allocation pointer is adjusted. The allocation pointer will now point to the end of the new object. For this reason, the oldest objects are at the base of the generation, while the newest objects are toward the top. See Figure 7-1.

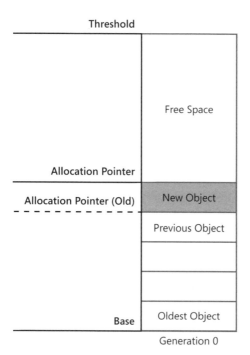

FIGURE 7-1 An example layout of Generation 0 after a new allocation.

When garbage collection occurs, objects on the affected generations are invalidated. A memory tree is rebuilt beginning with the root objects and their object graphs. The root objects are composed of the global, static, and local variables. The object graph includes all the other objects that are referenced either directly or indirectly by the root object. Creating the memory tree marks those objects that are reachable. Objects not in the tree are considered unreachable and available for collection. Unreachable objects have no reference variable or a field referring to them. The Garbage Collector compacts the reachable objects on the managed heap. Compacting the heap prevents fragmentation and maintains the stack model.

Although unadvisable, the *GC.Collect* method of the .NET Framework Class Library (FCL) can be used to force garbage collection. The parameterless version of the function performs a full collection. The single argument version of the function targets a specific generation, which is identified by the parameter. *GC.Collect* can interfere with the normal practice of the Garbage Collector. First, forced garbage collection is expensive. Second, calling *GC.Collect* frequently can harm the performance of your application.

Managed Wrappers for Native Objects

Managed classes sometimes wrap native objects. The managed class is an interface between the managed application and the native resource. In this way, the managed class abstracts the native resource. There are plenty of examples of this in the .NET Framework Class Library: the *FileStream* class abstracts a native file, the *Socket* class abstracts the Berkeley sockets interface, the *Bitmap* class abstracts a bitmap, and so on.

Problems can occur when there is a disparity between the size of the managed class and the native resource that it represents. For example, a managed wrapper could be a few kilobytes in size, while the native resource represented by the wrapper is several megabytes in size. The Garbage Collector will track the memory for the managed wrapper. However, the memory for the native resource is unseen. You could have plenty of managed memory available, while unknowingly running out of native memory. This creates a situation where an application crashes for lack of memory, while the Garbage Collector believes there is plenty. Native memory is the invisible elephant in the room. As instances of the manager wrapper are allocated, the elephant is getting bigger, while the room appears nearly empty.

The *GC.AddMemoryPressure* and *GC.RemoveMemoryPressure* methods help the Garbage Collector account for native memory. This is especially useful for classes that wrap heavy native resources. *GC.AddMemoryPressure* applies artificial memory pressure to the managed heap, while *GC.RemoveMemoryPressure* reduces memory pressure. Each method has a single parameter, which is the amount (bytes) of pressure to apply or relieve. In the constructor for the wrapper class, call *GC.AddMemoryPressure* and apply memory pressure equal to the amount of native memory required for the native resource. This will force additional garbage collections, where instances of the wrapper object and native resource can be released. In the *Finalize* or *Dispose* method, call *GC.RemoveMemoryPressure* to remove the additional pressure.

The following class demonstrates the proper way to implement a managed wrapper for a native resource that uses a disproportional amount of native memory.

```
public class Elephant
{
    public Elephant()
    {
      // Obtain native resource and allocate native memory

      GC.AddMemoryPressure(100000);
    }

    ~Elephant()
    {
      // Release native resource and associated memory

      GC.RemoveMemoryPressure(100000);
    }
}
```

GC Class

The GC class, which is in the System namespace, is an interface between the user and the Garbage Collector. Table 7-1 lists each method with a description.

TABLE 7-1 GC Methods

GC Method	Description
GC.Collect	Forces a garbage collection cycle. The default *GC.Collect* forces a full garbage collection, which is essentially Generation 2. For a more granular garbage collection, use the one-parameter *GC.Collect* method. The parameter stipulates the generation that should be collected (i.e., 0, 1, or 2).
GC.WaitForPendingFinalizers	Suspends the current thread until the finalization thread has called the finalizers of the objects waiting on the *FReachable* queue. Call this method after *GC.Collect* to provide ample time for the finalization thread to finish its work before the current thread resumes.
GC.KeepAlive	Keeps an otherwise unreachable object from being collected during the next garbage collection cycle.
GC.SuppressFinalize	Removes a reference to a finalizable object from the Finalization queue. Remaining overhead related to the finalizer is avoided. *GC.SuppressFinalize* is usually called in the *Dispose* method. Because the object has been disposed, finalization is no longer required.

GC Method	Description
GC.AddMemoryPressure	Applies additional memory pressure to the managed heap. This is typically used to compensate for native resources in managed code.
GC.RemoveMemoryPressure	Removes memory pressure from the managed heap. Like GC.AddMemoryPressure, this is typically used to compensate for native resources in managed code.
GC.CollectionCount	Returns the number of times garbage collection has occurred for the specified generation.
GC.GetGeneration	Returns the generation of the provided object.
GC.GetTotalMemory	Returns the number of bytes allocated on the managed heap.
GC.ReRegisterForFinalize	Reattaches a finalizer to an object. This is usually called on objects that have been resurrected to assure proper finalization.
GC.RegisterForFullGCNotification	Registers the application to be notified when a full collection is likely to happen and after it has occurred.
GC.CancelFullGCNotification	Unregisters the application from receiving notifications about impending full garbage collections.
GC.WaitForFullGCApproach	Notifies an application if a full garbage collection is impending.
GC.WaitForFullGCComplete	Notifies an application that a full garbage collection has completed.

Large Object Heap

The Large Object Heap holds large objects. Most large objects are arrays rather than the assemblage of non-array members of a class. Larger objects are longer lived and typically migrate to Generation 2. Promoting large objects from Generation 0 and eventually to Generation 2 is expensive. Placing really large objects immediately on the Large Object Heap is much more efficient. The Large Object Heap is collected during a full garbage collection, which is Generation 2. During garbage collection, memory for large objects on the Large Object Heap is freed. However, the Large Object Heap is never compacted. Sweeping and consolidating large objects on the Large Object Heap would be expensive. Therefore, that step is skipped. Garbage collection for the Large Object Heap entails these steps:

- Memory for unreachable objects is released.

- Memory from adjacent and unreachable objects is combined into a free block.

- Memory for unreachable objects at the end of the Large Object Heap is released back to Windows.

Because the Large Object Heap cannot be compacted, it can become fragmented. Allocating and releasing disparate-sized large objects on the Large Object Heap makes fragmentation more likely. You are unable to place large objects in the free space from unreachable smaller large objects—unless combined with contiguous space from another free object. The Garbage Collector is forced to search the individual free spans for holes large enough for the pending allocation. Collectively, the free spaces of the Large Object Heap may have enough memory to honor the request but not in a contiguous area.

If you use disparate-sized objects, one possible solution is a buffer of like-sized large objects that can be reused. This keeps the large objects in contiguous memory and could prove to be more efficient. You conserve memory, when the number of instances would otherwise exceed the pool, minimize fragmentation, and reduce the number of full collection operations. Full collections are especially expensive. The downside is when the simultaneous instances are consistently less than the size of the pool. That would waste memory resources and require fine-tuning the pool.

The following code demonstrates how to create and manage a buffer of large objects. In our example, the buffer contains 10 large objects, as shown below.

```
static BigObject[] bigobjects = {  new BigObject(),
                        new BigObject(),
                        new BigObject(),
                        new BigObject(),
                        new BigObject(),
                        new BigObject(),
                        new BigObject(),
                        new BigObject(),
                        new BigObject(),
                        new BigObject()};
```

The *BigObject* class below contains a byte array of 200,000 elements. For this reason, the byte array but not the *BigObject* class is placed on the Large Object Heap. The code for the class is minimally implemented because the concepts are simple. If an object in the buffer is available for use, the *bAvailable* field is set to *true*. The *Initialize* method initializes an object and makes the status available. The *Reset* method is called to reset an object from the object pool that is already being used. The reinitialized object is then returned.

```
public class BigObject
{
    // other data

    public void Initialize()
    {
```

```
        // perform initialization
        bAvailable = true;
}

public BigObject Reset()
{
    Initialize();
    bAvailable = false;
    return this;
}

public void Update()
{
}

public bool bAvailabled=true;
byte[] data = new byte[200000];     }
```

I run the application and create 15 objects. This exceeds the pool limit. Therefore, 10 objects are actually created. The additional five objects reuse objects that are already in the pool. Using Windbg, I have listed instances of the byte array. Windbg is a debugging tool that is discussed more thoroughly in Chapter 9, "Debugging." In the following listing, *MT* refers to the method table of a class. A method table is an array of methods that belong to a particular class. Instances of the same type share the same method table. For this reason, you can list all instances of the same type from the address of the method table. In this way, the method table is more of a cookie of a particular type of object than an address. They are shown in bold in the following listing. As expected, there are exactly 10 instances of the large byte array, not 15. Five of the instances reuse large objects from the object pool.

```
!dumpheap -mt 7912dae8
  Address       MT       Size
014aad34 7912dae8     1036
014ab140 7912dae8     1036
014ab54c 7912dae8     1036
014ab958 7912dae8     1036
02486bc0 7912dae8   200016
024b7920 7912dae8   200016
024e8680 7912dae8   200016
025193e0 7912dae8   200016
0254a140 7912dae8   200016
0257aea0 7912dae8   200016
025abc00 7912dae8   200016
025dc960 7912dae8   200016
0260d6c0 7912dae8   200016
0263e420 7912dae8   200016
```

Finalization

Finalization occurs during garbage collection. The finalizer is invoked during finalization to clean up resources related to the object. Non-deterministic garbage collection is performed on a generation or Large Object Heap when the related threshold is exceeded. Because of this, there may be some latency between when an object becomes unreachable and when the *Finalize* method is called. This may cause some resource contention. For example, the action of closing a file in the *Finalize* method may not occur immediately. This may cause resource contention because, although the file is not being used, it remains unavailable for a period of time.

Non-Deterministic Garbage Collection

Place cleanup code for the non-deterministic garbage collection in the *Finalize* method, which is implicitly called in the class destructor. The class destructor cannot be called on demand. As mentioned, there may be some latency in the *Finalize* method running. The class destructor is the method of the same name of class with a tilde (~) prefix.

```
class XClass {
    // destructor
    ~XClass() {
        // cleanup code
    }
}
```

For certain types of resources, non-deterministic garbage collection is inappropriate. You should not release resources that require immediate cleanup. Also, managed objects should not be cleaned up in a *Finalize* method. Order of finalization is not guaranteed. Therefore, you cannot assume that any other managed object has not been already finalized. If that has occurred, referring to that object could raise an exception.

Non-deterministic garbage collection is neither simple nor inexpensive. The lifetime of objects without a *Finalize* method is simpler. For these reasons, the *Finalize* method should be avoided unless necessary. Even an empty destructor (which calls the *Finalize* method), harmless in C++, enlists the object for the complete non-deterministic ride—a very expensive ride. For the purposes of this chapter, objects with destructors are called finalizable objects.

The additional cost of having a *Finalize* method begins at startup. At startup, objects with a *Finalize* method have a reference placed on the Finalization queue. This means, when the object is otherwise unreachable, there is an outstanding reference being held on the queue, which will prevent immediate garbage collection.

When the finalizable object is no longer reachable and there is a garbage collection event, the object is not removed from memory. At this time, a normal object that is unreachable would be removed from memory. However, the finalizable object is moved from the Finalization to FReachable queue. This keeps the finalizable object in memory. The current garbage collection cycle then ends.

The FReachable queue holds finalizable objects that are waiting for their *Finalize* methods to be called. Finalizer thread is a dedicated thread that services the FReachable queue. It calls the *Finalize* method on the finalizable objects. After the *Finalize* method is called, the reference to the finalizable object is removed from the FReachable queue. At that time, there are no outstanding references to the finalizable object.

During the next garbage collection, finalizable objects that have been removed from the FReachable queue can finally be removed from memory at the next garbage collection cycle. Unreachable normal objects are removed in one garbage collection cycle. However, unreachable finalizable objects require at least two garbage collection cycles. This is part of the expense of using finalizable objects. Finalizable objects should not have a deep object graph. The finalizable object is kept not only in memory but also in any object it references.

Figure 7-2 shows the garbage collection cycle for two groups of objects. F is a finalizable object that references objects G and H. I is a non-finalizable object that references J and K. G, H, J, and K are non-finalizable objects.

The *IDisposable.Dispose* method is an alternative to the *Finalize* method in non-deterministic garbage collection. Contrary to the *Finalize* method, *IDisposable.Dispose* is deterministic, called on demand, and has no latency.

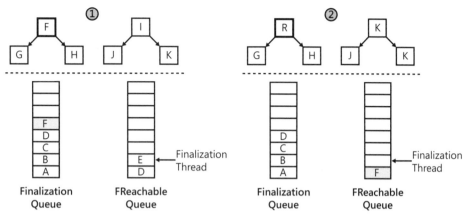

F is the only finalizable object and references objects G and H.

Finalization Thread calls destruction on object F.

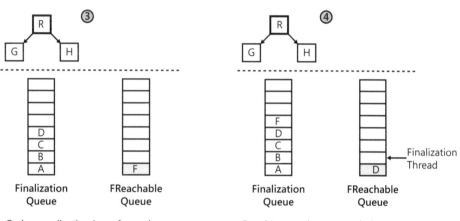

Garbage collection is performed.
I, J, and K removed from memory.
F reference moved to FReachable Queue.

F and I are no longer needed.

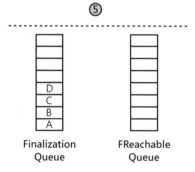

Garbage collection is performed.
K, G, and H removed from memory.

FIGURE 7-2 Garbage collection cycle for finalizable object.

Disposable Objects

Disposable objects implement the *IDisposable* interface, which has a single method—*Dispose*. The *Dispose* method is called deterministic or on demand. In the *Dispose* method, you can clean up for resources used by the object. Unlike the *Finalize* method, both the managed and unmanaged resources can be referenced in the *Dispose* method. Because the *Dispose* method is called on demand, you know the sequence of cleanup. Therefore, you know which objects have been previously cleaned up or not.

You can implement the *Dispose* method without inheriting the *IDisposable* interface. That is not the same as implementing the *IDisposable* interface and the resulting object is not a disposable object. The *IDisposable* interface is a marker indicating that the object is disposable. The Framework Class Library (FCL) relies on this marker to automatically call the *Dispose* method. For example, some .NET collections detect disposable objects to perform proper cleanup when the collection is disposed.

The method name *Dispose* is not the most transparent in all circumstances. Long-standing terminology or domain-specific phraseology may dictate using a different term. Most frequently, the alternate method name is *Close*. Whatever name is chosen, the method should delegate to the *Dispose* method. The user had the option to use the alternate name or the standard name, which is *Dispose*. The *File.Close* method is an example of using a different method name for deterministic cleanup. Avoid using alternate names for disposal unless there is a close affinity of the term with that type of object.

You can implement both the *Finalize* method for non-deterministic garbage collection and the *Dispose* method. Because you can clean up both managed and unmanaged resources there, the implementation of the *Dispose* method is usually a superset of the *Finalize* method. The *Finalize* method is limited to cleaning up unmanaged resources. In the *Dispose* method, call the *GC.SuppressFinalize* method. This method will remove the reference to the current object from the Finalization queue to avoid further overhead related to finalization. When both are implemented, the *Finalize* method is essentially a safety net if the *Dispose* method is not called.

To avoid inadvertently not calling the *Dispose* method on a disposable object, employ the *using* statement. Disposable objects defined in the using statement are automatically disposed of at the end of the *using* block. The *Dispose* method is called on those objects as the *using* block is exited. See the following code. In this code, *obj1* is a disposable object. The *Dispose* method is called after the *using* block is exited.

```
using( XClass obj1) {
}
// obj1 disposed.
```

Next is a more complex *using* statement. You can list more than one disposable object within a comma-delimited list in the *using* statement. Within a single *using* statement, you can define multiple instances of the same type. For disposing different types, precede the *using* block with more than one *using* statement—one for each type. In the following code, there are two *using* statements. There is one *using* statement for the *XClass* type, while the other is for the *YClass*. In total, three instances are defined. The *Dispose* method of the three objects is automatically called at the end of the *using* block.

```
using( XClass obj1=new XClass(),
            obj2=new XClass())
using (YClass obj3 = new YClass())
{

}
// Dispose method called on obj1, obj2, and obj3
```

Dispose Pattern

Implementing proper disposal in a managed class can be non-trivial. When there is a base and derived types that are both disposable, the implementation can be even more complex. The dispose pattern is more than a pattern for implementing the *Dispose* method. It is the best practice for implementing deterministic and non-deterministic behavior and cleanup for a base and derived class. This relationship must be considered to implement the proper cleanup behavior. For easier understanding, the base and derive class implementation of the dispose pattern are presented separately in this chapter.

The dispose pattern has four primary goals: correctness, efficiency, robustness, and code reuse. Correctness is the goal for every pattern. The dispose pattern is the perspective from Microsoft on the correct implementation of the *Dispose* and *Finalize* methods. A disposed object is probably not immediately collected. For that reason, it remains available to the application. You should be able to call the *Dispose* method and other methods on a disposed object with predictable results. The dispose pattern provides robust behavior for disposed objects. The dispose pattern is refactored for code reuse to prevent redundant code. Redundant code is hard to maintain, and it is a place where problems can flourish.

The base class (*XParent*) implementation for the dispose pattern is as follows:

- In the dispose pattern, the base class implements two *Dispose* methods. The protected *Dispose* method performs the actual resource cleanup. At the start of the method, a flag (disposed) is set to indicate that the object is disposed. The only parameter (disposing) indicates whether the cleanup is deterministic or non-deterministic. If disposing is true, it is deterministic and the *Dispose* has been called programmatically. You can clean up both managed and unmanaged resources. If false, you are restricted to the cleanup of unmanaged resources.

- The second *Dispose* method, which is part of the public interface for the class, is called to initiate deterministic cleanup. It delegates to the one-parameter *Dispose* method to perform the actual cleanup. The parameter is set to *true* to indicate deterministic garbage collection. Because the cleanup has been performed, the *Dispose* method invokes *GC.SuppressFinalize* and removes a reference to a disposed object from the Finalization queue. This prevents further costs from finalization.

■ *BaseFunction* represents any method of the class. Methods of a disposable object should be callable even after the object is disposed. In the method, check if the object is disposed first. If so, throw the object-disposed exception. This is demonstrated in *BaseFunction*.

■ The base class destructor (*~XParent*) delegates to the one-parameter *Dispose* method also. However, the parameter is false to indicate non-deterministic garbage collection.

```
// Base class

public class XParent: IDisposable {

    // Deterministic garbage collection

    public void Dispose() {

        // if object disposed, throw exception.

        if (disposed) {
            throw new ObjectDisposedException("XParent");
        }

        // Call the general Dispose routine

        Dispose(true);

        // Collection already performed. Suppress further finalization.

        GC.SuppressFinalize(this);
    }

    // dispose property true if object has been disposed.

    protected bool disposed = false;

    // Deterministic and non-determenistic garbage collection
    // disposing parameter = true ( determinstic )
    //                       false (non-deterministic)

    protected virtual void Dispose(bool disposing) {

        disposed = true;

        if (disposing) {

            // if deterministic garbage collection, cleanup
            // managed resources.
        }
```

```
            // cleanup unmanaged resources.
        }

        // Representative of any base class method

        public void BaseFunction() {

            // if object disposed, throw exception.

            if (disposed) {
                throw new ObjectDisposedException("XParent");
            }

            // implement method behavior
        }

        // Non-deterministic garbage collection

        ~XParent() {

            // Call the general Dispose routine

            Dispose (false);
        }
    }
```

The child class (*XChild*) implementation is as follows.

- The child class inherits the public *Dispose* method (parameterless) and the disposed property.

- The one-parameter *Dispose* method is overriden in the child class to clean up for child resources. The overriden function is almost identical to the version in the parent. The only other difference is that this version calls the base class *Dispose* method. This affords the base class an opportunity to clean up for its resources.

- *DerivedFunction* represents any method of the child class. In the method, you must check whether the object is disposed. If so, throw the *object-disposed* exception.

- The child class destructor (*~XChild*) delegates to the one-parameter *Dispose* method for proper cleanup.

```
    // Derived class

    public class XDerived: XParent {

        // Deterministic and non-determenistic garbage collection
        // disposing parameter = true ( determinstic )
        //                        false (non-deterministic)

        protected override void Dispose(bool disposing) {
            disposed = true;
```

```
        if (disposing)
        {
            // if deterministic garbage collection, cleanup
            // managed resources.
        }

        // Call base class Dispose method for base class cleanup.

        base.Dispose(disposing);

        // cleanup unmanaged resources of derived class.

    }

    // Representative of any derived class method

    public void DerivedFunction() {

        // if object disposed, throw exception.

        if (disposed) {
            throw new ObjectDisposedException("XChild");
        }
        // implement method behavior
    }

    // Non-deterministic garbage collection

    ~XDerived(){

        // Call the general Dispose routine

        Dispose(false);
    }

}
```

Weak References

There are strong and weak references. Until now, this chapter has focused on strong references. Both weak and strong references are created with the new operator. The difference
is how a weak reference is collected unlike a strong reference. A strong reference cannot
be collected unless unreachable. This is within the control of the application and not the
Garbage Collector. A weak reference, unlike a strong reference, can be collected at the discretion of the Garbage Collector.

In managed code, strong references are the default reference. There is a strong commitment
from the Garbage Collector to keep the associated object in memory—no exceptions or flexibility. Conversely, a weak reference has a weak commitment from the Garbage Collector. The
Garbage Collector has the flexibility to remove the weakly referenced object from the managed heap when memory stress is applied to the application and more memory is needed.

Weak references represent the best of both worlds. Both the application and the Garbage Collector can access the weakly referenced object. If not collected, the application can continue to use the object referenced by the weak reference. In addition, the Garbage Collector can collect the weak reference whenever needed.

Weak references are ideal for objects that require a lot of memory and are persistent in some manner. For example, you could have an application that maintains large spreadsheets that is cached to a permanent or temporary file. Large spreadsheets that consist of hundreds of rows and columns are memory intensive. Naturally, the application performance improves when the spreadsheet is memory resident. However, that applies considerable memory stress. The Garbage Collector should have the option to remove the spreadsheet object if necessary. The spreadsheet object is the perfect candidate for a weak reference. This would keep the spreadsheet object in memory, and accessible by the application, but also collectible by the Garbage Collector, if needed. If collected, the application could easily rehydrate the spreadsheet from the backing file.

Weak references are also ideal for maintaining caches. Cache can be memory intensive. The weak reference can be used to vary the lifetime of the cache based on a time-out, variables, or other criteria. For example, a cache may have a time-out. Before the time-out, the cache could be maintained as a strong reference. When the cache expires, it would be converted to a weak reference and be available for collection, if needed. If the cache is backed by a persistent source, such as a Microsoft SQL database, associating the cache with a weak reference is done to conserve memory resources as required.

There are two types of weak references: a short and long weak reference. A short weak reference is the default. With a short weak reference, the strong reference is released before finalization. For long weak references, the reference is tracked through finalization. More than extending the lifetime of the object reference, it allows the object to be resurrected.

Following are the steps for using a weak reference:

1. Create a strong reference.

2. Create a weak reference that is initialized with the strong reference. The default constructor creates a short weak reference.

3. Set the strong reference to null.

4. The weak reference is accessible from the *WeakReference.Target* property.

5. If the *WeakReference.Target* property is *null* and the *WeakReference.IsLive* property is *false*, the weak reference has been collected and is no longer available.

6. If the weak reference is available, assign the *WeakReference.Target* property to a strong reference, and then use the object.

7. If the weak reference is no longer available, rehydrate the data from a persistent source. When you are finishing using the updated strong reference, reinitialize a weak reference with the new strong reference.

The following code is a partial listing from an application that uses a weak reference. The program displays an array of names that is read from a persistent file. The array is assigned to a weak reference. The *hScrollBar1_Scroll* function scrolls through the names. First the function creates a strong reference. This is the *WeakReference.Target* assignment. If null, the *names* array has been collected, and the weak reference is no longer available. If that occurs, the array is rehydrated with the *GetNames* function. At the end of the function, the names reference is assigned null. This negates the strong reference, which leaves the weak reference to control the lifetime of the array.

```
Name[] names = null;
WeakReference wk;
List<byte[]> data = new List<byte[]>();

private void hScrollBar1_Scroll(object sender, ScrollEventArgs e) {
    names= (Name[]) wk.Target;
    if (null == names) {
        MessageBox.Show("Rehydrate");
        names=GetNames();
        wk.Target = names;
    }
    if (e.NewValue > names.Length) {
        return;
    }
    txtItem.Text = names[e.NewValue].first+" "+
        names[e.NewValue].last;
    names = null;
}
```

Pinning

Unmanaged code expects normal pointers, which are assigned a fixed address. For example, a pointer parameter in a native function call is a fixed pointer. A reference in managed code is an abstraction of a moveable pointer. When calling a native function via interoperability, you must be careful about passing references as parameters where pointers are expected. Because the reference is movable, the native call may behave incorrectly or even crash the application. A reference can be fixed in memory, which is called pinning. The referenced object is then considered a pinned object.

Pinned pointers can interfere with normal garbage collection. The Garbage Collector cannot move the memory associated with the pinned objects on the managed heap. Therefore, the generation with the pinned object cannot be fully compacted into contiguous memory. For this reason, pinning is the exception where a generation can possibly become fragmented. Objects that would otherwise fit comfortably in the combined free space do not because of fragmentation. This translates into potentially more garbage collection, which is expensive and harms the performance of the application. Keep pinning to a minimum to avoid this behavior. If possible, pin objects for a short duration—ideally within a garbage collection cycle. This avoids most of the problems in garbage collection related to pinning.

If possible, pin older objects and not younger objects. Older objects are objects that have been promoted to Generation 2. Generation 2 is collected less frequently. Therefore, the Garbage Collector is less likely to have to work around pinned objects. Objects on Generation 0 and 1 are more volatile and move frequently. Pinning objects in these generations creates considerable more work for the Garbage Collector. If an application pins objects regularly, particularly small or young objects, create a pool of pinned objects. Fragmentation is limited because the pinned objects are in contiguous memory and not scattered about the managed heap. This will allow the Garbage Collector to compact storage into contiguous free space more effectively. Performance of the Garbage Collector and application will improve.

There are three ways to pin an object:

- During interoperability, pinning sometimes occurs automatically. For example, passing strings from managed code into a native API as a method parameter. The managed reference for the string is automatically pinned.

```
[DllImport("user32.dll", CharSet = CharSet.Auto)]
public static extern int MessageBox(IntPtr hWnd,
    [MarshalAs(UnmanagedType.LPTStr)] string text,
    [MarshalAs(UnmanagedType.LPTStr)] string caption, int options);

static void Main(string[] args) {
    string message = "Hello, world!";
    string caption = "Solid Code";

    // pinned
    MessageBox(IntPtr.Zero, message, caption, 0);
}
```

- The *fixed* statement is used to obtain a native pointer to a reference. In the *fixed* block, the reference is not moveable and the related pointer can be used.

```
public class TwoIntegers {
    public int first = 10;
    public int second = 15;
}

unsafe static void Main(string[] args) {
    TwoIntegers obj = new TwoIntegers();

    // pinned
    fixed(int *pointer=&obj.first) {
        Console.WriteLine("First ={0}", *pointer);
        Console.WriteLine("Second={0}", *(pointer+1));
    }
}
```

- You can also pin objects using the *GCHandle* type, which is part of the *System.Runtime. InteropServices* namespace. *GCHandle* holds a reference to a managed type that can be used in unmanaged code or an unsafe block. As the method name implies, *GCHandle. AddrOfPinnedObject* returns the address of the pinned object.

```
static int[] integers = new int[] { 10, 15 };
unsafe static void Main(string[] args)
{
    GCHandle handle = GCHandle.Alloc(integers, GCHandleType.Pinned);
    IntPtr ptrRef= handle.AddrOfPinnedObject();
    int *pointer=(int*)ptrRef.ToPointer();
    Console.WriteLine("First  = {0}", *pointer);
    Console.WriteLine("Second = {0}", *(pointer+1));
}
```

Tips for the Managed Heap

These are tips for interacting with the managed heap. Some of these tips, such as avoiding the *GC.Collect* method, have been articulated previously in this chapter. However, they are included here for completeness.

- Do not program contrary to the garbage collection paradigm in the managed environment. Small objects should be short lived, while larger objects should be long lived. Objects are expected to communicate with like-sized objects.

- Avoid boxing. Frequent boxing, as occurs when using non-generic collections with value types, flood Generation 0 with small objects. This will trigger extra garbage collections.

- Because of the cost of finalization, use a *Finalize* method only when imperative. Furthermore, empty destructors are not innocuous as in C++. You still incur the full cost of finalization.

- Classes that have a *Finalize* method should not have deep object graphs. Finalizable objects are kept in memory longer than normal objects. Objects referenced by the finalizable objects are also kept in memory longer.

- If possible, do not refer to other managed objects in the *Finalize* method. First, those objects may no longer exist. Second, you may inadvertently create a back reference to yourself and resurrect the current object. Resurrected objects can be problematic.

- Define disposable objects in the using statement, which will automatically call the *Dispose* method and guarantee cleanup.

- Do not call *GC.Collect*. This is especially true for a complete garbage collection, which is expensive. Allow garbage collection to occur naturally.

- Keep short-lived objects short lived. Do not reference short-lived objects from long-lived objects. That links the lifetime of the two objects, and both are then essentially long-lived objects.

- Set objects as class members and local objects to null as early as possible. This allows them to be collected as soon as possible.

- Do not allocate objects in either hashing or comparison methods. When sorting or comparing, these methods can be called repeatedly in a short period of time. If the methods contain allocations, this could result in considerable memory pressure on the managed heap and additional garbage collection activity.

- Avoid near-large objects. These are objects that are close to 85 KB in size. As near-large objects, expect those objects to migrate to Generation 2. Add a buffer to the type and increase the near-large object to a large object. This will place the object immediately on the Large Object Heap and avoid the overhead of promoting the object through to Generation 2.

- Keep code in a *Finalize* method short. All *Finalize* methods are serviced by a separate thread—the finalizable thread. An extended *Finalize* method prevents a thread from servicing other *Finalize* methods and releasing the reference to the related object.

Even after adhering to every tip, don't be surprised to have the occasional memory problem. The CLR Profiler from Microsoft is helpful in those occasions. This tool allows developers to diagnose issues with the managed heap.

CLR Profiler

> *Look up in the sky! It's a bird! It's a plane! It's the CLR Profiler!*
>
> *—Donis Marshall*

The CLR Profiler is an excellent diagnostic tool that monitors an executing managed application and collects data points on object allocation, the managed heap, and garbage collection. The tool is available from Microsoft. If you suspect problems related to the managed heap, the CLR Profiler is an effective tool for diagnosing and pinpointing particular issues. The results of the CLR Profiler are available in a variety of text reports and graphs (mostly histograms). In addition to specific data on the managed heap, the CLR Profiler can provide information on methods in detailed call graphs. Information can be reported during program execution and post mortem. For example, you can obtain a memory summary of the managed heap while the application is executing. Conversely, you can also get a list of objects allocated while the application was running at program completion.

I have great reverence for the CLR Profile as the previous quote would indicate. CLR Profiler is one of the best written .NET applications. The breadth of information and level of detail pertaining to the managed heap and garbage collection is invaluable:

- An easy-to-understand summary of the managed heap.

- A comprehensive overview of object allocations.

- A list of methods that allocate memory on the managed heap, which includes the percentage of allocation attributed to each method.

- A variety of call graphs.

- Ability to track the lifetime of the Garbage Collector: when garbage collection occurs, the duration between garbage collections, which objects were affected by a particular garbage collection, and more.

- A list of finalized objects.

- A wide variety of graphs that paint an accurate description of managed memory for non-developers, which is helpful for meeting with managers.

Download the current version of the CLR Profiler from the Microsoft downloads Web site: *www.microsoft.com/downloads*. You can download both the 32- and 64-bit versions of the application. Once installed, the target application can be launched from within the CLR Profiler. The CLR Profiler is intrusive and will adversely affect the performance of the application. For this reason, do not use the product in a production environment.

The CLR Profiler is a complex tool. The following walkthrough provides an introduction to the product. This is not a comprehensive review of the CLR Profiler. Refer to the reference material on the CLR Profiler from Microsoft for additional details.

CLR Profiler Walkthrough

This walkthrough demonstrates the fundamentals of the CLR Profiler. The NoBigPool and BigPool applications are used during the walkthrough. BigPool was described earlier in this chapter. The application maintains a pool of 10 large objects, which are reusable. A large object is defined as an object that resides on the Large Object Heap. The NoBigPool is identical to the BigPool application except it does not maintain a pool of large objects. We assert that BigPool is more efficient because of the pool. In the walkthrough, CLR Profiler will confirm this assertion or force me to rewrite this chapter. We will create 20 big objects. Depending on the application, this will require either releasing or reusing 10 of the big objects. CLR Profiler will allow us to compare the result of the managed heap for both applications.

Each application randomly places secondary large objects, which are increasingly larger, on the Large Object Heap. These secondary objects are occasionally freed. As mentioned previously, during a full garbage collection, the Large Object Heap is swept but not compacted. For this reason, the disparate-sized objects have the potential to slowly fragment the Large Object Heap of both the NoBigPool and BigPool applications. This is being done to simulate a normal pattern of allocation.

Start the CLR Profiler to begin the walkthrough. See Figure 7-3. The Allocations and Calls check boxes should be selected by default. If not, select them to profile the managed heap and function calls, respectively.

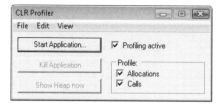

FIGURE 7-3 CLR Profiler window.

1. We start the walkthrough by profiling the NoBigPool application. Press the Start Application button. Browse to the folder containing bigpool.exe, and select the assembly. The CLR Profiler will start the application, and the NoBigPool user interface will appear momentarily.

   The NoBigPool application is shown in Figure 7-4. The Get Large button creates a large object on the Large Object Heap. The Clear Object button sets the reference to a large object to null, which makes the object unreachable and a candidate for future garbage collection. The spin control specifies the big object to clear. Adjust the spin control before pressing the Clear Object button.

FIGURE 7-4 The user interface for the NoBigPool application.

2. For the walkthrough, create 10 large objects. Press the Get Large button 10 times. Using the spin control and the Clear Object button, clear the 10 objects. Create another 10 objects. You have now touched 20 big objects in some manner.

3. Using the CLR Profiler, we can now examine the details of the managed heap for the NoBigPool application. Click the Show Heap Now button in the CLR Profiler to collect current heap information pertaining to the application. The Heap Graph window is displayed. Close the window.

4. We are more interested in displaying a text summary of the managed heap. From the View menu, select Summary. In the Summary window, find the Garbage Collector Generation Sizes group. This is where the size of the Large Object Heap is displayed. For our example, the size of the Large Object Heap is 4.5 megabytes (MB). See Figure 7-5. This number may vary based on several factors, such as the version of the .NET Framework.

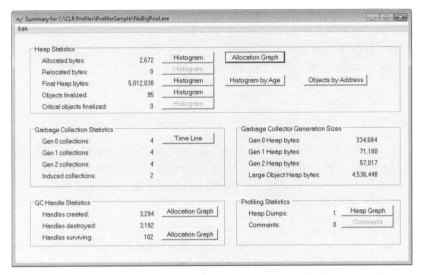

FIGURE 7-5 The Summary window of the managed heap for the NoBigPool application.

When the managed heap is larger than expected, the CLR Profiler offers a variety of helpful reports to diagnose the problem. For example, you can request list objects and their sizes that have been allocated. You can also view a report that lists the methods where significant allocations are occurring. The list can be sorted by total allocation per method, which is particularly helpful.

5. From the Summary window, you can display the allocated objects that are currently on the managed heap. In the Heap Statistics group of the Summary window, press the Histogram button next to the Final Heap Bytes value. The Histogram By Size For Surviving Objects window will be displayed. See Figure 7-6.

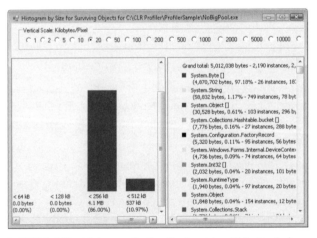

FIGURE 7-6 The Histogram By Size For Surviving Objects window.

6. The Histogram By Size For Surviving Objects window is separated into two panes. The left pane displays a graph of allocated objects—grouped by size. Scroll the pane right to displayed larger objects, such as objects that are on the Large Object Heap. The right pane is both a legend for the left pane and a sequential listing (descending order) of types that are on the managed heap. In our example, *System.Byte* arrays account for almost 97 percent of the allocated memory, which is worth further investigating. It would be helpful to know where *System.Byte* arrays are being allocated. That would be an important first step in diagnosing a potential problem. In the right pane, open a context menu (right-click) for the *System.Byte* array item in the legend. Select Show Who Allocated from the menu. An Allocation Graph is displayed, as shown in Figure 7-7.

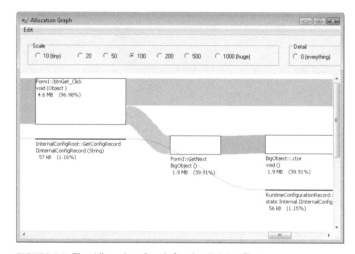

FIGURE 7-7 The Allocation Graph for the CLR Profiler.

Scroll to the right of the Allocation Graph window to view the actual method, or nearest, of the allocation. The graph shows *Form1.GetNext* as the method where the large object byte array is being allocated. This pinpoints the location of the potential problem, which is helpful. You now know what source code to investigate first.

7. Let us create 20 objects using the BigPool application and then compare the results with the NoBigPool application. First, close the CLR Profiler and the NoBigPool application. Restart the CLR Profiler. Use the Start Application button to launch the BigPool application from within the CLR Profiler. In the BigPool user interface, press the Get Large button repeatedly to use the 10 objects in the pool. This exhausts the object pool. Clear 10 objects using the spin control and the Clear Object button. Finally, get another 10 objects using the Get Large button. You have now touched 20 big objects.

8. Let us view the impact of this activity on the Large Object Heap. Press the Show Heap Now button to collect current heap information about the application. Close the Heap Graph window when displayed. Choose View from the menu, and select Summary. The

size of the Large Object Heap is reported as 4.2 MB, which is about 8 percent less than the NoBigPool example. See Figure 7-8. This is a significant difference considering the minimum number of objects that were allocated. If that was hundreds of objects, the difference would be substantial.

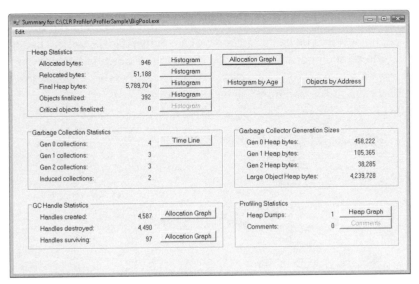

FIGURE 7-8 Summary of the managed heap for the BigPool application.

Summary

The Common Language Runtime provides several services to managed applications, such as the Garbage Collector (GC). The developer is responsible for allocating memory for reference types on the managed heap using the new operator. However, the Garbage Collector is responsible for freeing managed objects on the managed heap.

The managed heap is organized in generations: Generation 0, 1, and 2. By partitioning the heap into generations, partial garbage collections can be performed to avoid the overhead of collecting the entire heap. There is also the Large Object Heap, which holds large objects. Because large objects typically live longer, this avoids the expense of promoting large objects between generations.

Garbage collection is initiated when a new allocation would cause the memory threshold for Generation 0 to be exceeded. A full garbage collection is a Generation 2 collection, which also collects Generations 0 and 1. Conversely, a garbage collection of Generation 1 also collects Generation 0. Finally, a collection of Generation 0, which is a minimum collection, only collects that generation. Garbage collection is performed on the Large Object Heap during a full garbage collection. Memory for objects on the Large Object Heap can be reclaimed. However, the Large Object Heap is not compacted.

There is sometimes a disparity between the size of a native resource and a managed wrapper class for that resource. Use the *GC.AddMemoryPressure* and *GC.RemoveMemoryPressure* methods to account for the differences.

Non-deterministic garbage collection occurs when additional memory is needed for Generation 0, which is somewhat unpredictable. This can delay the cleanup of resources associated with unreachable objects. For the deterministic cleanup of resources, implement the *IDisposable* interface. The *IDisposable* interface has a single method—the *Dispose* method. Call the *Dispose* method on a disposable object to immediately clean up related resources. If the base and derive classes are both disposable, implement the dispose pattern.

Use the CLR Profiler to diagnose memory issues in managed applications. The CLR Profiler offers a variety of graphs and reports that detail the current or historic state of the managed heap of a managed application. This information can be helpful in resolving difficult memory problems.

Key Points

- The managed heap is segmented into Generations 0, 1, and 2 and the Large Object Heap.

- The assumption of the memory model for the managed environment is that small objects are short lived, while large objects live longer. In addition, objects of like size are likely to communicate with each other.

- Garbage collection in .NET is non-deterministic. You can force garbage collection with the *GC.Collect* method. However, this is not recommended.

- *GC.AddMemoryPressure* and *GC.RemoveMemoryPressure* apply artificial pressure to the managed heap. This is useful to account for the difference in size between a managed wrapper and the native resource.

- The Large Object Heap is collected, but not compacted, with a full garbage collection.

- Finalizable objects implement a *Finalize* method. Disposable objects implement the *IDisposable.Dispose* method. Implement the dispose pattern to properly define a base and derive a class as disposable.

- Weak references can be reclaimed at the discretion of the Garbage Collector.

- References abstract moveable pointers. Pin the reference to fix the pointer, which can then be safely passed to native code.

Chapter 8
Defensive Programming

If you take care of the small things, the big things take care of themselves.

—Anonymous

Defensive programming is a coding style that proactively prevents problems. As a coding practice, defensive programming is an amalgamation of small goals such as writing readable code, proper naming conventions, checking the return value of all functions, and employing design patterns. With defensive programming, it is all about the details. The bottom up approach makes the overall application more robust, correct, and extensible. Candidly, defensive programming consists mostly of common sense practices. For example, look at the following expression:

```
price=price*1.05;
```

The previous code statement has a simple problem. It is not fully readable and is an example of poor programming practice and a common sense problem. The problem is the literal 1.05. What is the context of this number? The number 1.05 could be a price increase, taxes, service charges, or even royalties. The context of the literal is important. Without that understanding, a maintenance programmer could improperly change the formula or use the results incorrectly. Literals, as used in the above formula, are difficult to optimize. That is the second problem. The following code is an excellent example of defensive programming. It corrects both concerns and is an example of self-documenting code.

```
price=price*priceIncrease;
```

Programs do not inherently have problems. A correct program is correct tomorrow, next week, and into subsequent years. What introduces code problems, now and in the future, are developers. Correct code requires programmer discipline. Defensive programming is a set of coding standards that apply a consistent programmer discipline for creating correct code. In many cases, defensive programming prevents future problems of the inadvertent nature. Look at the following code:

```
if(a>5)
    a+=5;
```

The truth condition of the preceding *if* statement is a single statement (*a+=5;*). Defensive programming dictates placing that statement in a code block. It is not compelling but nonetheless important. If not, someone might add a second statement to the truth condition and forget the block. The code would still compile. However, you have now introduced a subtle bug to the application. Rigorous testing would hopefully, but may not, uncover the problem.

This is one example of the detail that constitutes defensive programming. Here is the corrected code:

```
if(a>5) {
    a+=5;
}
```

Defensive programming starts with reasonable deadlines. You must have time to *think* about programming. The belief that writing coding is an entirely technical process is a myth. Great programmers are creative and require time for analysis and innovation. Short deadlines leave less time to think and be creative. Consider adding a task called "Thinking" to your project plan. To avoid raising eyebrows with management, call the task something inventive, such as Cerebral Exploration of Future Profits through Solid Applications, or simply Playing the Xbox in the Employee Lounge.

Defensive programming tends to add code to your application. But what is the objective of product development: fewer lines of code or correct code—particularly if performance is not measurably different? Regardless, I would attest that customers prefer correct code over a suspect application that performs a nanosecond quicker.

"Assume the worst case scenario in all circumstances" is an important tenet of defensive programming. The worst problems occur when developers assume otherwise. Code as if anything is possible. For example, always code the default case in a switch statement, even if the probability is remote. In the worst case scenario, the error handling in the default case is never used. In the best case scenario, you handled a future problem correctly.

Defensive Programming and C#

C# was designed with defensive programming in mind. C++ is akin to the wild wild West, where literally anything goes. Developers have enormous flexibility in C++, which is both good and bad. Developers are given plenty of rope. You know what some people can do with a long rope. C# has attempted to rein in the freewheeling environment of C++. For this reason, developers can focus mostly on resolving business problems and less time wrestling with the nuances of the language. The assignment problem is a perfect example of this. In C++, the following code is valid:

```
int a=5;
if(a)
{
        // Do whatever
}
```

In C++, *true* is a non-zero value, and *false* is zero. This means an integral value can be substituted as a Boolean value in expressions, as shown previously. Using an integer value for a Boolean accords considerable flexibility but can also result in an error if done incorrectly. One reason is that developers often forget the rules. The definition of *true* and *false* varies between languages, which can cause confusion for even experienced developers. In addition, the code is not very readable. In C#, Boolean expressions are limited to Boolean values (*true* or *false*), which is clearer. Clarity prevents potential problems. This is an example of a rule that forces defensive programming in C#.

Here is another example. The following code is allowed in C++. A transfer of control statement, such as a break statement, is not required with each case statement. For that reason, the following code is a nifty way to calculate a factorial. C# expects transfer control statements between each case statement and would not compile similar code. Why? Omitting the break statement in a switch block is a common C++ error. Preventing this error in C# is a form of defensive programming.

```
int factorial=5;
int result=1;
switch(factorial){
    case 5: result*=factorial--;
    case 4:result*=factorial--;
    case 3:result*=factorial--;
    case 2:result*=factorial--;
}
```

Warnings

Sometimes more is more. That is something Yogi Berra would say. Set and keep the warning level at the highest level. More warnings during compilation are the result. You must then commit to investigating every warning, which is an element of defensive programming. It is better to resolve reported problems early instead of later at run time or during deployment. You should always prefer to find problems before the customer. Fortunately, the default warning level is 4, which is the highest level. Lowering the warning level will assuredly lead to quieter compilations. However, in this circumstance, silence is not golden.

You may also consider treating warnings as errors. This mandates that every warning must be recognized and resolved before a successful compilation. This is important for defensive programming because problems cannot be deferred to later. Current compilers are sophisticated and not prone to generating extraneous warnings. For that reason, no warning is a nuisance and every warning is worth investigating. The Treat Warnings As Errors option enforces this policy. Unfortunately, this option is sometimes not practical for legacy applications, where the challenge to address every warning is not always possible. However, it is important to retain this option as long as possible. Alternatively, you can redline specific warnings using the pragma error warning statement. This would allow the continued use of the Treat Warnings As Errors option, while accepting some warnings.

Set both the Warning Level and Treat Warnings As Errors options in the Project Properties dialog box. In the Properties window, open the Build pane. From there, the Errors And Warnings and Treat Warnings As Errors option groups are available. See Figure 8-1.

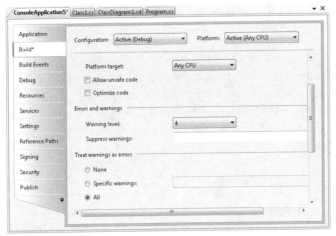

FIGURE 8-1 The Build pane with the Warning Level and the Treat Warnings As Errors options.

Code Review

Code review is a first line of defense in defensive programming. Proofread a business document or personal letter that you have written, and then have someone else proofread the same document. The other person will almost assuredly find more problems than you. Why? At a subconscious level, you read *what you think* was written, which is often different than the actual text. Developers have the same challenge when examining code. It is difficult for them to see errors in their own code.

Some time ago, I was employed at the National Climate Center in Asheville, North Carolina, which is part of the National Oceanic Atmospheric Administration (NOAA). NOAA is a unit of the U.S. Department of Commerce. My manager asked that I write an inventory system. At that time, they had a Univac 1100/60 mainframe. Okay, maybe this was more than some time ago. I decided to write the inventory system as an online application—even though the customer had not requested this. However, it was cool! Unbeknownst to management, I ordered the technical manuals for the computer terminals. Using a combination of COBOL, FORTRAN, and assembler routines, I eventually completed the online inventory system. A few months later, I left the National Climate Center without documenting the application. Yes, I should have been drawn and quartered.

A couple years later, the National Climate Center bought replacement terminals for the old units. The new terminals were from a different vendor. Shortly thereafter the online inventory system crashed. For a small fee, I was coerced into returning to resolve the problem. I made the appropriate changes (basically rewriting the entire application) to correct the problem. In the meantime, they had hired someone to *comment other* people's code. I was obligated to review the code—line by line—with this individual. This was a precursor to what is now called a code review. During the review, numerous problems were uncovered. Because of the code review, the final version of the application was much more stable and correct.

Have a formal process of code reviews at a minimum of two milestones: checking source into source control and product deployment. Informally, have a code review as often as reasonably possible. For informal code reviews, find someone outside your immediate team— someone who has a different perspective and maybe different assumptions. This will provide a fresh set of eyes on the code.

Software Testing

Software testing is the formal process of evaluating an application. Testing compares expected results to actual results, where a deviation indicates that the test failed. Testing can test the correctness of an application but is also used for validating security, scalability, and customer expectations. Typically a software test accepts inputs as the parameters of the test. You execute the test, which exercises the application. The output is then compared with the expected result. Input can be functional parameters, user interaction, database input, and so on. Test failures, if any, are recorded in a bug tracking system. Except for the simplest application, more than a single test is required to adequately test an application. A test suite consists of multiple tests, where each test verifies or validates a different aspect or perspective of the application. In this manner, the test suite provides a complete analysis of the application. Testing is verification and validation. Verification verifies that some part of the application is technically or functionally correct. For example, verification would confirm the return value of a specific function. Validation validates the expectation of the application. A test of the user interface against customer expectation would be an example of a validation test.

When possible, test suites should be automated. This creates a convenient and consistent means of executing a series of tests. Consistency is important for benchmarking and comparing a series of tests over a period of time. Database-driven tests are useful for increasing consistency. Each data record would contain input parameters for a single test. This is ideal for consecutive tests with multiple input values. Tests can also be automated using scripts. There are a variety of products available for this.

Both software testers and developers build tests. Actually, the collaboration of software testers and developers often result in the best tests. However, developers are sometimes solely responsible for generating tests. This is the case in a test-driven programming methodology. In that methodology, developers write a test first and then the code to pass the test second. With the test-driven approach, testing is an integral part of the coding process.

Testing should begin early in the software development cycle. As soon as there is enough of an application to be hoisted into a test harness, testing should start. You must accurately access and incorporate in the project plan time for testing. This includes the initial tests and later regression tests. Problems found later in the software development life cycle may require re-architecting the application, which is expensive late in the development process. This is one reason to use a test-driven development (TDD) approach, where testing starts even before coding and continues throughout the development process. Excluding the TDD, you should begin testing after the code base is stabilized. Testing an application before then can be daunting because the code base is constantly changing.

What is a regression test? The pesticide paradox, as defined by Boris Beizer, states, "Every method you use to prevent or find bugs leaves a residue of subtler bugs against which those methods are ineffective." Regressions tests test previously working software for failures. There are several reasons to run regression tests:

- Changes made to the code because of a previous failed test
- Changes to the testing environment
- Changes to the operating environment
- Refactoring

Creating a test is usually straightforward. However, creating tests that reflect the real-world operating modality (stress, user interaction, data input, and more) can be more challenging. This is especially important because developers often have an ideal development environment: computers faster than lightning, a monitor the size of a Volkswagen, and disk storage capacity best described as redefining the bounds of the nature. This can be significantly different from the production environment where an application is deployed. For example, when testing a high-traffic Web application, creating an environment that accurately reflects the typically load can be difficult. For intensive database applications, simulating the breadth and randomness of data content can be challenging. Visual Studio offers some assistance in this area and supports Web, load, unit, and manual tests.

You should test functional and non-functional activities. A common test provides input to a function and compares the output to a known result. Any discrepancy is an indication of a bug. However, some tests are less conventional. For example, sometimes external factors needed to be considered. You could have an application that predicts earthquakes by detecting subtle tremors through remote sensors. This type of application might require a manual test. It is hard to automate an earthquake. Here is one potential test. Start the application, leave the office, and jump up and down in the middle of the street. Assuming that you are not hit by a car, you can return to the office and verify whether a tremor was detected by the software application. Manual tests are supported in Visual Studio. Other categories of tests are scalability, usability, security, and more. It is important to test the various aspects of your application.

Although testing should be rigorous, you cannot test everything. Testing every permutation in some circumstances is impossible. Look at the following formula, which is a simple equation:

```
x=y+z;
```

Assuming *x*, *y*, and *z* are integers, there are several million permutations of the preceding equation. You cannot, and it is not necessary, to test each of these permutations. You should determine and test the limits of the equation, where failure is much more likely. This is a handful of tests, which is more manageable.

Testing is a feature of Visual Studio Team System. It is convenient to have the test harness (test project) and code project saved in the same solution. This is particularly convenient for a test-driven development approach to programming.

Test-Driven Development

TDD is a test first and code second approach to programming. You create a test for an outstanding requirement or some portion of a requirement (each test should comprise only a few lines of code). The test will initially fail because the code is not implemented. Implement the code and rerun the test, which should now pass. If so, you can proceed to the next test. This is an incremental approach to creating an application and melds testing and development. This is not a different style of testing but a different style of programming. Test-driven programming is the reverse of traditional programming, where code is implemented first and then tested.

In TDD, you create a test suite incrementally that provides coverage for the entire application. Most of the test suite consists of unit tests that test specific code in the application. However, it can also include acceptance tests. Acceptance tests reflect customer expectations of the product and encompass processes as compared with specific code. In an accounting system, an acceptance test could be entering an accounting transaction.

There are several advantages to the TDD programming methodology:

- Reliability is enhanced since all code is encompassed by a test. Naturally, 100 percent code coverage reduces the probability of a bug.

- The emerging test suite provides continual feedback on the stability of the application.

- TDD promotes compiling and testing code in small increments, which emphasizes decomposition.

- TDD also promotes implementing and testing components separately. This enforces a high level of isolation and reduces dependencies between classes and components.

- Increased awareness of the requirements means developers are more knowledgeable about the code.

- Finally, each test further documents the code. This is helpful in maintaining the application into the future.

Test-driven development is more of a challenge for graphical user interface (GUI) applications. The primary focus of TDD is functional tests. With an advanced GUI application, there is a portion of the application that is user driven and outside the scope of a functional test. Functional tests are typically code based and discrete, while GUI tests are process related and span one or more functions. For TDD, it is more appropriate to have a functional foundation with the user interface as a thin veneer. This makes it easier to emulate the user interface in relation to functionality. Another drawback to TDD is the expanded code base. TDD requires an extensive testing infrastructure, which translates into considerably more code. This code must also be maintained and kept current with the implementation.

TDD requires a higher level of discipline and commitment. Developers must adhere to the test first and then code philosophy. You create a test to move the development process forward, rather than write code. This is foreign to most developers. In addition, developers dislike writing tests and may be tempted to subjugate the process. The temptation is heightened when faced with an impending deadline. Management must be included in the decision to adopt TDD and understand the value proposition for the development team. Management needs to adjust developer assessment and incentives to reward developers for properly executing the TDD process.

Here are the details of the test-driven development process. First, evaluate the current requirement. Next, write a failed test for that requirement, which is added to the test suite. Stub the code to confirm that the test fails. Implement minimal code to make the test pass. Remember, each test should encompass only a handful of code. After the test passes, refactor the code. Refactoring includes removing redundancies, optimizing algorithms, or otherwise improving the code. Next, rerun the individual test. If the test passes, run regression tests to validate the overall health of the application. Repeat the process for the next requirement. TDD is divided into three phases: Red, Green, and Refactor. In the Red phase, the test fails. In the Green phase, the code is implemented and the test passes. In the Refactor phase, the code is perfected. Figure 8-2 shows the TDD process.

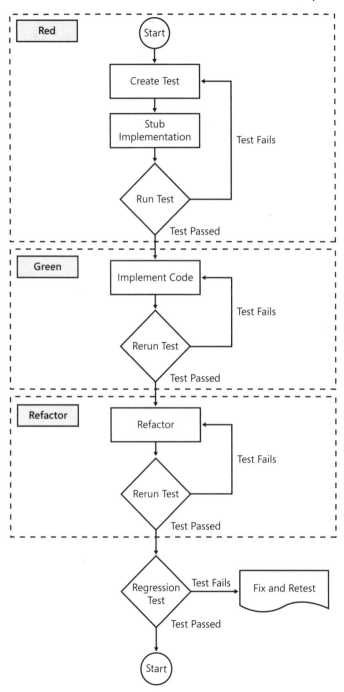

FIGURE 8-2 Diagram of the TDD process.

Code Coverage

Testing is as effective as the percentage of code touched. Testing that does not exercise a larger portion of your code does not provide quality assurance. For this reason, defensive programming requires that the majority of your code be tested. Code that is not tested may contain uncovered problems. As the percentage of untested code increases, so does the likelihood of undiscovered problems. Code coverage reports how much code is included under the testing umbrella. Code coverage is considered white-box testing and not black-box testing. White-box testing is testing on the internals of an application and requires code-level understanding of the application. White-box testing is also referred to as glass-box testing. It's called "glass box" because you are seeing through the exterior of the application to test the details. Black-box testing is essentially functional or aspect testing. With black-box testing, inputs are defined, functionality is executed, and then outputs are compared with expected results. This requires little or no knowledge of the internal workings of the application. Black-box testing is also called functional testing.

Technically speaking, code coverage does not test an application. It does not explicitly improve the reliability or correctness of an application. Code coverage is not a direct indicator of problems in an application. Therefore a high percentage of code coverage does not guarantee a quality application. Conversely, low code coverage is not a definite indicator of a buggy application. Code coverage is simply a barometer of the breadth of testing relative to the overall application. Code coverage highlights possible lapses in testing (code that is not touched). You can then design additional tests for those areas of the program. It is better to view code coverage as an indirect confirmation of the reliability of an application. High code coverage indicates that the majority of the program is covered by a test. This means the vulnerabilities are much more likely to have been discovered now and into the future. Low coverage means potential problems may lurk simply because the code has never been tested.

Code coverage can be more or less granular depending on the level of code coverage desired. Here are the more commonly types of code coverage:

- **Functional coverage**   Functional coverage reports on whether a function is exercised and the frequency. You are basically testing function inputs and outputs.

- **Statement coverage**   Statement code coverage reports on whether a line of code is touched and how often.

- **Path coverage**   Path code coverage reports on whether paths of execution have been exercised. In a typical application, there are multiple paths of execution.

With the exception of TDD, you should not expect 100 percent code coverage. For a normal application, code coverage of 85 percent to 90 percent is viewed as adequate. Reaching code coverage at this level is not easy. The appropriate level of code coverage depends on the type of application. For example, mission critical applications may indeed require 100 percent code coverage. In these circumstances, an error in a single line of code could cause serious problems (even beyond the application). Software for the main system of the space shuttle might require 100 percent code coverage. Software for a heart monitoring system might require similarly high code coverage; a single mistake in a heart monitoring system could be fatal. However, 100 percent code coverage is typically not possible or necessary. If you are writing a game application, that level of code coverage is probably not required. The level of code coverage should be set before programming begins. This level of code coverage must be communicated to and agreed upon by everyone on the team. *For source control, source code not meeting that standard should not be checked in.*

Code coverage is available in Visual Studio Team System and as command-line tools. The command-line tools are located in the *install directory*\Microsoft Visual Studio 9.0\Team Tools\Performance Tools directory. Command-line code coverage tools are convenient for scripting and automating the test environment. Following is a list of the tools.

- **VSInstr.exe**   VSInstr instruments an application and .pdb file.

- **VSPerfCmd.exe**   VSPerfCmd can perform a variety of code coverage tasks, including starting code coverage, returning the current status of code coverage, and stopping code coverage.

- **VSPerfMon.exe**   VSPerfMon is the actual tool that collects code coverage data from instrumented applications that are running. This tool is called from VSPerfCmd to start code coverage.

- **VSPerfReport.exe**   VSPerfReport creates a report from the code coverage data, which is saved to a .vsp file.

- **VSPerfCLREnv.cmd**   VSPerfCLREnv sets environment variables in support of manual code coverage for .NET applications.

Self-Documenting Code

Many developers are less than passionate about commenting their code. For this reason, comments are provided but are often incomplete and most likely not maintained. One solution is self-documenting code. Self-documenting code is readable code. When you read self-documenting code, it reads like a story complete with plot twists and protagonists. The amount of separate commenting required for code is inversely proportional to the readability of that code. Basically, the more readable the code, the less comments are needed.

This is guaranteed. If you cannot understand your program, another developer will not. This leads to programming errors. Be kind to developers who might maintain your application in the future. Remember, one day *you* may be in the role of maintenance programmer. Most programs spend the majority of their lifetime being maintained. Therefore, self-documenting code is an important defensive programming technique.

Look at the following code. What does the code accomplish? The code is nearly unreadable because the variable names are abbreviated. Despite this, the code is correct. However, the context is lost. Maintaining this code would be difficult. Inadvertently introducing problems to this code would be easy.

```
int i= 1250;
double d= .05;
int u= 2;
int f= 100;
const double t= .065;
double t2= (i + u);
t2 = t2 - (t2 * d);
t2 = t2 * (1 + t);
t2 = t2 + (f* u);
```

Functionally, the following is identical to the previous code—except descriptive long names have been substituted for the short names. The expressions and the context are now both transparent, which makes the code clearer and more maintainable. Actually, an error is now apparent. This is an error that was impossible to detect in the preceding code. The expression *purchaseprice + units*, which calculates the total price, is incorrect. It should be *purchaseprice*units*. This is an example of defensive programming.

```
int purchaseprice = 1250;
double discount = .05;
int units = 2;
int installationfee = 100;
const double tax = .065;
double total = (purchaseprice + units);
total = total - (total * discount);
total = total*(1 + tax);
total = total + (installationfee*units);
```

Naming Conventions

Proper naming conventions enhance code readability and contribute to self-documenting code. These are helpful rules for naming elements of an application.

- Classes represent a person, place, or thing. As such, class identifiers should be nouns.

- Member functions imply some sort of action. For this reason, verbs are usually used as function identifiers. Verbs, such as start, stop, or delete, indicate action and are perfect for function names.

- Like a class, data members are also a person, place, or thing. Therefore, data members should be assigned a noun as the name.

- Namespace names should also be nouns.

Class and namespace names should be Pascal case, while class members should be camel case. For a complete explanation of capitalization of identifiers, refer to MSDN. The book

Code Complete (Microsoft, 2004), by Steve McConnell, also provides excellent information on naming identifiers. In general, *Code Complete* is also a great resource for techniques on defensive programming.

Use long names. Do not sacrifice readability to save a character or two. Not every developer is a good typist. Unbelievably, this is frequently the reason for short names. Take typing lessons! The overall cost of unreadable code is more expensive than a typing class and affects many others. Code should not require cryptanalysis to interpret. Of course, balance is the key. Your code should not read like a Tolstoy novel.

Prefixes further describe a variable or the name of a data member. As such, although optional, prefixes are a common artifact of many programs. Consistency is the primary benefit, which is important in a collaborative environment. When you have several people working on the same project, a common set of prefixes helps to avoid improper use of data members and variables. A type prefix indicates the type of the entity. For example, *nVar* indicates an integer variable. Context prefixes highlight the usage of a variable. For example, *gVar* indicates a global variable. Do not concatenate multiple prefixes at the start of an identifier. This can be confusing. You do not want developers to spend their valuable time deciphering alphabet soup. This is important—prefixes must be kept current. The refactoring feature of Visual Studio makes this easy. Prefixes document the code and benefit readability. Invalid prefixes are a form of misdocumentation and contribute to coding errors.

Pseudo Code

Most paintings start life as a rough sketch. An artist creates a sketch to explore a concept, dabble with a color scheme, explore different media (for example charcoal versus chalk), and more. The sketch, not the final work, is where the artist experiments. Artists will often refer back to the sketch as necessary while completing the actual work. In this way, the sketch documents what the artist intends. Pseudo code is to the developer what the sketch is to the artist.

Developers sketch their program in pseudo code. This should be done in an incremental manner as portions of the software application are written. What is pseudo code? Pseudo code is a blend of natural language and software language, with an emphasis on substance. It may have some but not all the detail or syntax of a programming language. Pseudo code is intended to be informal. There is no reference manual or universal set of rules to follow. The most important rule is that pseudo code should be readable. However, there should be sufficient details to make translation from pseudo code to programming language trivial.

Pseudo code fulfills a role similar to flow charting—except developers will actually use pseudo code. Most developers abandon flow charting as an integral part of the development process once they leave the hollowed grounds of the university parking lot the final time. However, developers will sketch algorithms on the back of a napkin at lunch, write a complex formula on the palm of their hands while in yet another boring meeting, and write stored procedures with crayons on the back of furniture while playing with their kids. All of this is pseudo code and is useful for documenting an application.

Here are the steps for using pseudo code:

1. Write the pseudo code first.

2. Use the pseudo code as a roadmap to writing the actual code. The names of identifiers for classes, variables, and other entities can be derived from the pseudo code. Because pseudo code is a mixture of an informal description and programming syntax, the translation should be straightforward.

3. Insert pseudo code into the source code as comments.

For developers who loathe writing detailed comments, pseudo code is a reasonable solution for code-level comments. The following is pseudo code for sample code presented earlier in the chapter:

```
initialize the variables
total = purchase price * number of units
total = total minus any discount
total = total + tax rate
total = total plus any installation fees
display results
```

The following is the actual code with pseudo code inline as the comments. I did not have to write any additional comments. I took the pseudo code, which already existed, and converted them to comments. This is defensive programming with a bonus. Pseudo code is a best practice for defensive programming. Converting that into comments, which is convenient and quick, is a bonus.

```
// initialize the variables

int purchaseprice = 1250;
double discount = .05;
int units = 2;
int installationfee = 100;
const double tax = .065;

// total = purchase price * number of units

double total = (purchaseprice + units);

// total = total minus any discount

total = total - (total * discount);

// total = total + tax rate

total = total*(1 + tax);
```

```
// total = total plus any installation fees
total = total + (installationfee*units);

// display results
```

Comments

Comment, comment, and more comments. If in doubt, add even more comments. Source code cannot have too many comments. Comments are the narrative for source code. Write comments for the future maintenance programmer, the person conducting the code review, and, most important, yourself. Have you ever reviewed your own code after a few months? Without comments, you might as well be reading Galwegian Gaelic—an extinct language once spoken in a region of Scotland. Despite all efforts to improve the readability of code, source code is often neither readable nor clear. When this occurs, it can be as difficult as interpreting an extinct language. Comments solve this problem.

The Hong Kong Airport is more of a shopping center than an airport. There are so many stores that it is sometimes difficult to find the gates. I remember wandering the airport looking for my gate, lost among an impressive menagerie of stores: Christian Dior, Lanvin Paris, Gucci, Giordano, Bvlgari, Tiffany and Company, and many more. Surround your source with comments equally well. The comments should almost be a nuisance.

Ample comments are necessary. However, comments should not simply repeat source code. This often occurs when programmers are attempting to close out a project and must add comments in haste. Comments, but not effective comments, are added. More thought must be put into commenting. Comments should add the context, assumptions, limits, and, in general, clarity as to the intent of the code.

Keep the format simple and comments close to the documented code. I have seen beautiful comments, where a developer obviously invested considerable time in the format. However, someone must maintain that format. This can be time consuming when the code base changes regularly. For comments, invest your time in clarity and not formatting. Even if you have a sophisticated tool that automatically formats comments, keep the format simple. Your successor may not have access to that tool.

As a convenience, some developers place comments at the top of a source file. This creates a single location where all comments can be found and maintained relative to that file. The problem is that a particular comment may not be near the related source code. As the source file grows, this problem will only worsen. A disconnect is created between the comments and the source code, which will inevitably cause problems.

Do not comment hacks. Change the code! Honestly, hacks still retain some value in C++. For performance and brevity, sometimes a C++ hack may have benefit. However, that is becoming less true as compilers improve. For C#, no hack is a good hack. Focus on the solution and leave everything else to the C# compiler and the Common Language Runtime (CLR). Every team has a developer who has perfected the art of hacks. Send that person for sensitivity training. From a defensive programming perspective, hacks are inevitably hard to maintain and also hurt productivity, which is expensive.

Every important aspect of the program should be commented. Ask yourself this question. Without this comment, is the code transparent? If it is transparent, a comment is probably unnecessary. However, make sure it is transparent to *someone else*. If in doubt, always add a comment.

At a minimum, comment these areas of a program:

- **Program**   Comments should describe the application and application design. In addition, the comments should include company information, copyright, build detail, and a brief description of the project files.

- **Source file**   Comment on the version control information, the context of the file, and the relationship of classes defined in the file.

- **Classes**   Comment on the purpose of the class, the class interface, assumptions, and dependencies.

- **Functions**   Comment on the behavior, parameters, return value, assumptions, and any limitations.

- **Fields and properties**   Comment on the extents of the data, initialization, and code usage. Also, document scope and visibility if applicable, such as whether the member is global or static.

- **Algorithms**   Comment on the basis of the algorithm, such as academic references. Also, document the reason this particular algorithm is used, any assumptions, and limitations.

- **Transfer of control**   Comment on possible criteria and potential paths.

- **Performance**   Comment areas of code that might affect performance or scalability. List the performance factors and measurements.

Comments must be kept current. If not, the related comment should be removed. Alternatively, the comment can be deprecated if clearly indicated. Outdated comments are misleading at best and can contribute to programming errors.

Documentation Comments

In Microsoft Visual C#, you can create documentation comments with triple forward slashes (///). Each documentation comment has a standard XML tag. The XML tag holds the specific comment. There are documentation tags for various aspects of the source code. For example, the *<param>* documentation tag describes a function parameter. In this way, documentation comments provide consistency to commenting. All classes, parameters, functions, and so on are documented in the same manner with separate XML tags. This is particularly important when several developers are collaborating on a project. Developers often have wildly varying styles of commenting, which can be confusing when combined in a single project. Documentation comments alleviate some of this inconsistency. Also, documentation comments augment IntelliSense with information on user-defined types, functions, and parameters. For library developers, this provides users with helpful added documentation.

Documentation comments precede the code that is being referenced. Visual Studio provides automatic insertion of documentation comments for certain language elements, such as classes and functions. Simply type **///** on the source line prior to the target element. This was done in following code. Visual Studio then automatically inserts the summary comment. You can then complete this comment and add additional XML documentation tags as needed.

```
/// <summary>
///
/// </summary>
class TestClass
{

}
```

As mentioned, from the documentation comments, you can create an XML documentation file. Open the project properties to create the file. Choose the Build pane. In the Output group, select XML Documentation File and specify the path and file name. See Figure 8-3. The XML documentation can then be formatted and published as documentation for the application. This is another nice feature for developers supporting libraries and users.

FIGURE 8-3 Select XML Documentation File to export documentation comments to a file.

Several XML tags are defined for documentation comments. Table 8-1 lists the primary tags.

TABLE 8-1 Primary XML Tags and Their Descriptions

Name	Description
Example	The *<example>* tag, and *<code>* sub element, assigns sample code to a comment.
Exception	Each *<exception>* tag identifies an exception that can be thrown. The specific exception is identified with the *cref* attribute.
Include	When the XML documentation file is created, the file referenced by the *<include>* tag is inserted inline.
Param	Each *<param>* tag documents a function parameter.
Permission	The *<permission>* tag describes the security permissions of a type member. The specific permission set is identified with the *cref* attribute.
Remarks	Use the *<remarks>* element to provide a description of a type.
Returns	The *<returns>* tag describes the return of a method, which includes properties.
Seealso	The *<seealso>* lists a secondary reference for a comment. The reference is set with the *cref* attribute.
Summary	Use the *<summary>* element to describe a member of a type, such as a field or property.

We started the chapter with a reference to small things. Let us expand upon that conversation.

Defensive Programming with Classes

When implementing a class, defensive programming should be considered. These techniques are likely to make your program *not* compile, which is a benefit. Problems are isolated at compile time and not later. Early discovery is always better. This is an example of not taking shortcuts simply to compile your program. Fight that temptation. Instead, force problems to compile time. It is less expensive to have the compiler find your problems than a customer—and definitely better for your brand.

The fully abstract class is an important concept in object-oriented analysis and design (OOAD). It is also important for defensive programming. A fully abstract class exposes an interface and hides the details. The interface is the public functionality of the class. Controlling access to the state of a class prevents inappropriate usage of the details (i.e., data members). Exposed data members can be changed far away from the class implementation, where the context is missing. This is where a mistake is likely to occur. A fully abstract class prevents this. Data members must be changed in member functions. In the member function, which is implemented in the class, the context is obvious.

Modifiers

Proper modifiers on a class are an important step in defensive programming. Class modifiers form an invaluable check on the intent of the class designer and developer. For example, a class designated as abstract in design should be decorated with the abstract modifier at implementation. Any attempt to create an instance of the abstract class will now cause a compile error, which is appropriate. Another example would be members with static content. Prefix those members with the *readonly* or *const* modifier, depending on when initialization occurs. If you later forget the intent of the member and assign the member a value, an error will occur at compilation. You catch the problem early.

Interfaces

The separation of interface and implementation is an important tool in defensive program-ming. A clear view of the interface is helpful in using the type correctly. Separating the inter-face from the implementation provides that. The code from the implementation, particularly for a large class, distracts from the interface, which can lead to improper use of the class. The interface should be clearly visible. For C++ developers, header files provided this clarity. This is the reason why header files are consistently used in C++ code, even though header files are technically optional.

For developers of libraries, there is an extra benefit to using the interface. You can expose the interface and not the actual object. This limits access to the actual object.

You can also expose a subset of available behavior of an object through an interface. Exposing discrete interfaces allows a developer to expose behavior based on context. If there was an *Amphibious* class, it would have two interfaces: *IAuto* and *IBoat*. Based on the usage (land or water), you could expose one of the two interfaces. (See the following code.) Limiting behavior to a specific context with an interface is a good defensive programming technique. This restricts the object to proper behavior based on the usage. Any attempt at other behav-ior would cause a compile error.

Look at the following sample code. The *Amphibious* class has *ICar* and *IBoat* interfaces.

```
public interface ICar {
    bool Start();
    bool Accelerate();
    bool Turn();
    // other methods
}

public interface IBoat {
    bool Start();
    bool Accelerate();
```

```
        bool Turn();
        // other methods
    }
    internal class Amphibious : ICar, IBoat {
        // interface method implementation
    }

    public abstract class Boat {
        public static IBoat GetBoat() {
            return new Amphibious();
        }
        public static ICar Convert2Car(IBoat obj) {
            return (ICar) obj;
        }
    }
}
```

Here is the *Amphibious* class being used:

```
IBoat myBoat = Boat.GetBoat();
myBoat.Start();
ICar myCar = Boat.Convert2Car(myBoat);
myCar.Turn();
```

Defensive Programming Without Examples

As mentioned, defensive programming is about small things. Some of the effects of defensive programming are rather subtle. For example, group related code with spaces. See the following code.

```
int number=0;
int factorial=0;
Console.WriteLine("Enter number:");
string snumber=Console.ReadLine();
number=int.Parse(snumber);
for(factorial=1;(number-1)>0;--number) {
    factorial*=number;
}
Console.WriteLine("Factorial is {0}.", factorial);
```

In the following code, spaces have been added. The resulting code is more readable. This change is both simple and subtle. Admittedly, the difference between the two versions is not dramatic. However, together all the details of defensive programming will dramatically improve the quality of your program.

```
int number=0;
int factorial=0;
Console.WriteLine("Enter number:");
string snumber=Console.ReadLine();
number=int.Parse(snumber);
```

```
for(factorial=1;(number-1)>0;--number) {
    factorial*=number;
}
```

```
Console.WriteLine("Factorial is {0}.", factorial);
```

The following is a list of other points that should be considered for defensive programming. Most of this reflects common sense programming. Nonetheless, each item is worth mentioning. You might want to create a "to do" list, which is checked during code development.

■ At the start of a function, check parameters for correctness. Confirm that parameters fall within an acceptable range of values. Remember the conventional programming adage: "garbage in, garbage out."

■ After a series of related expressions, check the correctness of affected variables. A series of expressions can alter the state of the application. Confirm that the resulting state is correct.

■ When possible, resolve problems with error handling and not exception handling.

■ When possible, functions should return something—not *void*. Functions that return nothing cannot be verified with exception handling.

■ Always check the return value of functions. Regardless of how unlikely, do not assume that a function will not fail. Improper assumptions are a primary contributor to errors at run time.

■ When porting code, convert pointer algorithms to references. Pointers interfere with normal garbage collection. Defining an unsafe block and keeping the pointer algorithm may be quicker. However, spending time to remove the pointers will make the application safer.

■ Do not write unsafe code. Operations that require an unsafe block are inherently dangerous and should be avoided.

■ Do not use literals. Repeated use of a literal cannot be optimized. As shown earlier in this chapter, literals are not readable code. Use a *const* variable instead. *Const* variables are named, while literals are not. This makes the code more readable.

■ Except when switching on an enumeration, always add the default statement to a switch block. The worst case scenario is that the default case is not used, which is better than the alterative.

■ Do not catch the general exception type. Catching *System.Exception* masks the specific exception and origin of a problem. By catching *any* exception, you cannot respond to a specific exception.

■ Do not special case exceptions. To "special case exceptions" means to catch *System. Exception* and, in the exception handler, handle specific exceptions. The problem is that other exceptions are filtered and then not handled with unpredictable results.

- Avoid defining or using object types. Using object types may unintentionally cause boxing or downcasting to a specific type. Boxing and downcasting adversely affect the performance of your application.

- Repetitive code is the breeding ground of future problems. Refactor code into reusable blocks or functions.

- Always used generic collections instead of standard collections. Standard collections are collections of object types, which cause boxing. Boxing is expensive.

- Use arrays when possible and not collections. Arrays may be old-fashioned when compared with vectors, link lists, dictionaries, and so on. However, arrays are simple and typically quicker than a collection. Less complexity means fewer problems.

- Do not use a native application programming interface (API) for functionality that exists in the .NET Framework Class Library (FCL).

- The *for* statement is preferred to other types of loops. *For* loops are structured and enforce programmer discipline. That structure prevents inadvertent errors. *While* and similar loops are flexible, but that openness can foster unattended errors.

- Unused objects should be set to *null*. You can then reliably check the status of the object. This also helps with garbage collection.

Defensive Programming with Examples

Avoid stupid complexity. Every team has a developer who specializes in writing code that is unreadable. If it looks like a hack, it probably should be rewritten. This was mentioned earlier, but it is worth repeating. Needlessly complicated code is more prone to have bugs, is harder to maintain, and is most often unreadable. Importantly, complex code does not generally run any quicker than the simpler version. Look at this code. It calculates a factorial within a single line of source code.

```
for(result=factorial;--factorial-1;result*=factorial);
```

The following example is simpler. It is several source lines, but it is more readable and just as effective.

```
for(result=1;number<factorial+1;++number)
{
    result=result*number;
}
```

When you have the option, always use a block and not a single statement. This prevents a common mistake of adding a statement later that should be part of a block but is not. Here is an error waiting to happen:

```
for(int var=0;var<10;++var)
    ++locala;
```

This easily becomes the following code, which is an error. The increment of *localb*, which should be controlled by the *for* statement, is outside the *for* loop.

```
for(int var=0;var<10;++var)
    ++locala;
    ++localb;
```

This simple change would have avoided the problem.

```
for(int var=0;var<10;++var)
{
    ++locala;
}
```

Decompose complex expressions. Separate a complex expression into individual expressions. If there is a problem in the following code, can you identify where?

```
double var=(((product+(product*priceDiscount))*(1+taxes))+(freight*units))*(1+regionCost);
```

This is more readable, and errors, if any, are more transparent.

```
double var=0;
var=product+(product*priceDiscount);
var=var*(1+taxes);
var=var+(freight*units);
var=var*(1+regionCost);
```

Parentheses add clarity to code. Look at the following equation. I often teach programming classes. In some of those classes, students are asked to manually calculate the result to the following equation. There are four common answers, in order of popularity: 110, 100, 101, and 11.

```
int i=10*10+10/10;
```

The correct answer is 101. The problem is that not everyone knows the order of precedence for operators. Parentheses can add clarity even when not changing the result. I am sure most everyone could obtain the correct answer from the following equation. The only difference is the added parentheses.

```
int i=(10*10)+(10/10);
```

Adhere to the guidelines of the Common Language Specification (CLS). This is especially important if you are writing code to be used by other developers. Case sensitive names would be an example of this. In the CLS, there is a specification about avoiding case sensitive names. The reason is that some .NET languages are case insensitive. The following code works perfectly in C#. This code is admittedly contrived but does convey the problem. Notice that there are separate *funca* and *FuncA* functions. The names are case sensitive. However, in a case insensitive language, these names would be ambiguous. For example, Visual Basic .NET is a case insensitive language.

```
public class XClass{
    public void funca(){
        // code
    }
    public void FuncA(){
        // code
    }
}
```

The preceding code is published as a library. It can then be referenced from another project, such as a Visual Basic .NET project. In that project, you could create an instance of the *XClass* type. However, neither *FuncA* method would be visible. Because the functions are ambiguous in Visual Basic .NET, both functions are not available. Your telephone is ringing because that Visual Basic developer is calling you at this very moment. For them, this is a bug—a bug that could have been avoided by following the guidelines of the CLS.

Many types expose properties that define the extents of that type. For primitive types, these are the *MinValue* and *MaxValue* properties. Use these properties in error checking to protect from overflows and underflows. This is less expensive than handling an exception. Look at the following code. The *IntegerMultiply* function calculates the product of two variables. The result is passed out as an integer variable, which is a parameter of the function call. The *Int. MaxValue* property checks for an overflow in the calculation before returning the result.

```
public static bool IntegerMultiply(int val1, int val2, out int result) {
    bool resp = int.MaxValue > (((long)val1)*val2);
    if (resp) {
        result = val1 * val2;
    }
    else{
        result = 0;
    }
    return resp;
}
```

Loops should be refactored. Expensive operations must be removed from the loop. Actions, such as unnecessary input/output, can throttle the performance of an application. Unnecessary boxing in a loop is another example of something that should be removed. This can fragment the heap, exert memory pressure, and cause premature memory collection, which is expensive. For boxing, box the value above the loop or create a wrapper class, which is a reference type. Look at the following code. In the loop, boxing occurs at the assignment to *reftype*. This means boxing will occur 1,000 times.

```
int number = 5;
object reftype;
for (int a=0; a < 1000; ++a ) {
    reftype = number;

    // do something with referencetype
}
```

The following code is modified to avoid the unnecessary boxing. The number variable is boxed before the loop. Therefore, boxing occurs only once instead of 1,000 times. This is considerably more efficient.

```
int number = 5;
object value = number;
object reftype;
for (int a=0; a < 1000; ++a ){
    reftype = value;

    // do something with referencetype
}
```

For defensive programming, enumerations are better than open integers. Assigning an invalid value to an enumeration is automatically detected at compile time and not run time. You do not have to write the logic to detect the invalid value. It is automatic. Filtering invalid integral values occurs at run time and relies on code logic and programming discipline. This code uses an integral value in the switch block. The default statement protects from invalid values. However, the default statement is executed at run time.

```
switch (value) {
    case 0:
        break;
    case 1:
        break;
    case 2:
        break;
    default:
}
```

This code uses an enumeration. Notice that the default statement is omitted. Why? Because an enumeration represents a discrete set of values, the default statement is not needed. An invalid value is trapped at compile time. This is another example of employing defensie programming.

```
static void Main(string[] args) {
    classgrade grade=classgrade.fail;
    switch (grade){
        case classgrade.fail:
            break;
        case classgrade.pass:
            break;
        case classgrade.incomplete:
            break;
    }
}
```

Avoid needless recursion. Yes, it is fun. However, recursion is expensive, which is amplified for small functions. Internally, each function has a function call site, prolog, and epilog. This infrastructure adds overhead to the function. For short functions, the execution of this infrastructure may exceed the code of the actual function. Finally, recursive functions are inherently more complex, which can lead to inadvertent errors. The following is a recursive function that calculates a factorial.

```
static public long Factorial(long val1) {
    if (val1 > 1) {
        val1 *= Factorial(--val1);
    }
    return val1;
}
```

This code also calculates a factorial. Instead of using a recursive function, a simple *for* loop is used. Both approaches were benchmarked. The *for* loop is about 50 percent quicker.

```
for (factorial = currentvalue; --currentvalue-1 > 0; factorial *= i) ;
```

Design Patterns

From the start of the computer age, developers, engineers, scientists, hobbyists in the garage, and others have written a large body of code. Most every programming problem has been addressed in some manner in this code. You might consider your problem unique, but it is not. At a macro level, your problem may appear to be unique. However, when decomposed, the application is a composition of familiar algorithms, formulas, input, and output. Design patterns are the representation of this knowledge. For example, a singleton is a common but complex construct required in a myriad of applications. A hundred developers would implement a singleton a hundred different ways—some incorrect. Why not create the perfect singleton from the collective knowledge of all developers? The perfect singleton could then be reused. This is a quicker and more robust approach. That is the purpose of the singleton pattern.

A design pattern is a formal description of a general solution to a common software problem. This includes defining the relationship between classes and objects necessary to implement the solution. Although general, design patterns are adaptable to specific purposes. A design pattern is also both language and platform independent. Design patterns are essentially agnostic and reusable solutions.

Instead of creating an application from nothing, first analyze the application design for potential patterns: composite pattern, decorator pattern, façade pattern, singleton pattern, and others. These patterns become the building blocks for constructing your application. Wrap and bind these building blocks with a thin layer of logic and user interface, if necessary. The thin layer represents the truly unique aspects of the application. See Figure 8-4.

Design Patterns: Elements of Reusable Object-Oriented Software, by Erich Gamma, Richard Helm, Ralph Johnson, and John Vlissides (Addison-Wesley Professional, 1994), is an excellent book on design patterns. There are also design patterns books specific to managed languages, such as C#. At Microsoft's Web site, *www.microsoft.com/patterns*, you can find a variety of information on design patterns and implementation for managed code.

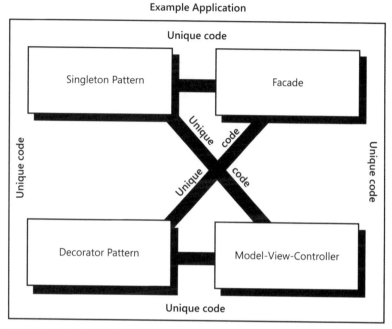

FIGURE 8-4 The Example Application is a composite of design patterns and truly unique code.

There are several benefits to design patterns. Each of these benefits contributes to defensive programming:

- A design pattern is a tested best practice.

- A design pattern is a documented solution for a common software problem, which also makes your application more maintainable in the future.

- Because it is a documented solution, a design pattern provides a basis of understanding for everyone working on a common project.

- You can focus on the larger problems that are unique to your application. Ultimately, this will lead to a better application for you and your client.

- Reusing solutions as described in a design pattern should make product development quicker.

Some of the common design patterns are shown in Table 8-2:

TABLE 8-2 Common Patterns and Their Descriptions

Pattern	Description
Builder	The builder pattern abstracts the creation of an object, where different implementations of the objects can be constructed.
Composite	The composite pattern allows a group of objects to be treated as a single entity or individual objects.
Decorator	The decorator pattern makes a class extensible allowing additional class members to be added dynamically.
Facade	The façade pattern publishes a refined interface for a large body of code. The façade pattern is frequently used with libraries.
Factory method	The factory method pattern abstracts the creation of an object using one or more methods of a base class that can be overridden in derived classes for a refined implementation.
Singleton	The singleton pattern creates a single instance of an object. One instance of the target object always exists—no more and no less.

Summary

Writing solid code is more than good intentions; it also entails defensive programming. Defensive programming is a proactive approach to diagnosing and preventing software problems and bugs. It provides a framework that enforces consistent programmer discipline to write quality code.

Problems discovered at compile time are easier to fix and less expensive to resolve. One problem is that unit testing is not guaranteed to isolate all runtime problems. Furthermore, unit testing tests features, user interface, usage patterns, and more, but most often it does not test individual lines of source code. Therefore, the responsibility of writing solid code remains firmly with the developer and not the tester. Best practices such as raising the warning level to four; treating all warnings as errors; and applying appropriate modifiers to classes, methods, and other entities moves the discovery of possible software problems from runtime to compile time.

Code is not perfect and must be revisited on occasion. This is typically the role of the maintenance programmer. Documentation documents code for the maintenance programmer and yourself. Documentation can be accomplished in several formats. For example, UML diagrams created for software modeling can document an application. You can also document code with pseudo code. Finally, you can add conventional comments. Self-documenting code mitigates the need for extensive comments.

Programmers create errors. No program is innately error prone. *You* place errors in the application. Independent reviews are helpful in finding programmer mistakes. Code reviews and unit tests are the best techniques for finding these kinds of problems. Automated unit tests are particularly useful for consistent and comparative results. Testing is only as effective as code coverage. You should strive for 85 to 90 percent code coverage. Remember, code that is not touched is not tested. For 100 percent code coverage, consider test-driven development (TDD). With TDD, you create the test first, which will fail. You then write the code to make the test pass.

Design patterns provide known, as well as tested, solutions for established software problems. The solutions are published as patterns and are not generally environment or language specific. Wherever possible, use patterns when available for a specific problem. This will help you create quality code quicker.

Key Points

- Defensive programming is about details, such as refactoring loops, avoiding unsafe code, adhering to CLS, and using parentheses.

- Leave the warning level at 4, which is the highest. If possible, compile with the Treat Warnings As Errors option.

- Code reviews are an important challenge to the correctness of the code base.

- Strive for code coverage of 85 to 90 percent during testing. For test-driven development, the goal is 100 percent coverage.

- With test-driven development, create the test and then the code that passes the test. When the test passes, you then refactor the code.

- Self documenting code is more readable. Abiding by proper naming conventions and pseudo-code also improves code readability.

- Comments, comments, and more comments. Documentation comments provide consistency and can be exported to an XML documentation file.

- Design patterns are reusable patterns excavated from the universal code base. Design patterns are documented, reusable, and perfected solutions to common programming problems. There is no need to re-create a solution to a known problem, and possibly introduce issues, when you can rely on a design pattern.

Chapter 9
Debugging

I write perfect code.

—*Anonymous*

If you write perfect code, skip to the next chapter. This chapter is for everyone else—those who do not write perfect code. There is one *other* person who writes perfect code: the source of the quotation. Why did I make it anonymous? I have kept the person's name anonymous because an experienced developer would never claim to write perfect code. The perfect developer does not exist, which is an unfortunate truth. The perfect developer can be found in the annals of history next to the abominable snowman, big foot, and other mythical figures. Perfect code is not the goal of this chapter or this book. That is not possible. However, minimizing potential problems and bugs is a valid goal and achievable by following certain best practices and policies, some of which are described in this chapter. This chapter is about embracing your bugs. Debugging is another perspective that should be considered in the software development life cycle, like security and deployment. It should not be left as an oversight, waiting for the first crisis situation to occur.

When planning a software project, time is often not set aside for debugging—a major omission since debugging is a significant portion of application development, deployment, and ongoing maintenance. Fifty percent (on average) of the effort to maintain a software application is debugging. Furthermore, debugging is an iterative process. This means debugging is a non-trivial task. Not setting this time aside means problems tend to be uncovered later in testing or, even worse, at deployment, which can be costly. Table 2-1 in Chapter 2, "Class Design and Prototyping," highlights cost savings from resolving problems early in the software development life cycle.

Effective debugging is about creating and maintaining a stable, robust, efficient, and correct application. A stable application will not fail with little impetus or indiscriminately. A robust application handles exceptional events at run time in a stable manner. Efficient applications scale either as users or throughput increases. A correct application responds as expected to user interaction and other inertia. Effective debugging is similar to being an auto mechanic. An auto mechanic is responsible for keeping a car running well through preemptive and reactive maintenance and repair. You are the software mechanic responsible for keeping your software application running well.

Some debugging techniques are universal and applicable to both desktop and Web-based applications. For example, debugging an overflow exception is virtually the same for Web-based and desktop applications. You check local variables and parameters for invalid values, validate results of expressions, and so on. However, there are circumstances where debugging a Web-based versus desktop application is different. Tracing, for example, can inadvertently display sensitive information of a Web-based application—information that is inappropriate to present to a remote user. This chapter focuses primarily on Web-based applications, such as ASP.NET applications. We have already mentioned one debugging difference. Here are other differences between debugging a Web-based versus desktop application.

- Web applications reside within an application domain of the worker process, which affects how the application is debugged. Desktop applications are isolated applications.

- Unhandled exceptions are handled differently in a Web application. Unhandled exceptions are routed to the page, application, and possibly a custom error page. This is somewhat different from resolving unhandled exceptions in a desktop application.

- Automatic recycling of the worker process, which hosts Web-based applications, can make debugging deadlocks and memory leaks more challenging than with a desktop application.

As mentioned, this chapter focuses on debugging Web applications. I suggest the *Debugging Microsoft .NET 2.0 Applications* book (Microsoft Press, 2006), written by John Robbins, for a comprehensive discussion of debugging. In addition to being technically superior, the book contains several interesting and fun war stories from John's experience in the trenches debugging with customers.

Debugging a developmental version of a Web application differs from debugging a production version. A developmental version is probably a debug version and used during active product development. It runs on a local machine and not on a production server. A production version of a Web application should be a release version that is deployed to a production server. Developers typically use the developmental version of a Web application, while remote users are the primarily clients of a production version. For these reasons and more, there are salient differences in debugging a developmental version of a Web application and debugging a production version. For example, requests on the developmental version (debug version) of a Web application do not time out. This provides an opportunity to debug an errand request. However, production versions (release versions) of a Web application set a time-out on requests to prevent stalling the application. Here are additional differences:

- Production versions are optimized, which can make debugging more challenging.

- Production servers may not have debugging tools, including Visual Studio, which, of course, makes debugging more difficult to accomplish on the local server.

- A production server is often less accessible. This may require remote debugging, with related security issues, to debug the Web-based application.

- Production debugging of a Web-based application is typically done post-mortem, while development debugging may entail live debugging.

Beneath the managed layer of a managed application is a native application. Understanding the native underpinning of a managed application can be helpful when debugging. Debugging at this level may be challenging. However, it can provide important information when debugging. The Shared Source Common Language Infrastructure 2.0 (project name is Rotor) is an open source version of the Common Language Runtime (CLR). *Shared Source CLI Essentials*, by David Stutz, Ted Neward, and Geoff Shilling (O'Reilly, 2003), is an excellent book on this topic. "Production Debugging for .NET Framework Applications" is an article published on the Microsoft Developer Network (MSDN) and another source of excellent information on the topic, which you can find here: *http://msdn.microsoft.com/en-us/library/ms954594.aspx*.

For example, when a managed application deadlocks, the native perspective can contain a wealth of helpful information. Windbg is a native debugging tool that is discussed in further detail later in the chapter. The following listing is the native call stack of a managed thread. From this information, I know that this thread was waiting on a *Monitor* when the program hung. A *Monitor* is a managed class and wrapper for a critical section, which is a native construct. Toward the top of the call stack is the *ntdll!ZwWaitForMultipleObjects* method call, where *ntdll* is the module name and *ZwWaitForMultipleObjects* is the method. From the arguments of this method, the number of objects being waiting on and their related handles can be found. As expected, the thread is waiting on one object. This is only a peek into the sort of information available when native debugging a managed application. There is much more.

```
ChildEBP RetAddr  Args to Child
03bcf110 77aa0690 76927e09 00000001 03bcf164 ntdll!KiFastSystemCallRet
03bcf114 76927e09 00000001 03bcf164 00000001 ntdll!ZwWaitForMultipleObjects+0xc
03bcf1b0 79ed98fd 03bcf164 004b8dd0 00000000 KERNEL32!WaitForMultipleObjectsEx+0x11d
03bcf218 79ed9889 00000001 004b8dd0 00000000 mscorwks!WaitForMultipleObjectsEx_SO_
TOLERANT+0x6f
03bcf238 79ed9808 00000001 004b8dd0 00000000 mscorwks!Thread::DoAppropriateAptStateWait+0x3c
03bcf2bc 79ed96c4 00000001 004b8dd0 00000000 mscorwks!Thread::DoAppropriateWaitWorker+0x13c
03bcf30c 79ed9a62 00000001 004b8dd0 00000000 mscorwks!Thread::DoAppropriateWait+0x40
03bcf368 79e78944 ffffffff 00000001 00000000 mscorwks!CLREvent::WaitEx+0xf7
03bcf37c 79ed7b37 ffffffff 00000001 00000000 mscorwks!CLREvent::Wait+0x17
03bcf408 79ed7a9e 004cb148 ffffffff 004cb148 mscorwks!AwareLock::EnterEpilog+0x8c
03bcf424 79ebd7e4 c6efd76b 00000000 0139916c mscorwks!AwareLock::Enter+0x61
03bcf4c4 009a03f6 013627f4 793b0d1f 013991a0 mscorwks!JIT_MonEnterWorker_Portable+0xb3
```

Some things begin at birth and continue to the grave: aging, relatives wanting to *borrow* frequent flyer miles, and, my personal favorite, taxes. Debugging falls into this category. Bottom line, you are debugging an application from cradle to grave. This is an activity that does not end when an application is placed into production. Actually, most applications are in production for a period of time much longer than the initial development. During this time, you are receiving support calls from customers, building the next release of the product, and of course continuing testing. These activities will undoubtedly uncover a few more bugs and require resolution. In addition, the deployment location is typically dynamic. Operating system upgrades, service packs, hardware upgrades, and more can cause unanticipated problems and necessitate debugging. For these reasons, post-production debugging must be planned, budgeted, and have resources reserved. Otherwise, the shiny new polished application you delivered to clients may eventually run off its wheels.

The culture at your company should not place the focus entirely on new product development, where current products are essentially abandoned at product release. The key word is *current*. Your current products, not future products, have a greater impact on your profitability, brand, and customer satisfaction. Therefore, if only for self-preservation, you should have a credible plan for debugging those products into the future. In design and implementation, plan for debugging released products. Plan to reinvest 10 percent to 15 percent of time back into the code base for fixing and enhancing problem areas. Here are some examples:

- Design and implement a plan for reporting the health of the application.

- Have a plan to enable and disable instrumentation when needed.

- Plan to incorporate hooks in your application to be used when debugging. For example, build in the ability to dump the state of various important components.

This chapter provided concrete steps, practices, and policies for effective debugging. However, debugging is as much philosophical as it is tactical. A debugging for quality mindset must be adopted by everyone on the team and reinforced by management. You don't wake up one morning and decide to be concerned about debugging. It must be ongoing and intrinsic to product design, development, and deployment, where every member of the team participates. Management must have an equal commitment to debugging for quality and supporting the software team in this goal. The software architect should ask important questions during the design phase. Can the product be designed in a manner to proactively prevent future problems? What remote functionality is required to debug the application on a production machine? When implementing the product, the developers must also ask important questions. If the application crashes, is there way of collecting and reporting critical information on the problem? The point is you need to think about debugging throughout the software development life to be properly prepared to resolve the inevitable bug.

Not being prepared to handle software problems can cause great harm to your business. The following sections showcase two stories from recent history where software bugs received widespread attention. Yes, software bugs can be headline news and extensively reported. Loss of product sales can be the least of your problems. The long-term harm to the overall brand of the company could be more damaging. The two software problems have become known as the Overflow Bug and the Pentium FDIV bug.

Overflow Bug

In December 2004, thousands of travelers were stranded in airports across the country because of an overflow in a field of a software application. The problem was widely reported during the holiday season, which is peak travel time for airlines. Here is what happened. Comair, a commuter for Delta Airlines, was forced to cancel hundreds of flights and strand angry passengers over the Christmas holiday. The core of the problem was a snowstorm that forced the rescheduling of airline crews. This caused an abnormally high number of crew reassignments, which caused an overflow in a field. This caused an essential software system to crash and otherwise perform incorrectly. The software system was a legacy application that was written in Fortran. Few at Comair understood the legacy application or the language, which complicated problems. The cost to Comair was $20 million. Furthermore, the Overflow Bug and the ramifications of it led to the resignation of two career executives. "Comair's Christmas Disaster: Bound to Fail" is an excellent article about this event: *www.cio.com/article/112103*.

Pentium FDIV Bug

This bug is interesting in the breadth of the media coverage and the actual scope of the error, considering the Pentium FDIV Bug never affected the vast majority of people. The bug was caused by an incorrect lookup table, which caused rare errors in floating point division. Pentium FPU is an Intel microprocessor, and the problem occurs during FDIV instructions (FDIV are floating point instructions). The problem was uncovered in 1994. Despite the limited scope of the problem, the bug received disproportionate coverage. It was reported on television, in newspapers, and literally just about everywhere. Pentium chips became the target of derision from engineers, a core audience for Intel. Jokes about the reliability of Pentium chips became commonplace. Therefore, although the direct financial harm was relatively minor, the impact on the brand was enormous. "The Truth Behind the Pentium Bug" is a great article about the problem and aftermath: *http://www.byte.com/art/9503/sec13 /art1.htm*.

Symbols

Whether debugging a release or debug version of an application, symbols make debugging more user friendly. With symbols, you don't have to manually interpret addresses for function names or line numbers for source code. Symbols provide symbolic names, source code line resolution, and other information when debugging. The symbol engine uses this information to convert symbolic information into memory addresses and vice versa. The source code information in a symbol file facilitates the setting of breakpoints using line numbers. When debugging a managed application, some of this symbolic information is available via reflection. However, reflection cannot provide everything, such as the names of local variable and source code information. Here are two partial listings of a call stack. Both listing were done in Windbg. For this example, Windbg was attached to Notepad. The first listing displays a call stack when the appropriate symbols are not available. Each row of information represents a stack frame or generally a method call. Each row ends with an offset that references the function relative to the module (Notepad). Is the function name apparent? No.

```
ChildEBP RetAddr  Args to Child

000bf950 00941971 00940000 00000000 000d316f notepad+0x149c

000bf9e0 76983833 7ffdb000 000bfa2c 77bea9bd notepad+0x1971
```

Next is the call stack when the symbols are available. The function name is apparent and appears at the end of each row. The call stack is more readable and that makes debugging easier. This highlights another benefit of symbols—increased productivity. Symbols allow you to focus on debugging rather than the challenges of interpreting low-level memory addresses.

```
ChildEBP RetAddr  Args to Child

000bf950 00941971 00940000 00000000 000d316f notepad!WinMain+0xec

000bf9e0 76983833 7ffdb000 000bfa2c 77bea9bd notepad!_initterm_e+0x1a1
```

The debugging engine and symbol server are required by any application needing symbol resolution. The debugging engine is dbghelp.dll, while the default symbol server for Windows is symsrv.dll. You can download a complimentary copy of both from the Downloading Tools for Windows Web site (more about this later). The debugging engine and symbol server are also distributed with some compilers and debuggers, such as Visual Studio.

Program Database (PDB) files are the current format for symbol files. In the past, there have been several formats for symbol files, such as COFF, Codeview, and C7. Some of these formats embedded the symbols in the binary. The PDB format stores symbols in a separate file. Placing the symbols in a separate file reduces the footprint of the application. However, this creates a potential version problem when matching a symbol file with an incorrect application. To help prevent this problem, the application contains the fully qualified name and path for the related PDB file. This is a hard-coded path. For versioning, an identical globally unique identifier (GUID) is placed in the assembly and PDB. You can display the GUID of the assembly with the dumpbin utility: dumpbin /headers *assemblyname*. This GUID is checked to confirm that version of the symbol file is correct for the target assembly or binary. When looking for a symbol file for an application, debuggers generally first check the embedded symbol path for the correct symbols. Second, the directory from where the assembly loaded is checked. Visual Studio will not allow you to use the incorrect version of a symbol file. That is also the default behavior of Windbg. However, you have the ability in Windbg to override this behavior and use a disparate version of an assembly and symbol file. This is done with the *symopt* command.

Convenient debugging requires both product and operating system symbols. You provide the product symbols, while Microsoft provides the operating system symbols. The Microsoft symbols can be downloaded from the Debugging Tools for Windows Web site. The link is provided later. Alternatively, most debuggers can be configured to download the operating system symbols automatically.

You may also need symbols for any third-party assemblies or binaries that are integrated in your application. It is important to check for availability of symbols before acquiring third-party products. Do not assume that symbols are automatically provided. This is a frequent mistake. Some vendors do not provide symbols to avoid disclosing proprietary information. Alternatively, they may provide public (stripped) symbols, which contain enough information to accurately depict a call stack but not much more.

For native debugging, there is the concept of public versus private symbols. The differences are as listed in Table 9-1. Private symbols are created by a company for their employees, partners, and others with a close relationship with the company. Because of the closeness of the relationship, there is a high level of trust. For this reason, private symbols are not filtered and contain full symbols necessary for debugging. Specifically, private symbol files contain both private and public symbol information. Conversely, public symbol files are for customers and are stripped of nearly everything. For this reason, public symbol files are also called stripped symbols. A public symbol file only includes the public symbols. You can configure Visual Studio to create a stripped symbol file. From the Project menu, choose Properties. From the Linker item, select the Debugging pane. Enter the location to create the stripped symbol file in the Strip Private Symbols option. Alternatively, you can also create stripped symbols using the PDBCopy tool, which is included in the Debugging Tools for Windows. PDBCopy can create a public symbol file from private symbol file.

TABLE 9-1 A Comparison of Private versus Public Symbols

Private Symbols	Public Symbols
Static and non-static functions	Non-static functions
Global variables	Global variables
Local variables	
Source file and line number information	
User-defined type information	

Maintain separate symbols for each public or released version of a product. This means having symbol sets for all versions of the product available to customers. Customer support problems, and there will be some, may necessitate debugging a specific version of the product. You need the specific symbols for that version. Re-creating symbols for that version after the fact may be difficult, if not impossible. For example, the original compiler that created the application may no longer available. Of course, maintaining multiple versions of symbols could be a challenge. Symbol servers to the rescue!

Symbol Server

A symbol server locates required symbols, which are then downloaded to a local cache. You can download from multiple symbol stores. It is recommended to download symbols from the closest symbol store first. Download from the furthest symbol store last because it is the least efficient. The symbol path sets the search path to locate and download missing symbols. Each debugger has a specific way for setting the symbol path. However, you can also set the symbol path using the _NT_SYMBOL_PATH environment variable. Most debuggers read this environment variable to obtain the default symbol path. This provides a convenient location to set the symbol path once for multiple debuggers. The following is the syntax for setting the symbol path.

```
SRV*downloadcache*symbolstore1*symbolstore2*symstore3
```

The first item of the symbol path is SRV. SRV refers to the symsrv.dll symbol server. The next item is the download cache. A debugger will load the symbols first from the download cache. If required symbols are not found there, the symbol server will attempt to download those symbols from symstore^1 to the download cache. From there, the debugger can access the symbol. For symbols in neither the local cache nor symstore^1, symstore^2 is searched, and so on. Here is a typical symbol path.

```
SRV*c:\symbols*f://symbols/ossymbols*http://msdl.microsoft.com/download/symbols
```

Microsoft has made available a symbol store, which contains operating systems' symbols and some binaries. The address is *http://msdl.microsoft.com/download/symbols*. This symbol store contains only public, or stripped, symbols.

You should also enter the symbol path directly into Visual Studio. From the menu, choose Tools and then Options. From the Options dialog box, select Debugging, and then select Symbols. The Symbols pane will appear. (See Figure 9-1.) Enter the location of the local cache in the Cache Symbols From Symbol Servers To This Directory text box. Add the search paths in the Symbol File (.pdb) Locations list box. The symbol server will search the list top-down.

Vendors, such as Microsoft, provide symbol stores that are connected to by symbol servers. A symbol store is a repository of symbols for an operating system or product. The repository contains a set of symbols for each version and iteration of the product. Before the advent of symbol servers, you were responsible for finding and downloading the correct symbols. This can be daunting for a product such as an operating system. For most of us, that is Microsoft Windows. There is a variety of sets of symbols for the various iterations of the operating system over a span of several years. Furthermore, there are occasions when the symbols required are not the ones for your local operating system. This is often true with dumps, which may have been created on another machine in a different operating environment. In these situations, having the correct symbols automatically downloaded from a symbol store is invaluable.

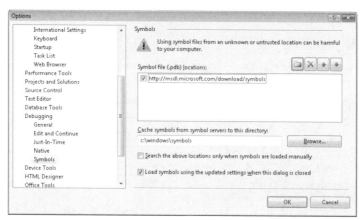

FIGURE 9-1 Enter the symbol path and the download cache in the Symbols pane.

You can create a symbol store for your product to download the appropriate symbols to peers, partners, or clients. Symstore.exe is a utility provided by Microsoft. Use this tool to create a symbol store for your product. You can then publish the symbol store as a public share or a server available outside the local domain. Download symstore.exe at the Debugging Tools for Windows Web site.

Source Servers

In addition to symbols, effective debugging often requires the source code files. Without appropriate symbols, you sometimes must convert arcane memory addresses while debugging. Without the source code files, debugging code requires reading disassembly, which can be equally arcane. The source server can automatically download source files related to a particular assembly.

The default location of source code files are written into the PDB file. The PDB file contains the fully qualified path and name of each source file in the project when the assembly was built. Using source control tools, the version number can be added to the source file reference. In addition, statements for retrieving the source file from source control are written into the PDB file. The process of adding this information is called source indexing. The debugger uses the information written into the PDB file to automatically retrieve the correct source files from the related source control program. This assumes your source control program is known to the source control tools provided by Microsoft. If not, these tools are extensible. Using Perl, you can extend the existing source control tools to update a PDB file with commands to retrieve code from most any source control program. The following source control programs are supported by default.

- Visual Sourcesafe
- Subversion

- Perforce

- Microsoft Team Foundation System

Srvsrc.dll is the standard source server and is installed with the Debugging Tools for Windows. The source server depends on indexed PDB files. Source control tools for indexing a PDB file are installed with the Debugging Tools for Windows. They are placed in the srcsrv subdirectory of the install directory. The following is the list of source control files and tools:

- **Srvsrv.ini**   Srvsrv.ini is a configuration file for the source server (srvsrc.dll). The source server reads this file, if available, at startup for proper configuration instructions. Some of the information included in the configuration is the location of source servers.

- **SSIndex.cmd**   SSIndex.cmd is a Perl script. SSIndex first assembles a list of source files from the target project. Second, it compares this list with the list of source files in each PDB file. All matches are recorded. Finally, SSIndex uses PdbStr to actually index the PDB file with this information, including the commands necessary to retrieve those files from source control.

- **SrcTool.exe**   SrcTool.exe is a tool that reads from a PDB file the list of indexed source files. The list includes the fully qualified path, version number, and other information pertaining to the indexed file.

- **PdbStr.exe**   PdbStr.exe writes the stream that indexes a PDB file.

John Robbins has written a helpful article about source indexing and using the various source control tools. Here is the link: *http://msdn.microsoft.com/en-us/magazine/cc163563.aspx*.

The source path is a list of directories and it lists in what order to search for source files. Each debugger has a different procedure for setting the source path. Alternatively, you can create the _NT_SOURCE_PATH environment variable. Some debuggers, such as Windbg, will check this environment variable at startup for the default source path.

We have now discussed symbol and source servers as part of the preparation for debugging. It is time to discuss actual debugging. This chapter is as much about preventing problems as it is about finding bugs after the fact. Any problem you preempt early may prevent a crisis later. Taking a preemptive approach to debugging can translate into substantial time and financial savings.

Preemptive Debugging

Benjamin Franklin once said, "An ounce of prevention is worth a pound of cure." This is especially true of creating a software system. Good practices and policies early in product development can reduce future problems. Instead of the normal avalanche of bugs, you only have a trickle. You can spend less time debugging and more time developing new products, learning state-of-the-art technology, or playing the latest Xbox game (only for intellectual stimulation, of course).

Preemptive debugging is not defensive programming. Defensive programming consists of best practices and policies that developers apply to coding. For example, the coding style of 1==x instead of x==1 is an example of defensive programming. Preemptive debugging is a macro approach to preventing bugs. Many of the techniques do not apply to a particular role, such as a developer, but to everyone working on the project.

As mentioned several times in this book, do not short circuit the software development life cycle. Completely fulfill the requirements and analysis, design, and other phases. This means most of your application development is spent on modeling and not coding. This modeling is the blueprint for drafting your application. If the blueprint is abbreviated or hastily created, everything derived from it is suspect. Figure 9-2 shows the trend of spending less time with coding and more with design. This figure was from the master thesis titled "Formalizing Use Cases with Message Sequence Charts," presented by Michael Andersson and Johan Bergstrand. Today it is expected that 70 percent of the software development life cycle is dedicated to modeling (everything before coding).

	Requirements Analysis	Preliminary Design	Detailed Design	Coding and Unit Testing	Integration and Test	System Test
1960s–1970s	10%			80%	10%	
1980s	20%			60%	20%	
1990s	40%		30%		30%	

FIGURE 9-2 Comparative ratio of time spent in each phase of the software development life cycle.

Everyone has an opinion on the primary reason for software problems: lack of attention to detail, short deadlines, lack of knowledge, "code first, think later" approach to programming, and so on. From my experience working with customers with real world problems, the primary culprit is the lack of knowledge. Fifteen years ago, I could read *Programming Windows 3.1*, by Charles Petzold (Microsoft Press, 1992), and know everything about Windows programming. In 1,000 pages, you could learn everything needed to write a Windows program. It was the seminal text of its time. Now 1,000 pages is barely an introduction to Windows Presentation Foundation (WPF). The breadth of information that anyone must learn to program in the Windows environment has grown exponentially. With few exceptions, everyone is now a specialist. This verticalization creates a fertile breeding ground for bugs. How is this resolved?

- **Education**   You must encourage and support technical training for engineers. For this reason, time for learning must be included in the project schedule. This prevents bootstrapped solution or kluges that often lead to problems.

- **Extend deadlines**   Everyone needs more time to research and learn applicable technology. When there are deadline problems, time for research or learning is generally curtailed first with predictable results.

- **Know what you don't know**   Create an environment where developers are encouraged to collaborate and share expertise. That combined expertise can resolve the knowledge gap.

Know the problem domain. There should be a close relationship between the real world, software model, and your code. If not, the program may work flawlessly initially. However, the world is not static. If your code does not model the real world, incorporating future customer changes (the world is dynamic) will invariably lead to problems. Someone on the team should be a subject matter expert (SME). For large projects, there should be a customer liaison to facilitate communication between the software team and the customer. This additional knowledge of the problem domain leads to a better solution and fewer problems in the future.

Avoid feature creep to prevent future problems also. Each new feature adds potential complexity and a possible harbinger of trouble. Fight the temptation to add "cool" features to the product particularly near project completion. Instead, trim features as you near the project deadline. This provides additional time for the remaining features to be fully developed. You must lock down or freeze the code base a reasonable period of time before product release to allow for adequate testing. At that time, only bug fixes and other critical changes should be allowed. This should not be discretionary and must be enforced through management approval. Remember, when deadlines are looming, cut features—especially features that you are unable to test adequately in the remaining time. Customers prefer reliable products with fewer features over unstable products with some extra features.

Even after fully implementing the software development life cycle, addressing the lack of knowledge, and understanding the problem domain, you will still have bugs. However, there will be fewer problems than otherwise. The key is finding these remaining problems early, which is where proactive debugging can help.

Proactive Debugging

Proactive debugging is a strategy whereupon bugs are found as early as possible during development. These are problems that survived preemptive debugging. The later a bug is found, the more expensive to resolve the problem. Proactive debugging is another method to find bugs earlier. Visual Studio is a useful tool for proactive debugging. Managed Debugging Assistants (MDAs) and Code Analysis are two features of Visual Studio that are helpful in this regard.

Managed Debugging Assistants

At run time, MDAs isolate problems related to interoperability, such as PInvoke and COM wrappers. When a problem is detected, the MDA displays an informational dialog box and interrupts the application. For example, there is an MDA (*DllMainReturnsFalse*) that detects when DllMain returns false. DllMain is the entry point function for a dynamic-link library (DLL). If DllMain returns false, that is an indication of an error condition. Here is another example. The *DangerousThreadingAPI* MDA detects when the *System.Threading.Thread.Suspend* method is called on another thread, which may cause an ungraceful interruption of that thread. Because MDAs act at run time, the proper MDAs must be selected before the assembly is executed. MDAs are critical because they identify potential and complex problems that are otherwise difficult to find while debugging managed code.

The MDA does interrupt the debugger but is primarily informational and otherwise will not alter the execution of the application. MDAs are available in Visual Studio but not other debuggers, such as Windbg or DbgCLR. For Web applications, there are three ways to configure MDAs: Microsoft Visual Studio, environment variable, or the registry.

Visual Studio   From the Visual Studio menu, you can choose the appropriate MDA. Select the Debug menu and choose Exceptions. The Exceptions dialog box will appear. One of the groups is Managed Debugging Assistants. See Figure 9-3. Enable or disable a MDA category by selecting or clearing the Thrown check box to the right of Managed Debugging Assistants. Alternatively, expand the Managed Debugging Assistants category to view a specific MDA. You can then set the status of an individual MDA with the Thrown check boxes. With MDAs, the User-unhandled option is always set and not relevant.

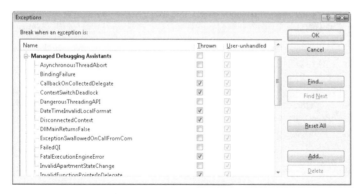

FIGURE 9-3 MDAs in the Exceptions dialog box.

Environment variable   Control the status of an individual MDA or category with the *COMPLUS_MDA* environment variable. Here is an example:

```
COMPLUS_MDA =0;DangerousThreadingAPI
```

COMPLUS_MDA is a semicolon-delimited string and can contain multiple elements. The string is also case sensitive. Each element identifies a specific MDA or special item. See Table 9-2 for a list of special items. Based on the following table, the preceding code example enables the *DangerousThreadingAPI* MDA, while disabling all other MDAs.

TABLE 9-2 SPECIAL ITEMS FOR THE COMPLUS_MDA ENVIRONMENT ELEMENT

Special Item	Description
0	Disable MDAs
1	Read MDAs from configuration file
managedDebugger	Enable MDAs that are implicitly enabled when managed application is started in debugger
unmanagedDebugger	Disable MDAs that are implicitly enabled when managed application is started in debugger

Registry   You can also use the registry to enable and disable MDAs as a group. This method will affect all .NET applications on the system. Of course, be careful when mucking around in the registry. Improper changes to the registry can adversely affect the behavior of the .NET Framework or operating system. Set the HKEY_LOCAL_MACHINE\SOFTWARE\Microsoft\. NETFramework key to control the status of MDAs. Add a string value named **MDA** to the key. Set the value to **1** to enable every MDA. Set the value to **0** to disable all MDAs.

MDA Example

The following code will cause an MDA to be invoked. In this code, one thread suspends another thread. This is done using the *System.Threading.Thread.Suspend* method. This behavior is potentially dangerous and will trigger the *DangerousThreadAPI* MDA at run time when *Thread.Suspend* is called. The program will then be interrupted, and a dialog box is displayed for the MDA. See Figure 9-4.

```
public partial class _Default : System.Web.UI.Page {
    protected void Page_Load(object sender, EventArgs e) {
        Thread t = new Thread(new ThreadStart(MyThread));
        t.Start();
        t.Suspend();
    }
    public void MyThread(){
        while (true){
            Thread.Sleep(1000);
        }
    }
}
```

```
public partial class _Default : System.Web.UI.Page
{
    protected void Page_Load(o
    {
        Thread t = new Thread(
        t.Start();
        t.Suspend();
        Thread.Sleep(5000);
    }

    public void MyThread()
    {
        while (true)
        {
            Thread.Sleep(1000)
        }
    }
}
```

DangerousThreadingAPI was detected   ✕

User code has attempted to call the following API:
'System.Threading.Thread.Suspend'. This may result in a deadlock in the process.

Troubleshooting tips:

Get information about MDA;.

Search for more Help Online...

Actions:
Copy the MDA message to the clipboard

FIGURE 9-4 The dialog box and message for the *DangerousThreadingAPI* MDA.

Code Analysis

Code Analysis is a set of rules for writing quality applications in .NET. Each rule represents a
best practice or policy for managed coding as defined in the *Framework Design Guidelines:
Conventions, Idioms, and Patterns for Reusable .NET Libraries*, by Krzysztof Cwalina and Brad
Abrams (Addison-Wesley, 2005), which is part of the Microsoft .NET Development Series.
Examples of rules are Do not initialize unnecessarily, Remove calls to GC.KeepAlive, and Do
not catch general exception types. Code analysis rules are grouped into categories, such as
Design, Globalization, Interoperability, and Maintainability rules. Code analysis inspects your
code during the build process. Any problems are displayed as warnings in the Error List window. Code Analysis is only available in Visual Studio Team System 2008 Developer Edition
and Visual Studio Team System 2008 Team Suite. The origin of Code Analysis is FXCop. FXCop
is a stand-alone tool that examines assemblies for coding problems. Code Analysis is beyond
the scope of this chapter; however, Chapter 10, "Code Analysis," presents a complete discussion on the topic.

Performance Monitoring

Use the Reliability and Performance Monitor tool to track system metrics and internal information on an application, group of applications, or operating system. The tool is located in
the Control Panel as part of the Administrators Tool group. As the name implies, Reliability
and Performance Monitor is separated into two components. The Reliability Monitor reports
on the health of the system and hardware. It also tracks key events, such as software installs
and uninstalls. Administrators could use the Reliability Monitor to monitor scalability and
plan future deployments. With the Performance Monitor, you can select and monitor performance counters on applications or the operating system. A developer could use the
performance monitor to track a variety of problems, including memory leaks and runaway
handles. The Reliability and Performance Monitor can present data in a variety of views,
such as a chart, dashboard, and report. This allows the display of even complicated data in
an easy-to-understand format. The Reliability and Performance Monitor collects data over

a period of time. Sometimes this can amount to a mountain of information. In this circumstance, you can save the data to a log file, print the resulting report, get a cup coffee, find a
deserted closet, and enjoy interesting reading.

With the Performance Monitor, you can select and monitor one or more counters. A counter represents a data point, such as the number of CLR exceptions that have been thrown,
the number of bytes on all managed heaps, or the number of finalization survivors. You can
select the desired counters and then the appropriate visual representation. There are several
counters for native and managed applications. There are even counters for ASP.NET. Counters
for managed applications are easily identified—they have the .NET prefix.

It is common to set several counters in the Performance Monitor. A Data Collector set is a
reusable collection of counters. This is a convenient way to save an assortment of counters
and reuse as needed. When a Data Collector is started, the Performance Monitor collects
data on the counters found in the set. You end the collection process by stopping the Data
Collector set. The Reliability and Performance Monitor comes with standard Data Collector
sets: LAN Diagnostics, System Diagnostics, System Performance, and Wireless Diagnostics.
You can also create user-defined Data Collector sets.

The Performance Monitor application programming interface (API) is available to managed code. You can use performance counters in your program. The *PerformanceCounter*
class in the *System.Diagnostics* namespace is a wrapper for the Performance Monitor API.
An instance of the *PerformanceCounter* class represents a single counter. With the resulting
object, you can read the value of the associated performance counter.

Performance Monitor example   As mentioned, performance monitoring is an excellent
tool for detecting potential memory leaks in managed applications. One of the first questions should be, "Is the memory leak in native or managed memory?" Performance Monitor
can plot a line graph of this comparison. When referring to native memory, this refers to
the overall memory of the application, including managed memory. Therefore a growth in
managed memory has an equal impact on native memory. Where n is native memory, m is
managed memory, and i^m is the increase in managed memory, this formula represents the
relationship $n + i^m = m + i^m$. If the relation between managed and native memory becomes
$n + i^m + x = m + i^m$, where x is a disproportionate increase of native memory, a leak in native
memory is implied. This is particularly true if the increase is continuous and does not plateau.
Conversely, if disproportionate growth is shown in managed memory, a leak in managed
memory is the likely problem.

For a Web application, you can set counters on the worker process to track memory requirements. For IIS 7.0, the worker process is w3wp.exe. In our example, two Performance Monitor
counters are selected for the worker process. First, in the .NET CLR Memory group, # Bytes
In All Heaps counter is selected. The instance is the w3wp.exe worker process. The # Bytes
In All Heaps counter returns the total amount of managed memory used, which is the sum

of Generations 0, 1, 2, and the Large Object heap. Second, in the Process group, select the Private Bytes counter. Specific steps for selecting these two counters are presented below. The instance is again w3wp.exe. Private Bytes is the total of native memory being used. Figure 9-5 is a line graph of these two performance counters. The top line is native memory; the bottom line is managed memory. As shown, native memory is growing disproportionate to managed memory. This indicates a leak in native memory. Actually, this is true. The Web application is calling a COM component, which is native code. The COM component periodically allocates memory that is never freed.

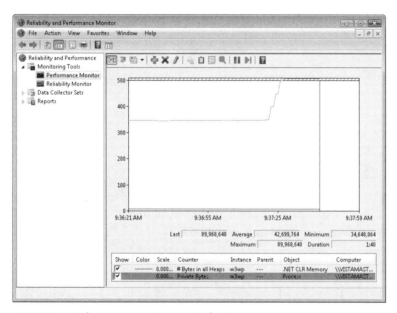

FIGURE 9-5 Performance Monitor graph of native versus managed memory.

These are the steps to create the graph shown in Figure 9-5:

1. Launch the Web application.

2. Start the Reliability and Performance Monitor from Administrator tools in the Control Panel.

3. The left pane of the Reliability And Performance Monitor is a tree control. The top node is labeled Reliability And Performance. Open the Monitoring Tools folder, and select Performance Monitor.

4. The right window is the graphing pane. On the toolbar, if not already selected, select View Current Activity. This is the first button on the toolbar.

5. Click the down triangle of the Change Graph Type button, which is the third button on the toolbar. Select Line as the type of graph.

The following are the steps to plot native and managed memory on the graph.

1. If there are counters already being plotted on the line graph, click the X on the toolbar to remove each line.

2. To add a counter for managed memory, click the + button on the toolbar. The Add Counters dialog box will appear. Expand the .NET CLR Memory counters (click the down arrow "v"). From the list, select # Bytes In All Heaps. Finally, choose w3wp as the instance. Add the counter to the graph with the Add button.

3. To add a counter for native memory, in the list of counters, find and expand the Process counters. Select the Private Bytes counter and w3wp as the instance. Add the counter to the graph with the Add button. Close the Add Counters dialog box.

4. Perform actions that you suspect cause a memory leak.

5. Observe the graph. Notice whether the lines are moving proportional to one another.

Debugging

Several best practices have already been provided that help prevent problems or at least eliminate bugs early in product development. Regardless, you will still deploy applications with bugs! Welcome to the real world. What is the next step? In *Debugging Microsoft .NET 2.0 Applications*, John Robbins suggests a nine-step process to follow, called the Debugging Process. The nine steps include tasks such as duplicate the bug, divide and conquer, and verify that the bug is fixed. Each of the nine steps is important and should be considered. The most important step is to consistently replicate the problem.

If the bug cannot be reproduced, you are unlikely to quickly or efficiently resolve the problem. Consider the difficulty of isolating a bug that occurs once a day, a week, or even a month. The longer the gap between occurrences, the more difficult it is to observe patterns and to create a hypothesis of the problem. Re-creating the problem consistently implies a degree of knowledge about the problem. In addition, it is much easier to discern patterns that create the problem. *Actually, you may have already uncovered the problem but don't realize it yet.*

Several common factors can make reproducing a bug more challenging:

- **Simulating real-world stress on the application can be difficult**   This is where a professional test apparatus is essential. There are a variety of products available on the market that can apply various stresses to a Web application.

- **Re-creating user input in a consistent manner is always a challenge**   For Web applications, WatiN is an open-source testing tool that provides some ability to re-create user input in a testing environment. For more information, visit the following Web site: *http://watin.sourceforge.net.*

- **Problems from deadlocks can sometimes be a challenge to re-create** This is particularly true since deadlocks most often occur in multi-threaded applications. For example, race conditions may disappear with the slightest change of environment. Deadlocks sometimes disappear when switching between production and debug versions of the product. The production application is a release version of the product, and it is optimized. Subtle changes in code from optimization may cause otherwise hidden bugs to appear.

- **The application with the problem is deployed to a production machine, where debugging on the production machine may not be an option** This is often the case with Web servers. For practical reasons, you may not want to potentially interfere with the execution of a production application. In addition, you may not have physical access to the production machine and remote debugging is required. All of this makes reproducing the problem much more of a challenge.

Many of these problems are more easily resolved with a dedicated test lab. In a dedicated test lab, you can run an application using different configurations and under various pressures. You could have a test machine for every deployment scenario. However, this is not always possible because of the sheer number of machines that might be required and the related costs. Not everyone can afford a dedicated test lab. One way to mitigate the hardware requirements and cost of a test lab is to use Microsoft Virtual Server, Microsoft Virtual PC, or Hyper-V. With these programs, you can install multiple platforms, including different service packs, on a single machine or a handful of machines. Most importantly, you can save an environment as an image, which can be retrieved at any time. This is ideal for resetting the test environment for repetitive tests.

Multi-threaded applications pose a special problem. This type of application can behave differently based on the type of system. For example, a multi-thread application may perform differently on a single- versus dual-core machine. In addition, differences in CPU speed can affect the operation of multi-threaded applications. It is important to test multi-threaded applications (both release and debug versions) on machines with single or multi-core machines. This can preempt future problems and debugging.

ADPlus is an essential tool for debugging random problems that cannot be consistently reproduced. You can download ADPlus with the Debugging Tools for Windows. ADPlus is configurable to capture a dump whenever a crash occurs, an exceptional event occurs, or the application hangs. The dump, which is a snapshot of an application at that moment, is typically made unattended. This will allow you to spend the day sailing. Later, perform postmortem debugging analysis of the dump or dumps to determine a pattern of problems that can help re-create the problem consistently or resolve the problem immediately.

Several tools, such as ADPlus, have been mentioned. Some of the tools are specialized debugging tools, while others are general purpose. Having the correct tools in your toolbox and knowing how to use them is important. Many of these tools are more complex and less documented than Visual Studio. These tools should be used for more complicated debugging scenarios. However, before reaching for the heavy arsenal, conduct lightweight debugging first in Visual Studio. Check that variables are initialized and within an expected range, confirm that acquired resources are being released, validate the return values of functions and APIs, review the call stack, and more.

Debugging Tools

You can perform minor car repairs with only a wrench and a screwdriver. However, that is wholly inadequate for fixing a major problem. Try replacing a transmission with only a wrench and screwdriver. It would be simpler to buy a new car. When debugging an application, you are the mechanic. Lightweight debug first. If a car is overheating, confirm the radiator has water before replacing the engine. Lightweight debugging a software application means using Visual Studio. Have a plan. Do not simply start by "kicking the tires." Debugging tools, especially the advanced debugging tools, can generate vast amounts of information. "Kicking the tires" would be akin to searching for a needle in a haystack. Start with a hypothesis. Validate that hypothesis, which narrows the cause of the potential problem and moves a step toward a solution. Based on what you have learned, refine the hypothesis. That should narrow the problem further. Continue on this path until the problem is resolved.

Let us review common debuggers, beginning with Visual Studio.

Visual Studio

Visual Studio has a feature-rich debugger. Most Windows developers are familiar with the Visual Studio integrated development environment (IDE). Microsoft has invested considerable time and resources to create a competent user interface in Visual Studio. Ease of use is an important feature of Visual Studio. This includes features such as IntelliSense, refactoring, the object browser, class diagram, and more. One of the major advantages of using the Visual Studio debugger is the polished user interface. Plus, it is a user interface that most developers are familiar with. Despite being the preferred debugger for lightweight debugging, Visual Studio is a complete debugger. You can set breakpoints, view the call stack, watch variables, inspect code, and more. Advanced features, such as trace points, visualizers, and debug methods or classes, means Visual Studio can also be used for more than lightweight debugging.

Visual Studio is a great tool for debugging Web applications. This includes debugging server-side and client-side code. You can even debug stored procedures. Open the Web site in Visual Studio to begin debugging. From the Debug menu, select Start Debugging. In the web.config file, a Web application must have the *<compilation debug="true" />* element and attribute to facilitate debugging. If this is not present, Visual Studio will alert the user with a dialog box explaining the problem when debugging is started. One option in the dialog box is Modify The Web.config File To Enable Debugging. Choose this option to automatically update the web.config file and continue debugging. Alternatively, you can open and update the web.config file manually.

You might also want to debug the client-side scripts of the Web application, such as being able to set breakpoints. Script debugging must first be allowed in Internet Explorer. From the Tools menu, select Internet Options. Click on the Advanced tab. In the Browsing group, clear the Disable Script Debugging (Internet Explorer) check box. If this option is selected, client-side debugging is disabled. When debugging, users will be notified with an alert message if the Disable Script Debugging option is selected. The dialog box will describe the problem and steps to follow to enable client-side debugging in Internet Explorer.

Production environment A debug version of an application can run differently than a release version. The debug version of a Web site has *<compilation debug="true">* in the web. config file. This is mostly because of optimizations. Debug versions of applications are not optimized, while the release versions are optimized. Other than optimization, here are three major differences between a release and debug version of a Web application.

- ASP.NET requests do not time out in debug versions of a Web application. When debugging, this provides an opportunity to debug an errant request. In a production environment, this could stall an application indefinitely. Requests on released versions of a Web application automatically time out at 110 seconds.

- There is no batch compilation for debug versions of a Web application. Batch compilation means that, when the first page is requested, the entire application is compiled into a handful of assemblies. For example, .aspx, .ascx, and .asmx pages would be batch compiled into separate assemblies. Each page is compiled into a separate assembly with the debug version of a Web application. The code behind is also compiled into a separate DLL. Batch compilation is more efficient than compiling each page into a separate assembly. This will result in many more assemblies, which can fragment virtual memory and apply memory stress on the application.

- For a debug version of a Web application, client-side code libraries and static images found in webresources.axd are not cached. They are downloaded with each page request. Developers avoid having to repeatedly flush the cache when debugging. For a release version of a Web site, these files are cached, which is more efficient.

For the aforementioned reasons, debug versions of a Web application will not perform or scale similar to a release version. This is a critical reason that debug versions of a Web site should not be installed on a production server. This is a common error and problem. You can disable this option on a production server by adding the *<deployment retail="true"/>* element to the machine.config file. This reverses *<compilation debug="true">* on all Web sites on the production server. Here is an example of the tag:

```
<configuration>
    <system.web>
            <deployment retail="true"/>
    </system.web>
</configuration>
```

.NET Framework Tools

Several debugging tools are installed with the .NET Framework. This includes DbgClr, Intermediate Language Disassembler (ILDASM), Son of Strike, mscorcfg, caspol, peverify, and more. The most useful of these tools for debugging are ILDASM and Son of Strike.

ILDASM   ILDASM is a popular managed debugging tool. ILDASM is the Microsoft Intermediate Language (MSIL) disassembler. You can also browse the internal structures of an assembly (.exe, .dll, .obj, and .lib) with ILDASM. This includes browsing IL code, metadata, and the manifest. Metadata includes namespaces, classes, methods, fields, attributes, and so on. ILDASM is both a graphical user interface (GUI) application and a command-line tool.

From the command line, you can perform round tripping with ILDASM. Round tripping is disassembling an assembly, making a change to the disassembled code, and then reassembling into a new assembly. When disassembling an application using ILDASM, you have the option to save the results to a text file. This text file represents a fully functional managed application. It is written in MSIL code. You can compile the text file and create a new assembly using the Intermediate Language Assembler (ILASM) tool. This is particularly useful for making minor changes when you do not have the original source code.

Reflector   Reflector is a free tool and similar to ILDASM. However, Reflector has some additional features not available in ILDASM. For example, you can still disassemble an assembly to MSIL code. But you can also reverse engineer the MSIL of the source code, such as C# or Visual Basic .NET. Reflector also supports third-party add-ons, such as AutoDiagrammer, CodeMetrics, and Diff. This makes the product extensible. ILDASM does not support add-ons. Reflector was created by Lutz Roeder, who has recently sold the product to Redgate Software. Reflector is now available at *www.red-gate.com*.

Son of Strike   Son of Strike (SOS) is the debugging extension for managed debugging, which is installed as part of the .NET Framework so it is on every machine. Debugging extensions are DLLs that expose debugging commands that can extend the behavior of a host debugger. The debugging extension for SOS is sos.dll. You simply load the debugging extension into a debugger. You can then access additional commands. Debugging extensions are standardized and must adhere to guidelines published by Microsoft. Both Windbg and Visual Studio support debugging extensions and consequently SOS. SOS exposes commands for advanced debugging of managed applications. This is accomplished through reading internal structures of the managed applications. The following is a list of some of the information available with SOS.

- Detailed information on each generation and the large object heap.

- A list of syncblk indexes, which is helpful in resolving deadlocks.

- A list of objects on the finalization queue. These are the objects waiting for the destructors to be called.

- Information on whether a method has been jitted.

- A list of all the objects currently on the managed heap.

In Windbg, the following command will load SOS. It is loaded from the same directory as the current mscorwks.dll module. Mscorwks.dll contains the CLR. This means you are loading SOS for the current version of the .NET Framework.

```
.loadby sos mscorworks
```

You can also load SOS from a specific directory regardless of the .NET Framework version. Here is the command:

```
.load drive:\directory\sos.dll
```

Debugging Tools for Windows

Debugging Tools for Windows has already been mentioned several times in this chapter. Many of the debugging tools introduced in this chapter are part of that package. The link to download the Debugging Tools for Windows is as follows: *http://www.microsoft.com/whdc/ devtools/debugging/default.mspx*.

Because the tools are updated regularly, download and install the Debugging Tools for Windows package periodically. These are some of the tools included with the Debugging Tools for Windows:

- **Windbg**   Windbg is an advanced kernel and user-mode debugger. In Windbg, load the SOS debugging extension to perform managed debugging. Windbg has graphical user interface.

- **Console debugger (CDB) and NT Symbolic Debugger (NTSD)**   Both CDB and NTSD are console applications and user-mode debuggers. For user-mode debugging, they have similar functionality to Windbg. There is one primary difference between CDB and NTSD. CDB runs in the current console window. NSTD starts a new console window.

- **Autodump + (ADPlus)**   ADPlus is a vbscript that automates CDB to create dumps. ADPlus has two modes: crash and hang mode. ADPlus is discussed in further detail later in the chapter.

- **Global Flags (GFlags)**   Use GFlags to enable and disable advanced debugging features. GFlags is especially useful for debugging memory problems, application startup, and module load issues. The tool primarily uses the registry to configure debugging features.

- **Srcsrv.dll**   Srcsrv.dll is the source server engine.

- **Symsrv.dll**   Symsrv.dll is the symbol server engine.

CLR Profiler

The CLR Profiler, formerly known as the Allocation Profiler, plots managed memory in easy-to-understand graphs. Using SOS, you can obtain a myriad of information on Generations 0, 1, and 2 as well as the Large Object heap. However, interpreting the data presented can be challenging. This is an occasion where a picture is probably worth a thousand words. CLR Profiler can provide that view and is most useful for debugging memory leaks. You can download the CLR Profiler at the "CLR Profiler for the .NET Framework 2.0" page, which is part of the Microsoft Web site.

Sysinternals

Windows Sysinternals is a Web site that hosts debugging, diagnostics, and other complimentary tools: *http://technet.microsoft.com/sysinternals*. Some of these tools are quite sophisticated. Other tools, such as BlueScreen, are just fun. Of course, you may have a practical usage for the BlueScreen screensaver that does not include scaring peers, friends, and family. Other tools, such as DebugView, ProcessMonitor, and the PSTools suite of tools, are helpful in debugging a variety of problems.

Sysinternals was created in 1996 by Mark Russinovich and Bryce Cogswell as part of Winternals LP. Mark is the co-author, with David Solomon, of the book *Microsoft Windows Internals*, 4th Edition (Microsoft Press, 2004). Sysinternals is now a unit of Microsoft (see above link).

The following is a list of some of the more important tools available at the Windows Sysinternals Web site. Visit the Web site for the complete list.

- **DebugView**   DebugView supports the viewing of debug output outside of a conventional debugger.

- **Strings**   The Strings tool can scan a binary file for a string or sequence of characters.

- **Handles**   The handles utility lists all the active file and directory handles. This includes listing the process that owns each handle.

- **Process Monitor**   Process Monitor is a tool for monitoring system, registry, process, thread, and DLL activity.

- **TCPView**   TCPView shows TCP and User Datagram Protocol (UDP) endpoints and which process owns each endpoint.

- **Process Explorer**   Process Explorer displays a variety of information on active processes, such as DLLs that are loaded into the process, the process identifier, and memory requirements. The tool will also track which processes have a handle to a file or directory.

Now that the toolbox is complete with the correct tools, you are ready to begin debugging. In addition to tools, tracing can provide extra or complementary information.

Tracing

Tracing, or instrumentation, is an important part of debugging. You can track events, display variable values, dump objects, and more.

Tracing a desktop application, as shown in Chapter 2, is different from instrumenting a Web application. For example, you may not want to display trace information to a remote user. Trace information for a Web application may contain data inappropriate for a remote user to view. Also, the execution path of a Web application tends to be more complex than a desktop application. The ASP.NET pipeline of a Web application, which controls if and when a module is executed, makes the execution sequence less transparent. The page handler may not even be called. This can happen when requesting a cached page. When problems occur, tracing can add some clarity to this complexity. Here are other differences between tracing in Web applications and desktop applications.

- Tracing is configured in a web.config file instead of the application configuration file.

- Tracing is page-centric versus document-centric. This includes tracking page events, such as *page load, page error, page unload,* and so on.

- The Web application may be running on a local or remote server, which can affect tracing in a variety of ways.

Web Application Tracing

A *TraceContext* object is used to trace in Web applications. This is different from desktop applications, which use a *TraceSource* object. *TraceContext* is exposed as the *Trace* property of the *Page* object (*Page.Trace*) and provides server-side tracing. The most relevant methods are the *TraceContext.Write* and *TraceContext.Warn* methods. The *Warn* method displays trace information in red, while the *Write* method outputs in black. Otherwise, the commands are identical.

You can enable or disable tracing per Web directory using a web.config file. All Web pages in the same directory or sub-directory (without a separate web.config file) as the current web.config file. You can always confirm that tracing is enabled with the *TraceContext* *.IsEnabled* property. If the property is true, tracing is enabled for that Web page.

Page level tracing   Control tracing for a page using the trace attribute of the *@page* directive. If true, page level tracing is enabled. You can also use the *TraceMode* attribute to sort the tracing output. By default, trace information is rendered with the page and displayed at the bottom. The following is an example of the *@page* directive for a Web application. Page level tracing is enabled.

```
<%@ Page Language="C#" Trace="true" AutoEventWireup="true"  CodeFile="Default.aspx.cs"
Inherits="_Default" %>
This is the server-side code that traces in a Web application.
    protected void Page_Load(object sender, EventArgs e)
    {
        Trace.Write("page load trace");
    }
    protected void Button1_Click(object sender, EventArgs e)
    {
        Trace.Write("button trace");
    }
```

Tracing in the web.config file   Page directive enables trace for a specific page. Alternatively, you can enable tracing in a web.config file. The trace attribute of the page directive takes precedent over the web.config file setting. Therefore, if the page directive enables tracing, tracing will occur regardless of the configuration for tracing in the web.config file.

In the web config file, the *Trace* element enables or disables tracing for relevant Web pages. The *Trace* element has several attributes:

- **enable**   The *enable* attribute enables or disables tracing. By default, tracing is sent to the trace.axd page.

- **pageOutput**   The *pageOutput* attribute redirects tracing to a Web page and not trace. axd.

- **requestLimit**   The *requestLimit* attribute is the number of traces that can be cached.

- **traceMode**   The *traceMode* attribute stipulates the sort order of the trace information.

- **localOnly**   The *localOnly* attribute controls where trace information is displayed. If true, trace information is displayable on the local machine only. This prevents remote users from viewing trace information, which may include sensitive data. For example, trace information includes server variables and cookies collection. Tracing for a Web application typically occurs on the Web server only. This means you must browse to the Web application from the local server to see trace messages.

This is an example of the *Trace* element in a web.config file.

```
<configuration>
 <system.web>
  <trace enabled="true" pageOutput="true" requestLimit="40" localOnly="true"/>
 </system.web>
</configuration>
```

Exception Handling

An unhandled exception is often the event that prompts debugging. There are a variety of system exceptions, including access violations, divide by zero exceptions, and data access exceptions. You can also receive a user-defined exception that was created for a specific application.

There is a concept of a first and second chance exception. When an exception is thrown, it is called a first chance exception. If an application (debuggee) is being debugged, the exception is first sent to the debugger. Most debuggers will not handle the first chance exception and simply forward the exception to the application being debugged. This provides the application an opportunity to handle the exception. If the application does not handle the first chance exception, it is returned to the debugger as a second chance exception because the application is crashing. Debuggers will usually handle a second chance exception and interrupt the application at the location of the exception. If no debugger is attached to the application, the first chance exception is immediately sent to the application. A second chance exception might become an unhandled exception and crash the application. Figure 9-6 shows the sequence of events for handling an exception.

As diagramed, the Visual Studio debugger forwards first chance exceptions to the application. This is different from Windbg. Windbg will interrupt on the first chance exception. Both debuggers can be configured to handle exceptions differently. In Visual Studio, you can configure exceptions to be handled on a first chance. Catching first chance exceptions can help preserve the state of the call stack. This can be helpful when debugging. In addition, the application will be interrupted at the origin of the exception. Designate that exceptions be handled as first chance exceptions in the Exceptions dialog box. From the Debug menu, select Exceptions. There are two columns of options in the Exceptions dialog box. Set the Thrown option to handle an exception as a first chance exception.

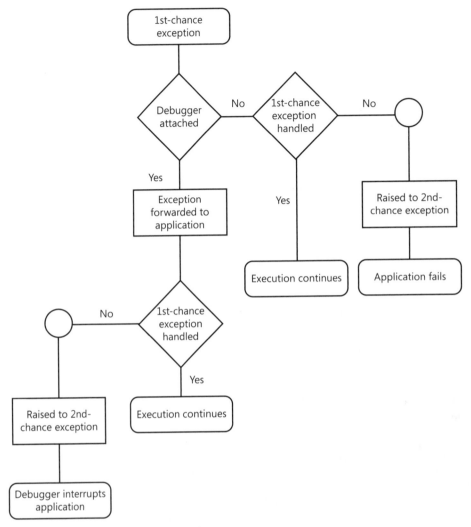

FIGURE 9-6 The logic for handling exceptions.

When an exception occurs, the correct handler must be found. If an appropriate handler is not found, the exception becomes an unhandled exception. Normally, this would crash your application. However, you can trap unhandled exceptions at the page or application level. At the page level, handle unhandled exceptions with the *Page_Event* event. *Page.Page_Error* is a handler for that event. Implement *Application_Error* in global.asax to handle unhandled exceptions at the application level. Page-level handling of an unhandled exception takes precedence over application-level handling.

For an unhandled exception, a user is automatically transferred to an error page. This occurs when an unhandled exception is not handled at the page or application level. Figure 9-7 shows the routing of an unhandled exception. The error page displays details of the exception, which may include information that is inappropriate to display to the user. You can control how the error page is displayed in the web.config file, with the *customErrors* element. *Mode* is the most important attribute of the *customErrors* element. Here are the possible values for the mode attribute:

- **RemoteOnly**   The *RemoteOnly* mode will display full exception information for an unhandled exception on the local server. Remote users are provided limited information.

- **On**   The *On* mode prevents the error page for an unhandled exception from being shown. If set, the custom error page will be shown instead.

- **Off**   The *Off* mode will display the error page for an unhandled exception—even if the custom error page is set.

The *defaultRedirect* attribute of the *customErrors* element identifies the custom error page. In the advent of an unhandled exception, this page will be presented in lieu of the default error page. Of course, you need to create the custom error page beforehand. The following is an example of the *customErrors* element.

```
<customErrors defaultRedirect="customerror.aspx" mode="On">
```

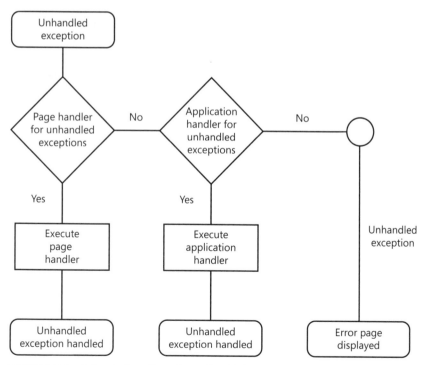

FIGURE 9-7 Logic for the handling of an unhandled exception.

In addition to exceptions, the custom error page can be used with HTTP status codes. Identify the specific HTTP status code with an error element. Identify the pertinent HTTP status code with the *statusCode* attribute of the error element. The redirect attribute names the error page. When the HTTP status code event occurs, you are transferred to the error page. This is an example of the error element.

```
<customErrors mode="remoteOnly">
    <error statusCode="404" redirect="error.aspx"/>
</customErrors>
```

Production Debugging

You have the choice between live or post-mortem debugging. With live debugging, the debugger attaches to a running application. Live debugging is intrusive, and the program may be modified in the process of being debugged. It can affect the performance or even interrupt an application. For example, applying a breakpoint will modify an application. An int 3 assembly instruction is inserted into the application for the breakpoint. Imagine the repercussions of hitting a breakpoint on a production Web application while it is servicing requests from hundreds of users. Disastrous is an apropos description. Live debugging is appropriate on a development or test machine, where customers are not likely to be affected. Post-mortem debugging uses a snapshot of the application. You can then debug the application from the snapshot. The most useful snapshot is a dump. Once the dump is generated, you can debug the application anywhere. You do not have to debug on the production machine.

Debugging from a dump (post-mortem) is different from live debugging. As you know, a dump is a snapshot and not the actual running program. Therefore, you cannot perform any task that would assume a running application. Here are some tasks that cannot be done when debugging a dump:

- Set a breakpoint
- Suspend a thread
- Change memory state
- Load modules

As with live debugging, symbols are useful with post-mortem debugging. However, symbols from the operating environment where the dump was created are needed. Based on that, the symbols required to debug the dump may be different from the symbols for the local machine. If you have dumps on your local computer created in Windows 2000 Professional, Windows XP, and Windows Server 2003, then symbols are required for those three operating systems. The easiest way to gather these symbols is to use the Microsoft public server to automatically download the correct symbols.

Not every dump is the same. Dumps can be created with varying amounts of detail. The terms *full dump* and *mini dump* are commonly used to describe dumps. A full dump minimally includes heap memory, thread information, and handle data. The primary difference is that mini dumps, unlike full dumps, do not contain heap memory. Mini dumps also do not usually have handle information. While full dumps can be gigabytes in size, mini dumps are a few megabytes or less.

You cannot create a dump for a managed application in Visual Studio. However, Windbg can create dumps for managed applications. The following command creates an appropriate dump for a managed application. Dumpname.dmp is the name of the new dump file. You must start a debugging session for the target application before creating the dump.

```
.dump /ma dumpname.dmp
```

MinidumpWriteDump is the native API for creating dumps. No wrapper exists for this API in the .NET Framework class library. However, *MinidumpWriteDump* API can be called directly via platform invocation. You would call the API to create a dump programmatically. This is helpful for saving dumps just in time at program failure, such as an unhandled exception. Another advantage is the ability to create various shades of dumps—not just full versus mini dump. *MiniDumpWriteDump* supports fifteen flavors of dumps, each with varying levels of detail. You should not call *MiniDumpWriteDump* on the current application. This may create a corrupt dump. *MiniDumpWriteDump* should be called from a separate application.

ADPlus is an alternative to writing custom code for the *MiniDumpWriteDump* API. ADPlus has the ability to create a dump just in time as an application crashes or hangs.

ADPlus

ADPlus is a debugging tool for creating dumps and log files on demand or just in time. You can download ADPlus from the Debugging Tools for Windows Web site, as described earlier. ADPlus is a vbscript that automates CDB, which is the console debugger. When using ADPlus, you are likely to see the CDB icon appear in the task bar. Do not close that CDB session! It is being used by ADPlus to create a dump for you.

ADPlus can operate in two modes: hang or crash mode.

- In crash mode, associate ADPlus with the application before it crashes. When the application raises an exception or crashes, ADPlus will create a dump just in time.

- In hang mode, associate ADPlus with the application before or after the application hangs. Deciphering when an application hangs is a subjective observation; you must decide that this has occurred. Open the related debugger session, and press Ctrl+C to create the dump on demand.

When ADPlus is started, several message boxes are displayed to the user. This includes notifying the user of the output directory where ADPlus files are written. If you run in the quiet mode (the –quiet option), ADPlus will not display any of the message boxes.

ADPlus can send you an alert when an application crashes. In crash mode, start ADPlus with the notify option. When the application crashes, you will be alerted via Windows messenger service. This is a convenient option that can improve your productivity.

ADPlus will create a mini dump and log file for most first chance exceptions. For second chance exceptions, a full dump is created. When an application crashes or hangs, ADPlus creates the following files.

- **ADPlus_report.txt** This file contains version information about ADPlus, command-line arguments and other status information on the debugging script.

- **Log file** The log file contains debugging commands run on the application. The log file contains the call stack for each thread and separately a complete list of modules.

- **Process_List.txt** This file contains the list of processes running at the time the crash or hang occurred.

A new feature of ADPlus is a configuration file. This allows you to create and save complicated ADPlus environments.

ADPlus Configuration File You can configure ADPlus from the command line. However, entering a complicated configuration from the command line is often inconvenient and sometimes not possible. Configuration files can save the day. You can enter in complicated configurations and save them for future reuse. Configuring ADPlus properly may be a challenge for administrators, testers, or support engineers. Developers can now configure ADPlus in a configuration file that is provided to non-technical staff. Finally, the configuration file extends the behavior of the command line. Conditional statements are just one example of an option available in the configuration file that is not available from the command line.

Here is a sample ADPlus configuration file:

```
<adplus>
  <settings>
     <runmode>crash</runmode>
     <option>quiet</option>
     <outputdir>c:\dumps</outputdir>
  </settings>
  <precommands>
     <cmd>.loadby sos mscorwks</cmd>
     <cmd>!eeversion</cmd>
  </precommands>
  <exceptions>
     <option>nodumponfirstchance</option>
     <config>
        <code>dz</code>
```

```
            <actions1>log;stack;eventlog</actions1>
            <customactions1>dd ebp</customactions1>
        </config>
        <config>
            <code>clr</code>
            <actions1>log;stack;eventlog</actions1>
            <customactions1>!stoponexception system.accessviolationexception 1;
                .if(@$t1==1){.dump /ma c:\\dumps\\mydump.dmp  }
            </customactions1>
        </config>
    </exceptions>
</adplus>
```

Let us examine the above configuration file:

- **<*settings*> element**   The *settings* element sets the operational mode of ADPlus. In the preceding example, ADPlus is set to run in crash mode, quietly, and the output directory is c:\dumps.

- **<*precommands*> element**   The *precommands* element sets commands to run when ADPlus is first attached to the application. In the example, SOS is loaded for managed debugging. Next, the version of the .NET runtime is displayed.

- **<*exceptions*> element**   The *exceptions* element defines exception handling. You can handle multiple exceptions, each described in a separate <config> section.

- **<*code*> element**   The *code* element defines the exception type. The *dz* type is the divide-by-zero exception, while *clr* is for Common Language Runtime exceptions.

- **<*actions1*> element**   The *actions1* element has the commands to be executed upon a first chance exception. This is the exception defined in the *Code* element. In our example, the *Log*, *Stack*, and *Eventlog* keywords are used. The *Log* keyword means to log the exception. The *Stack* keyword displays the call stack for the thread where the exception occurred. The *Eventlog* keyword means the exception is recorded in the event log. The *Actions2* element is similar but used with second chance exceptions.

- **<*customactions1*> element**   Enter specific debugging commands in the *customactions1* element. These commands will be run when a first chance exception occurs. The type of exception is defined in the *Code* element. The second *customactions1* in the example configuration file is more complex. It demonstrates how to trap specific managed exceptions. When a *System.AccessViolationException* occurs, the mydump.dmp is created. The double slashes (\\) in c:\\dumps\\mydump.dmp are translated into single slashes, which is appropriate for delimiting a path.

ADPlus and Web Applications   The perfect application does not exist. Historically, applications have been short run. You start an application, perform a discrete task, and then shut down the program. The application is restarted for the next task. In this scenario, the program does not execute long enough for problems to accumulate. For example, memory leaks do not have time to accumulate and potentially crash the program. However, the paradigm has changed with Web applications. Web applications run for an extended period of time—several days and even months. Small problems that were inconsequential before can accumulate and become a considerable issue. For this reason, the ASP.NET worker process may be recycled. Proactive recycling recycles an otherwise healthy application. This will periodically give you a fresh worker process to handle future requests. This is helpful in preventing denial of service attacks on a Web server. For example, the worker process can recycle after a specified number of requests. Reactive recycling recycles the worker process when a problem occurs. For example, the worker process can be recycled when memory exceeds a set threshold.

When the worker process recycles, current requests are completed by the active worker process. A new worker process is started that handles future requests. The old worker process exits after handling the final request. The recycling of the worker process is then reported in the event log. You can always check the event log to determine if the worker process has been recycled and the reason for it.

For IIS 6.0, worker process recycling is controlled by the *processModel* tag in the web.config file. The *processModel* tag is allowed solely in the root web.config file. In addition, the *allowDefinition* attribute of the tag must be set to *Everywhere*. Table 9-3 lists some of the relevant attributes.

TABLE 9-3 Attributes of the *ProcessModel* Tag That Affect Recycling

Attribute	Description
requestLimit	The number of requests allowed before the worker process is restarted. Default is infinite.
responseDeadlockInterval	The time allowed for outstanding requests not to respond before recycling the worker process.
memoryLimit	Percentage of virtual memory (relative to the system) that the worker process can use before it is recycled. Default is 60.
Timeout	The number of minutes before a worker process is recycled. Default is infinite.

For IIS 7, you configure worker process recycling through the application pool. First, start IIS 7.0. Open the context menu for a specific application pool. Select Recycling. The Edit Application Pool Recycling Settings window will open. Select the appropriate recycling options, and enter parameters in the related text box. See Figure 9-8.

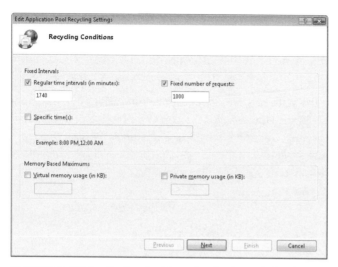

FIGURE 9-8 Edit Application Pool Recycling Settings window for configuring recycling of the worker process.

When a worker process recycles, that is usually, but not always, an indication of a problem. Getting a dump at the moment would be useful for post-mortem analysis. You can use ADPlus to create a dump when the worker process is recycled. The following ADPlus configuration file accomplishes this task. The *ExitProcess* function is called just before the worker process is recycled. You can set a breakpoint on that function and create a dump at that very moment.

```
<ADPlus>
    <Settings>

        <RunMode>crash</RunMode>
    </Settings>
    <Breakpoints>
        <NewBP>
            <Address>kernel32!ExitProcess</Address>
            <Type>bp</Type>
            <Actions>FullDump</Actions>
            <ReturnAction>G</ReturnAction>
        </NewBP>
    </Breakpoints>
</ADPlus>
```

Here are the specifics pertaining to the configuration file.

- The *NewBP* element sets a breakpoint.

- The *Address* element specifies a breakpoint at *kernel32!ExitProcess*. *ExitProcess* is located in kernel32.dll.

- The *Actions* element indicates that a full dump should be created when the breakpoint is hit.

- The *ReturnAction* element indicates that, after the dump is created, regular program execution should continue. "G" is for *go*. The worker process will then be recycled.

Finally, ADPlus can capture the state of a Web application. Run ADPlus in crash mode on the worker process, which is w3wp.exe. However, for the complete picture of a Web application, you should run ADPlus on inetinfo.exe and dllhost.exe also. Run ADPlus on these programs individually. Alternatively, run ADPlus with the IIS option. The following command will automatically attach to w3wp.exe, inetinfo.exe, and dllhost.exe.

```
adplus -hang -IIS
```

Summary

There is no perfect application. This chapter outlines strategies to mitigate software problems. It also discusses curing the bugs your application does have. The objective is to keep your application consistently stable, robust, efficient, and correct. One of the best practices to avoid future software problems and bugs is to fully implement the software development life cycle. Debugging desktop applications is different from debugging Web applications. For example, desktop applications are typically local applications and short lived. These differences make it more complex to debug Web applications. Also debugging a production application is different from debugging a developmental application. Production applications are typically a release version. Also, production applications are better suited for post-mortem debugging. Make sure the proper symbols are available before debugging. If not, you will be unable to debug with symbolic information, which is more transparent. Vendors such as Microsoft publish symbol stores available for download with the appropriate symbols for their products. Visual Studio has several features that promote proactive debugging. MDAs isolate potential interoperability issues in managed applications. Code Analysis evaluates managed code against the Framework Design Guidelines and warns of problems. For debugging, you can download several debugging tools from the Debugging Tools for Windows Web site. Windbg is probably the most powerful tool available in this package. Load the SOS debugging extension into Windbg to perform managed debugging. ADPlus, another tool from Debugging Tools for Windows, is used to create dumps when an application crashes or hangs. ADPlus is also useful for creating dumps when the worker process recycles.

Key Points

- Private symbols are full symbols and have the most details, such as local variable names.

- Public symbols have minimal information—just enough to basically re-create the call stack.

- Source indexing a PDB file inserts a list of source files and the commands to retrieve those files from source control into the file.

- Perform lightweight debugging with Visual Studio before using advanced tools. Check obvious things, such as the call stack, values of local variables, proper cleanup of resources, and so on.

- ADPlus can use a configuration file, which is the –c option. This is useful for creating complex and reusable configurations.

- Do not deploy a debug version of a Web application on a production machine. Place the *<deployment retail="true"/>* element in the web.config file to prevent this from happening inadvertently.

- For Web applications, you can handle unhandled exceptions first at the page level and then at the application level.

- Use *MiniDumpWriteDump* to write a dump programmatically.

- Set worker process recycling in the application pool of IIS 7.0.

Chapter 10
Code Analysis

Some of us will do our jobs well and some will not, but we will all be judged by only one thing—the result.

—Vince Lombardi

As you have probably guessed by now, writing solid code is about more than just writing application code. Investing in thoughtful designs, writing efficient programs, and incorporating development best practices are all important aspects of developing software applications. However, code requires exercise and analysis to ensure that the features and functionality being built work as expected. The users of our applications will, as the quote suggests, judge our efforts by the results that we deliver them. Therefore, it is important that we understand the quality of our application code before releasing it to them. By incorporating automated code analysis and testing into day-to-day engineering processes, we are better able to predict application quality and find and address bugs earlier in the release cycle.

Automated testing, sometimes referred to as test automation, is the use of software to control the execution of tests. This involves using programming frameworks such as the one found in Visual Studio or open source projects like NUnit to automate testing against various sections of the application code. These automated tests help to determine whether the targeted areas of code are functioning as expected. With these frameworks, developers and testers can programmatically control test preconditions, execution conditions, or post conditions such as automated bug filing when tests fail. Additionally, these frameworks provide the building blocks for developing a rich suite of automated tests. These suites of tests can be used to reduce the cost of application testing while improving the reliability and repeatability of the test effort.

Incorporating programmatic, or automated, testing within the application development process is fundamental to understanding how an application will perform when users interact with it. Manual testing remains a great method for discovering usability centric issues, or problems with complex user interaction flows, and should not be absent from the software-testing process. However, programmatic testing almost always helps find bugs earlier in the release cycle, which helps to improve overall code quality, especially when release cycles are short.

When automated code analysis, testing, and code coverage are applied within software development teams, the result is generally higher code quality, fewer regression bugs, and more stable application builds. Applying this level of automated rigor in the development process accrues value with every feature that gets added to the application. As software complexity increases, automated test execution and coverage keeps pace and helps maintain the quality of the application. Throughout this chapter, we will discuss the importance of investing in test automation and focus on tactics and tools for helping application development teams streamline their testing processes and address the quality of application code earlier in the release cycle. Additionally, we will highlight key metrics that can provide actionable indicators for code quality during the development cycle, which further helps to manage application quality. This chapter is for both developers and testers alike as both are equally critical to the process of managing application quality. Let's start by discussing ways to streamline the testing process.

Invest in the Test Process

Throughout this book, we have discussed the "cost" associated with finding and fixing bugs within the application development life cycle. In Chapter 2, "Class Design and Prototyping," we cited "The Economic Impacts of Inadequate Infrastructure for Software Testing" report as one example of the cost associated with finding bugs late in the development cycle versus earlier. These findings also correlate with the Windows Live Hotmail case study of Chapter 1, "Code Quality in an Agile World," which found that, as the team improved its testing during the development cycle, the team noted fewer bugs during the later phases of the release. As more development teams adopt increasingly agile development models and shorter release cycles, it is a significant challenge to ensure high levels of quality with less time to develop and test. To address this, software engineering teams must invest in building a set of automated test cases that will both increase the amount of test coverage being applied over a shorter period of time and improve the consistency and repeatability of the testing.

As with any investment in automation, the benefits of increased efficiency, productivity, and repeatability of the process being automated are more than worth the investment required to get there. We can simply look back at some of the large-scale successes of the industrial revolution in the United States to understand the benefits that the automation of the assembly line brought to automobile manufacturing. Investing in test automation has a very similar value proposition. Once a test framework is in place and the corpus of automated tests is established and running, evaluating changes to the application code requires significantly less work and is accomplished in a fraction of the time it would take to test manually. This not only reduces the overall cost of developing a feature, but it also increases the probability of finding issues very early in the feature development cycle. That said, automation does not represent a replacement for real, live, breathing, and thinking human testers and manual testing. There remain many testing scenarios, especially with user interfaces, where manual testing is the only way to find certain classes of bugs. Therefore, it is important to adopt the right balance of automated and manual testing within your overall testing philosophy.

There is clear value to application quality that originates from investments in testing processes and practices. Although we have briefly started discussing automated testing, there are also other ways to approach improving the testing process from an end-to-end perspective. Let's begin by discussing the importance of establishing a test rhythm for the team.

Define a Test Rhythm

For any software development team, clear processes and procedures help increase efficiency, control costs, and, in general, improve the quality of the output. This principle applies broadly across the overall software development process and is especially important to critical activities like testing. Defining a structured and repeatable test rhythm for your project team not only provides a framework for managing the project's quality gates but ultimately helps improve the consistency and repeatability of the testing effort. This involves identifying key points in the application development cycle and interleaving the appropriate testing processes so that specific quality objectives are achieved as a result of the testing. Accomplishing this requires that we first review some of the common types of testing that can be applied at various steps in the development process.

- **Unit testing**   This is a method for examining and verifying the functionality of the individual units of code that make up the system. Typically, unit tests are written to exercise individual methods and properties of a class to ensure that the functionality has been implemented as specified and is working correctly. Unit tests are generally written by the application feature developers and often used to verify the quality of a feature before it is checked in to source control. This is sometimes referred to as white-box testing.

- **Build Verification Testing (BVT)**   Typically, BVTs are represented by a suite of individual test cases that are collectively used to verify the quality of an application's build before being released for broader testing. The BVT test cases are often representative of major application functionality and focused on providing a quick examination of build quality. If an application build fails any of the test cases within the BVT suite of tests, the entire build is rejected from being tested any further. If an application build passes the BVT suite of tests, it is believed to be of sufficient quality to warrant broader, more focused testing. This type of testing is often referred to as black-box testing.

- **Functional testing**   This type of testing evaluates the entire application in the context of specific functional requirements. It is intended to examine the limits of the application features both from the design and customer perspectives and to essentially find the quality boundaries. This type of testing can be very broadly scoped and also include other aspects of testing like stress, security, or performance testing of the application features.

- **Load testing**   Sometimes referred to as scalability testing or stress testing, load testing is used to measure an application's ability to perform under an increased user load. This type of testing is predominantly used to determine the resource consumption behavior of an application, such as how much memory or CPU it utilizes, and its ability to scale out to meet increased user demand. Load testing is often performed a few times within a typical testing cycle and, when the outcome is compared with previous results, can inform development teams of the effects of recent feature additions on application performance overall.

- **Security testing**   This is a much more specialized form of testing that is designed to evaluate applications for flaws in security that could either compromise the integrity of a user's personal information or expose the user or software to other malicious attacks. In recent years, security testing has become increasingly important as software becomes more globally connected and subject to a wide variety of predatory practices. Security testing is often used in conjunction with functional testing to ensure that the key security concepts of confidentiality, integrity, authentication, authorization, availability, and non-repudiation are addressed. In Chapter 6, "Security Design and Implementation," we discussed threat modeling as a mechanism for analyzing application security threats during application design. The results of threat models are a valuable starting point for creating a security test plan and strategy and should be incorporated as part of the security testing effort.

- **Performance testing**   Also used in conjunction with functional testing, performance testing is utilized to determine the speed of an application or specific functionality within an application. In Chapter 4, "Performance Is a Feature," performance testing was mentioned in the context of measuring page load times or the speed at which Web application pages were being delivered to an end user's browser. While this is one application of performance analysis, other methods may evaluate the speed of connections to data sources or even the number of specific calculations over a given interval of time.

- **Integration testing**   This type of testing is broadly defined as the phase of software testing where all components of the application are brought together and evaluated for end-to-end quality. In some cases, this includes testing across all integrated systems upon which the application relies. The goal of this phase of testing is to ensure that functional scenarios are tested across the application and that all components of the system interact with one another appropriately.

Having reviewed a few of the common types of testing that can be applied during the development process, it's important that we examine how to apply them to a structured testing rhythm. As an example, let's consider the testing process illustrated in Figure 10-1.

This example illustrates how we can interleave testing into day-to-day application development processes as a means to not only improve quality but to maintain agility in feature development. In this diagram, you may notice the line that separates the testing processes that occur before feature check-in from those that occur after check-in. During feature development, specific testing procedures such as automated unit testing and check-in testing can be used to iteratively evaluate quality as a means to prevent low-quality code from being introduced into the application's source repository. Additionally, after feature code has been checked in, daily build verification testing and a regimen of functional and integration testing can be used to further evaluate the overall quality of the application. This balance of testing in our hypothetical process intends to achieve higher check-in and build quality, which translates into finding and addressing quality issues earlier in the release cycle.

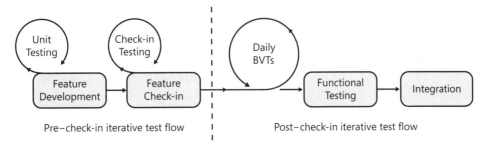

FIGURE 10-1 Hypothetical testing process.

It is important that the appropriate test processes and rhythms be established and incorporated into the overall software development life cycle within your organization. Without the correct mechanisms for finding, fixing, and tracking issues within your software applications, it will be nearly impossible to fully understand the quality level of your product. Because we have already established the need for a formal testing process that integrates into the day-to-day development efforts, let's discuss the importance of managing the test work load.

Establish Test Work Item Tracking

We have already established that delivering successful products that are of high quality is about more than just coding. It is very important to ensure that all aspects of the project are aligned so that the team members are assured that they have performed their jobs effectively. This implies that the requirements we identified, the code we wrote, and the testing we have completed all reconcile with one another. Effective project teams recognize this and establish the processes required to align work items across the program management, development, and test disciplines. Fortunately, Visual Studio Team Foundation (VSTF), which is part of the Visual Studio Team System suite of client and server products, allows teams to accomplish this with relative ease.

In VSTF, all team participants across the aforementioned disciplines can track their respective work individually and relate work items through linking. For testers on the project team, this means making sure that work items for each test case being written are clearly identified and entered into VSTF. These test work items can then be linked to other work items, such as those that represent the coding effort or the scenario that defined the feature. This allows test teams to make sure that they are building automated tests for each feature within the project. Additionally, this makes building queries to track test progress across all features, or within a specific feature, possible.

Note Visual Studio Team Foundation 2008 does not make a "Test Work Item" template available out of the box, which would be useful for tracking work item properties that are specific to test work items as opposed to more generic work items. Fortunately, VSTF extensibility allows you to create custom work item types for the project template your team is using. Thus, you can create custom work item types for coding, testing, or any other function that might require extended work item properties.

In addition to tracking test case development work items, test teams also need to ensure they are appropriately tracking any bugs found as a result of testing efforts. Bug tracking is perhaps the most important mechanism for understanding the state of quality in an application at any stage of the testing process. It is imperative that application teams have a process in place for logging application bugs and appropriately triaging and fixing them. To accommodate these practices, VSTF provides a "Bug" work item template as one of the default work item types. Like any other work item type within VSTF, bugs can be linked to other work items, dependent bugs, or the results of an automated test run. This allows a more granular level of quality tracking and reporting. Thus, teams can periodically review the bugs that have been logged, assess their priority, and assign them to other team members for resolution. An example of a bug that has been linked to an associative work item in VSTF is shown in Figure 10-2.

Thus far, we have established that defining a structured and repeatable test rhythm for your project team not only provides a framework for managing the project's quality gates but ultimately helps improve the consistency and repeatability of the testing effort. Accomplishing this includes defining a test rhythm and process that integrates into the development cycle in a way that pushes quality upstream. We reviewed an example of one such process in Figure 10-1, and we discussed the importance of leveraging different forms of automated testing at different stages of the development process. Investing in this type of process for your team will pay dividends in terms of team efficiency, effectiveness, and overall application quality. Tightly coupling a formal testing process with the appropriate tracking mechanisms will give the team a more granular understanding of its progress and thus help the team govern its efforts more effectively. Once the appropriate test rhythm and tracking mechanisms have been instituted, test teams can focus the bulk of their energy on the most important aspects of their job, which is evaluating application features and code and finding bugs. Let's review some common approaches to performing the code analysis necessary to find quality issues within the application code.

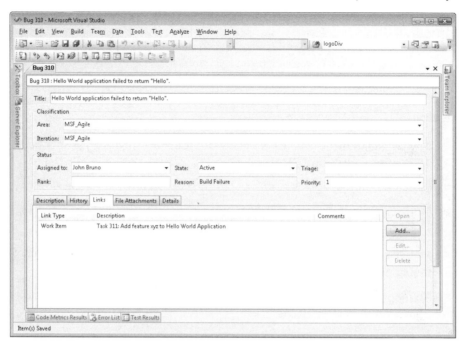

FIGURE 10-2 Bug work item example.

Incorporate Automated Code Analysis

The best way to ensure quality within your application is to invest in developing automated methods for validating the logic and algorithms within your application code. This invest- ment not only helps to find application bugs in new features early in the development cycle but also helps to prevent regression bugs in the quality of older code. Within Visual Studio Team System (VSTS), there are multiple features available for incorporating automated code analysis into your team's development life cycle. These features include tools for analyzing code based on predefined rule sets, a framework for developing unit tests, as well as tools for generating code metrics. When combined with some of the process management features in VSTF that were previously mentioned, these tools enable development teams to improve the efficiency and effectiveness of their overall application testing. Let's consider the various code analysis methods that we recommend incorporating into your development process.

Use Static Code Analysis Tools

Static code analysis is a technique for analyzing software application code without actually executing the code. This type of analysis is used to evaluate code against a specific set of rules or guidelines for which the code analysis engine has been preconfigured to use. There are free and commercially available static code analysis tools for almost any programming language, including all flavors of managed code, of course. The most common example for managed code analyzers is FxCop, from Microsoft.

FxCop is used to check .NET managed code assemblies against the Microsoft .NET Framework design guidelines to ensure that the code in question conforms to the set of pre-selected rules. Each of the rules present within FxCop are grouped into the following categories.

- **Design**   Rules that evaluate your code for proper library design as specified by the .NET Framework Design Guidelines

- **Globalization**   Rules that evaluate your code for determining world readiness

- **Interoperability**   Rules that evaluate your code for ensuring proper interoperability with COM clients

- **Mobility**   Rules evaluate mobile application code for efficient power usage. These should generally be applied to smart device applications

- **Naming**   Rules that check for adherence to the naming conventions of the .NET Framework Design Guidelines

- **Performance**   Rules that evaluate code to ensure high performance

- **Portability**   Rules that evaluate your application code's portability across processor architectures

- **Security**   Rules that promote safer libraries and applications

- **Usage**   Rules that ensure proper usage of the .NET Framework

From a process perspective, FxCop is designed to be an integrated part of the software development life cycle, specifically during the coding phase of the project. The tool can either be downloaded for free and run as a stand-alone application or leveraged directly through Visual Studio 2008. By default, the rule set within Visual Studio 2008 is extended to include the following categories.

- **Maintainability**   Rules that ensure library and application maintenance guidelines are followed.

- **Reliability**   Rules that evaluate code to ensure correct designs for library and application reliability, such as correct memory and thread usage.

FxCop users are able to configure the tool to run individual rules, all rules within a category, or all categories. The tool parses Microsoft Intermediate Language (MSIL) and performs call-graph analysis to compare your application assemblies against rules within the previously described categories. Upon completion of the analysis, the tool generates a report containing the various rule violations it encountered. When running within Visual Studio, the results are displayed within the Error List window.

Static code analysis is one of the best ways to find code issues early in the project life cycle. It helps to ensure that all project developers adhere to the common set of accepted coding guidelines provided in the default rule set. Additionally, the tools also support extending the default rules to include custom rules built by individual development teams. When these tools are incorporated directly into the build process, either through Visual Studio or the command-line interface of the stand-alone FxCop application, the overall quality of the application builds as well as the consistency of the application code can be improved. It is important, however, to follow some basic usage guidelines to help select and manage the appropriate analysis rules for your application. Let's review some basic guidelines.

Note For more information on creating custom FxCop or Code Analysis rules for integration into Visual Studio, I recommend reading the Code Analysis team blog at *http://blogs.msdn.com /fxcop/archive/2004/01/09/49287.aspx*.

If you are incorporating code analysis for the first time on an existing application, you may get quickly overwhelmed by the number of rules and number of warnings being generated by the analysis tool. In this scenario, it is best to follow these guidelines.

- First, enable all rules and run the analysis tool on the existing code.

- Evaluate the results generated by the analysis tool and determine which warnings are most effective to enable on your existing code base.

- Enable the subset of rules that you believe are most applicable and re-run the analysis.

- File work items or bugs to track the warnings generated by the analysis tools and assign them appropriately to be addressed.

By contrast, if you are including code analysis within your application development cycle for the first time on a new application, it is best to adhere to these practices.

- Enable all rules and run the analysis tools during the development process, preferably prior to each application build on local developer workstations.

- Address all issues identified by the code analysis tools before checking code into the source repository.

- Configure Visual Studio Team Foundation to enforce code analysis as check-in criteria.

If possible, do not wait until the end of the development cycle to run static code analysis rules. Running static code analysis late in the development cycle could potentially destabilize the product or introduce a large number of small changes into the code base that could be difficult to review and verify. This would put a large burden on the development and test team during a critical juncture in the project cycle. It is certainly more ideal to incorporate code analysis during the phase of the project where code is actively being written. This will allow the team to enforce rules on application code that has not been checked in and thus ensure better quality of code earlier in the development cycle. Sometimes, however, this is not always possible. In the event your application code base is pre-existing, it is best to follow the aforementioned guidelines, triage the issues that get uncovered, and prioritize fixing them whenever possible.

As mentioned, static code analysis does an excellent job uncovering a certain class of bugs within your application code. These issues, while very important, often have more to do with the structure of the code, API usage, and/or usage patterns. Static code analysis does not evaluate the logic of your application for conformity with the design specifications or to ensure it functions properly. The only way to examine these facets of your application is to develop test code that evaluates application code using the automated testing framework provided by Visual Studio 2008. Let's explore this in greater detail.

Write Application Test Code

In addition to leveraging static code analysis to drive higher levels of quality, application development teams should also invest in writing automated application test code. This generally means developing a corpus of different unit, functional, and integration tests across the application. The goal of this effort is to build out a set of tests that can be leveraged to examine and exercise individual features or broad portions of the application. Earlier in this chapter, we discussed the differences between the different types of testing, and we suggested how each should be applied within the testing life cycle. In this section, we will evaluate the specifics of the most common form of automated test—the unit test.

Unit tests are intended for examining code at the method and property level of a class, to ensure that the application functionality has been implemented as specified and is working correctly. Therefore, as a best practice, application developers should write unit tests when developing features to ensure that the code they are writing works as intended. To accomplish this, developers should consider following these guidelines. First, they should build a broad scope of tests to ensure that all possible conditions are examined before checking in the code. This should include test cases that cover the following scenarios.

- **Positive tests**   These tests exercise the code in accordance with the specified rules and ensure that a positive result is returned.

- **Negative tests**   This type of test is designed to exercise the code in a way that was not intended to ensure that it handles error conditions appropriately.

In addition to choosing the appropriate scope of testing, application developers should also ensure that their unit tests adhere to a set of principles that will drive continued efficiency and effectiveness of the testing. These principles include the following.

- **Tests should be well structured**   For maintainability, it is important to ensure that tests are structured appropriately. Much like application code, test logic should be organized and written using standard .NET Framework design guidelines and object-oriented principles.

- **Tests should be self-documenting**   Unit tests should be specific about what test case is being applied, what inputs are being utilized, and what the expected result should be. Additionally, tests should be named appropriately so that there is a clear understanding about the goal of that test.

- **Keep unit tests simple and fast**   Unit tests should be run against application prior to being checked into the source repository. Therefore, the tests you design should be optimized for fast, repeated use.

- **Unit tests should be automatic and repeatable**   Tests should not require human interaction to either manually execute or evaluate results. They should be 100 percent repeatable and reliable in their outcome.

- **Unit tests should be simple to execute**   For tests to be effective, they need to be able to execute on multiple machines by either command line or button click.

- **Tests should be independent**   Tests should not depend on other tests to complete successfully. They should be self-contained and able to be run independently or as part of a larger group. This will keep them robust and maintainable.

Adhering to this set of guidelines and principles will help developers remain focused on the goals of unit testing, which is to build an automated, repeatable, robust, and reliable set of tests that can be used throughout the life of the application code to ensure quality. Let's look at the anatomy of a unit test in greater depth and discuss the application of these guidelines and principles.

Anatomy of a Unit Test

Unit tests begin as Test projects within Visual Studio. Similar to other projects, Test projects can be stand-alone or incorporated as part of a larger solution. They generally include standard project artifacts such as *.cs files, and they will include references to the application assemblies being tested and the Visual Studio unit testing framework. In addition to these files, you will also notice a *.vsmdi file, which is a test metadata file. This file maintains the data for test lists, which can be used to group a specific set of tests together for execution.

All test classes within the test project are adorned with the *[TestClass()]* attribute, which signifies that the class contains test methods. Furthermore, each method within the class that is a test should be adorned with the *[TestMethod()]* attribute. Certainly other methods and properties can exist within the test class and be leveraged by the tests themselves. Developers should write tests with the same object-oriented design principles that they would apply to their applications. This includes practices such as incorporating code reuse and not duplicating logic. The important thing is to apply the above principles within the test method itself.

In addition to the *[TestMethod()]* and *[TestClass()]* attributes we just discussed, the unit test framework also provides other attributes for enabling specific unit-test functionality. These attributes include *[TestInitialize()]* and *[TestCleanup()]*, which are used to designate methods that will perform initialization and cleanup logic for all tests within the test class. Designating a method with the *[TestInitialize()]* attribute is a great way to establish a specific runtime state for your test. By contrast, designating a method with the *[TestCleanup()]* attribute is the recommended best practice for incorporating logic that returns the test environment to the pre-test state. While both of these attributes are useful for maintaining the test environment, to verify that the specific state of the test has been reached, developers must incorporate the use of Asserts.

Asserts are methods within the VSTS unit test framework that developers should use within their test code to affirm a certain action or condition has been met within the test. By nature, unit tests result in either a passing or failing condition. In fact, unit tests are assumed by the test engine to be in a passing state until an assert triggers a failed or inconclusive state, or a unit test throws an exception that is not specified in the *ExpectedExceptionAttribute* attribute. Therefore, it is important to use Asserts appropriately and handle exceptions properly in order to confirm the intended conditions are achieved and thus avoid any false positives. Fortunately, there are a number of options for using asserts and handling exceptions within the tests that afford developers the flexibility to evaluate several types of conditions. These classes include the following, all of which are available from the *Microsoft.VisualStudio.TestTools.UnitTesting* namespace.

- **Assert**   This class provides methods for verifying true or false conditions within tests. It includes several methods for comparing values.

- **StringAssert**   This class contains a number of useful methods for comparing strings such as *Contains()* or *StartsWith()*.

- **CollectionAssert**   This class provides methods for comparing collections of objects and verifying the state of one or more collections.

- **AssertFailedException**   This is an exception that is thrown when a test fails either because of an unexpected exception or the failed result of a particular Assert statement within the test.

- **AssertInconclusiveException**   This is an exception that is thrown when a test returns a result of inconclusive. Typically, developers will add an *Assert.Inconclusive()* to their test method to indicate that it has not been completed yet. Visual Studio adds this automatically when you generate tests from your project.

- **UnitTestAssertException**   This class is primarily used as a base class for custom Assert exceptions that application developers wish to build for their specific purposes. Inheriting from this class makes it easier for developers to detect the exception as an Assert exception rather than an unexpected exception.

- *ExpectedExceptionAttribute*   This attribute is used to decorate test methods when developers want to test that a specific exception within their application code is being thrown appropriately.

Developers and testers should decide how best to leverage any of the above Asserts in their test code to measure the outcome of the test. Regardless of what logic they choose to include within the test, the Assert statements dictate the results of the test. Even tests that incorporate multiple Asserts are assumed to be in a passing state until one of those asserts encounters a failing or inconclusive state. Let's take a look at a code sample that demonstrates a simple unit test with multiple asserts. First, let's review the method that we will be testing.

```
/// <summary>
/// Simple method for returning a greeting.
/// </summary>

public  static String BuildGreeting(String name)
{
    return String.Format("Hello{0}",name);
}
```

As you may have noticed, this method is very simple. It accepts a name as an input string and returns a concatenated string with a greeting and the input parameter. Now, let's review the code for testing this method. We appropriately named this test method *BuildGreetingTest()* to indicate that it is a test for the *BuildGreeting()* method.

```
/// <summary>
/// A test for the BuildGreeting method.
/// This test ensures the proper string is returned.
///</summary>

[TestMethod()]
[DeploymentItem("SolidCode_Chapter_10.exe")]
public void BuildGreetingTest()
{
    string name = "John Doe";
    string expected = "Hello " + name;
    string actual;
    actual = Program_Accessor.BuildGreeting(name);
    StringAssert.Contains(actual, "Hello");
    Assert.AreEqual(expected, actual);
}
```

This test method accomplishes two objectives. First, it ensures that the actual string being returned from the *BuildGreeting()* method contains the word "Hello." Additionally, it examines the entire string being returned to ensure that the actual result matches the expected result. This is of course a redundant check and not necessarily required. However, the point of this code example is to demonstrate that the test actually fails on the second Assert and not the first. A bug has been intentionally inserted in the *BuildGreeting()* method to cause the Assert to fail. Notice that the actual result was "HelloJohn Doe" as opposed to "Hello John Doe," which was what we expected. Running this test in Visual Studio provides us with the feedback we are expecting, which is shown in Figure 10-3.

FIGURE 10-3 Test Results window from Visual Studio.

In addition to making this visually available through Visual Studio, the test results are also available in an XML format within the TestResults folder of your Visual Studio project as a *.trx file. The file contains some extensive information about the test results, for which a sample has been provided below.

```
<Results>
<UnitTestResult executionId="b9005e6f-d1da-4ec6-b06d-4c073353c5b9"
testId="d904ee09-1da5-dae8-1540-8fd41331ef42" testName="BuildGreetingTest"
computerName="DevComputer" duration="00:00:00.3799795"
startTime="2008-10-25T16:22:11.6950000-07:00" endTime="2008-10-25T16:22:12.5320000-07:00"
testType="13cdc9d9-ddb5-4fa4-a97d-d965ccfc6d4b" outcome="Failed"
testListId="8c84fa94-04c1-424b-9868-57a2d4851a1d">
<Output>
    <ErrorInfo>
      <Message>Assert.AreEqual failed. Expected:&lt;Hello John Doe&gt;. Actual:&lt;HelloJohn
      Doe&gt;
      </Message>
      <StackTrace> at SolidCode_Chapter_10Tests.ProgramTest.BuildGreetingTest()
        in C:\Visual Studio 2008\Projects\SolidCode_Chapter_10\SolidCode_Chapter_10Tests\
        ProgramTest.cs:line 78
      </StackTrace>
    </ErrorInfo>
</Output>
</UnitTestResult>
</Results>
```

Now that the test code is complete, running, and producing results, any new changes to the application logic can be checked very quickly for bugs. This allows us to continually measure the quality of this code for as long as it is being used within the application. Although this gives us a certain level of confidence in the feature being developed, it does not validate the quality of the entire scenario in which this method is a participant. As we move beyond testing at the unit level to testing at more of the functional or scenario level, we will need more than just single unit tests to validate quality. Fortunately, Visual Studio provides some options for testing beyond the *BuildGreeting()* method. Let's take a look at some of those options.

Testing with Visual Studio

Scenario-based testing or functional testing, as described previously, allows developers and testers to evaluate the application or feature of an application in the context of specific functional requirements. For example, if we consider the hypothetical console application that accepts the input of a person's name and outputs a greeting, there may be multiple specific requirements of this feature that should be tested. This requires that feature testing include a list or series of tests to validate each of the distinct attributes of the feature. In this elementary example, there are likely only a few distinct tests, but imagine a more complex feature that may require dozens of tests to validate the end-to-end quality. Visual Studio offers some options for how to approach this challenge.

- **Test lists**   Visual Studio allows the creation of test lists, which represent a collection of specific tests that are organized into groups. Test lists can be built from the set of available tests within your Visual Studio solution, as well as tests that were built outside the solution. They are created with the Test List Editor by selecting from the Test menu on the Visual Studio toolbar and choosing Create New Test List. Once created, the tests within the list can be run manually, as part of the build process, or through Visual Studio Team Foundation as part of a check-in policy. Test lists can help development teams organize their individual unit tests in a number of different ways and subsequently be used to execute sets of tests for feature-level validation, or perhaps even build validation.

- **Ordered tests**   Although test lists are very useful and can be used to group tests together, ordered tests actually can be used to ensure that tests are executed in a particular sequence. Ordered tests can be executed stand-alone, whereby all tests within the ordered test will be executed in the specified order, or they can run as part of test lists. This makes ordered tests a great solution for conducting scenario-based testing where developers or testers may be required to follow certain sequences of events to validate that the feature is functioning properly.

In addition to scenario-based or functional testing, there are other types of testing for which Visual Studio provides support. Scenario and functional validation are obviously very important for validating the quality of the feature or application. However, there are other facets of quality, such as load testing, that require analysis at the individual feature level or across the application. Let's review Visual Studio's support for load testing.

- **Load tests**   In Chapter 5, "Designing for Scale," we discussed the importance of building applications that can scale properly to large numbers of users. One way to measure how your application performs under high usage is to leverage load testing. Load tests allow application developers and testers to execute automated tests simultaneously using virtual users. Load tests can be configured in a variety of ways using the Load Test Wizard pictured in Figure 10-4. These configurations allow adjustments to parameters like load patterns, network settings, and which performance counters should be monitored. Additionally, tests can be run using a single computer or multiple computers. The test results are subsequently provided in a set of tables and graphs once the test run is complete. In general, load tests are an incredibly useful feature for both developers and testers to apply stress testing to their features or applications.

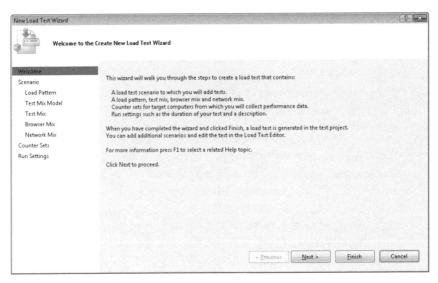

FIGURE 10-4 Visual Studio Load Test Wizard.

 Note As with many of the topics throughout this book, load testing requires a much deeper evaluation before jumping right into using the available tools. Although we have established here that it is an important facet to testing, we hardly scratched the surface of what is possible. I recommend taking a deeper look at load testing in Visual Studio at MSDN: *http://msdn .microsoft.com/en-us/library/ms182561.aspx*.

Use Metrics to Understand Quality

Thus far, we have discussed a number of methods for improving your team's testing processes and overall application quality. We evaluated both process improvements as well as testing tactics for measuring individual feature or application quality. If you were to incorporate some of the tactics mentioned into your existing processes, the quality of your code would certainly be improved. At the end of the day, though, these tactics largely focus on determining whether application testing passes or fails. Of course, automated tests that are passing or failing tell us a lot about the state of quality for that feature. However, there are other metrics we could incorporate that may actually tell us more about the code being built and tested across the team.

Visual Studio provides application development teams with a number of different metrics for understanding the quality of the application code as well as understanding the volatility, complexity, and even the maintainability of the code. These metrics are useful at various stages of the project and, when applied appropriately, can help to focus or prioritize the testing effort for the team. Let's review the specifics of these metrics.

Measuring Complexity and Maintainability of Code

As software applications grow with complexity, it becomes increasingly difficult to build maintainable and reliable code. While certain resources, such as this book, can help developers to improve the quality of their code, it is fundamentally difficult to evaluate code for both quality and maintainability without testing. In recent versions of Visual Studio, a code metrics feature was added to give developers an early indication of the complexity, or maintainability, of their code. The primary goal of these tools is to provide developers with a perspective on where their code might need additional testing or rework. Developers can use these features by selecting Calculate Code Metrics from the Analyze menu within Visual Studio 2008. These metrics provide insights into the following areas.

- **Maintainability index**   This metric is an index value between 0 and 100 that is an indicator for the ease of maintaining the code. The higher the number, the more maintainable the code is thought to be. The calculation is based on a combination of cyclomatic complexity, lines of code, and the Halstead Volume, which is a quantitative measure of complexity determined from the operators and operands in the code. Visual Studio provides green, yellow, and red color-coded ratings to help identify trouble spots within the code.

- **Cyclomatic complexity**   This is a measure of the structural complexity of the code. It is determined by calculating the number of different code paths present within the flow of the program. This calculation is determined by evaluating the various *do while*, *for each*, *if* blocks, or *switch* cases within the program. The result is a number that represents the complexity of control flow within the code. Areas of code that exhibit high cyclomatic complexity should be refactored into smaller, more granular blocks. Code that cannot be refactored should be thoroughly tested.

- **Depth of inheritance**   This metric is an indicator of the number of class definitions extended to the base class of the hierarchy. The depth of the hierarchy is an indicator of how difficult it could be to understand where particular methods or properties are defined or refined.

- **Class coupling**   Measures the coupling of unique classes to parameters, variables, return types, method calls, interface implementations, generic or template instantiations, base classes, fields defined on external types, and attribute decoration. Good design suggests that classes and methods have low coupling and high cohesion. The opposite, high coupling and low cohesion, is an indicator of a design that is difficult to reuse due to the number of dependencies.

- **Lines of code**   This measure is an approximation of the number of lines of Intermediate Language (IL) code. Because the measurement is based on IL, it is not an exact match against source code. This metric is unfortunately not very suggestive of a particular problem and may just be indicating that methods with a large number of lines be refactored into smaller parts.

When teams combine the use of these metrics with automated testing, they can quickly assess the risk areas of the application code and structure or prioritize their testing accordingly. For example, if the code being developed for a specific feature has a high cyclomatic complexity, the application developer should ensure that he or she has adequate unit tests to cover the variations in the logic effectively, assuming that the logic cannot be refactored. Additionally, the feature tester should make certain that the test plans or strategy prioritizes this area of the feature. While code metrics in and of themselves are interesting, it is more important to understand what they tell us about our application code, so we can take proper actions on them. They are great to apply at the individual feature level during the coding portion of the development life cycle and perhaps even early in the testing phase since they can help steer the direction of testing. Application developers and testers should leverage these tools as a means to understand more about the application code and validate that their approach to testing the feature or code is most effective.

Using Perspectives to Understand Quality

In the same way that code metrics are useful in understanding complexity and maintainability of application code at a feature level, there are other metrics that can be leveraged across the entire code base as a means to understand how application quality is trending. Because projects are very fluid with frequent feature check-ins, daily builds, and various levels of testing happening in real time, it is often difficult for teams to understand the state of the application quality. Fortunately, Team Foundation Server (TFS) provides insights into team progress and quality through data reporting, which are available within the analysis features of TFS. Let's enumerate some of the available metrics and discuss the value they provide for project teams.

- **Build perspective**   This represents a set of metrics focused around the application builds. It can be used to analyze various dimensions of build data such as the number of builds over time, the outcome of the build, who performed the build, and when the build was performed. This helps to understand how often builds are successful, how well teams are achieving their build quality goals, and whether the established build processes are effective.

- **Code churn perspective**   This provides metrics about the rate of change in the code in terms of how many files were changed and the number of lines changed, added, or deleted. This data can be analyzed a number of ways but is very effective when ana-lyzed in the context of specific builds. This can help teams, especially testers, identify the scope of code change between builds, which can help focus the testing efforts quite effectively. Also, it presents a good indicator of code volatility within specific areas of the code, which could help to identify certain risk areas that may require addi-tional testing.

■ **Code coverage perspective**   This provides the metrics about how many lines of code or blocks have been tested across test runs. These metrics can also be very helpful in evaluating how effective the automated test passes have been and help further guide test efforts.

■ **Load test perspective**   As described in the previous section, load testing is a great way to measure the performance of your application under stress and profile the effect that the application has on system resources. The load test perspective allows developers and testers to evaluate the results of load testing across multiple test runs. This allows teams to trend the results over time to ensure that comparable application builds or releases have not regressed in quality.

■ **Test results perspective**   Similar to the load test perspective, this set of results allows teams to track and trend the results of their test efforts across multiple application builds or releases. The data can be analyzed by test outcome, the specific build, the type of test, or other test dimensions. This data is very useful in showing how feature testing is progressing, as well as illustrating the completeness versus incompleteness of the testing effort.

■ **Current work item perspective**   This provides application development teams with analysis of the current work items and their respective statuses within Team Foundation Server. Despite this being largely used to understand overall project progress, it can be very useful in evaluating bug metrics and tracking progress on closing and resolving issues in the application.

Although this is not the complete representation of the perspectives metrics provided by TFS, it does represent the set that are most useful to the testing initiative. These metrics and reports are geared toward helping teams to evaluate their progress relative to the overall project, but especially with respect to testing. Incorporating the use of these tools within the testing process provides actionable data to development teams so that they can proactively manage the testing effort and ensure they are achieving their quality and testing goals. If these metrics do not precisely meet the requirements of your team, TFS makes it very simple to generate your own metrics by simply connecting to the TFS data warehouse with tools like Microsoft Excel. When development teams recognize the value that this data provides, they will very likely revisit their existing work-tracking processes and augment them to further increase the effectiveness of the resultant data. This is a testament to the flexibility and value that TFS provides application development teams and how, as an end-to-end toolset, it can help teams to manage and improve the quality of application code.

Inside Microsoft: Managing Quality for the Microsoft. com Web Analytics Platform

Microsoft.com is a large, public-facing Web site managed by Microsoft. In addition to being the corporate presence for the company, it is also used to showcase the many Microsoft products ranging from Xbox and Zune to Windows and Office. As of September 2008, Comscore reported that the sites under the Microsoft.com umbrella received around 124 million page views that month, which should provide an indication as to the popularity of the site.

Because the sites within the Microsoft.com umbrella are largely product information pages that are targeted toward consumers of Microsoft products, measuring the success and reach of those pages is critical to understanding the effectiveness of the site. This requires an investment in a business intelligence framework and data analysis toolset that can be used to collect and aggregate data about the usage of individual pages within the Microsoft.com sites. This is primarily the role of one of the Microsoft.com platform feature teams, which builds the logic, infrastructure, and tools for collecting, analyzing, and reporting Web site business analytics data. In addition to the Microsoft.com product-focused sites, the team is also responsible for collecting and aggregating data for such popular sites as MSDN, Codeplex, and Windows Update.

The Importance of Code Quality

For most platform teams at Microsoft, there are numerous other teams depending on the infrastructure, code, or services that the platform team delivers. The quality of their deliver-ables is expected to be high, and partner teams also require that platform components meet the greater percentage of their usage needs. Therefore, it is incumbent upon platform teams like the Microsoft.com Customer Intelligence team to ensure that their partners receive features and services that both address their needs and are of the highest quality. When con-sidering the scale and importance of the Microsoft.com Customer Intelligence partner teams, this can be a challenging goal to achieve. Fortunately, the team has invested heavily in build-ing strong, automated testing processes that help it produce higher quality deliverables.

The Test Investment

As an avid user and proponent of the Visual Studio Team Foundation (VSTF) and Visual Studio Team Suite (VSTS) products, the Microsoft.com Web Analytics team has built many of its processes, workflows, and quality metrics from the templates provided by VSTF. The team has been using VSTF since the early beta versions and believes strongly in the structure and value that the tool provides in terms of integrating workflow, project tracking, coding, testing, and reporting into one suite of tools. In some cases where the tool did not address the team's immediate needs, the team simply utilized the built-in extensibility model and extended the functionality. Overall, the team has invested a great deal in managing its end-to-end project tracking through VSTF, especially for its test work. Let's review some of the tactics the team has applied.

- **Automate as much as possible**   The team generally believes that investments in test automation wherever possible pays long-term dividends. Despite TFS lacking automated processes specific to its needs, the team has extended the TFS capabilities using the extensibility tools that are currently available and have increased the team's productivity as a result. The team recommends that other teams explore the extensibility options, including the Visual Studio Team Foundation Power Tools, and automate their processes wherever possible.

- **Use static code analysis**   Static code analysis is a great way to quickly evaluate code before it gets checked in for compliance with predefined best practices or custom rules. The Microsoft.com Customer Intelligence team is currently leveraging both predefined rules and custom rules within its static code analysis practices. The team has invested in developing these custom rules to ensure that certain design principles are consistent across the code base. The team recommends that teams incorporate the static code analysis rules within their processes, especially as part of check-in procedures.

- **Write automated tests and build test suites**   In addition to using static code analysis, the team also invests in building out a corpus of unit and functional automated tests. Generally speaking, developers on the team deliver unit tests as part of their feature work. These tests are generally very focused on specific functionality of the specific feature code. By contrast, testers author more functional tests, which often cover broader test scenarios. As automated tests are created, VSTF is used to create test lists or suites of test cases that can be applied at different phases of application testing.

- **Establish check-in policies**   Creating check-in policies allows application development teams to enforce a certain level of quality in the code being checked into source control. This ensures that a certain classification of bugs does not get introduced into the source repository, thus reducing the total volume of bugs likely to be found at the end of the development cycle. The team firmly believes that establishing check-in policies and enforcing them through VSTF affords the team increased control over the quality of code being checked in. Through these processes, the team gains increased confidence in the check-in since it can verify that certain test cases have been executed, static code analysis has been run, and code reviews have been conducted.

- **Automated build and test processes** The team automated its application builds and Build Verification Testing (BVT) processes using Visual Studio Team Foundation Build. This has allowed the team to ensure that each automated build that is initiated benefits from a BVT test pass. These processes have the intelligence built in to get application code from source control, copy to the appropriate lab server, execute the build, run through the appropriate test cases, and file bugs when builds fail. Additionally, the team extended the existing functionality of TFS in a way that allows it to correlate test case results to each specific build.

Managing Quality

In addition to the process and automation investments that the Microsoft.com Customer Intelligence team has incorporated within its engineering procedures, the team has also focused on integrating the appropriate quality metrics. The team primarily utilizes these metrics to understand test progress and manage the overall effectiveness of its efforts. Many of the metrics and reports it currently incorporates are available within the reporting capabilities of VSTF. Others have been custom built using tools like Microsoft Excel to query the data warehouse that VSTF makes available through its data analysis tier. Let's review some examples of the metrics that the team finds most valuable.

- **Code coverage metrics** The team uses the code coverage metrics within VSTF to understand the relative effectiveness of its testing efforts. It studies the combination of the code coverage results for blocks and cyclomatic complexity to better understand how much of the code is being covered by the automated testing. Achieving 100 percent coverage is generally unrealistic, so the team strives to achieve between 70 and 80 percent coverage and assumes that the remaining code will either be covered by manual testing or represent edge case scenarios that are lower priority.

- **Code churn metrics** To understand the quality of the code being checked in each day and appearing in the daily builds, the team relies on code churn metrics. This allows the team to understand the rate of change being introduced into the code each day and therefore be more predictive about the volatility or stability of the build. In an agile development process, code churn metrics help the team balance test priorities each day and manage its test efforts more effectively.

- **Build a test scorecard** To understand the overall quality of the application code, the team constructed a composite scorecard that is composed of multiple metrics. The team built this scorecard by creating Excel spreadsheets that connect to the TFS data warehouse and execute custom queries. These scorecards are then used to quickly evaluate the team's overall progress for the current release cycle by running one composite report as opposed to several.

Summary

As we have discussed throughout this chapter, the measure of code quality depends on the scope and results of application testing. In addition to implementing thoughtful designs and incorporating development best practices, application code requires analysis and exercise to understand whether the appropriate quality bar has been achieved. Application development teams should approach testing in a holistic manner and focus on the end-to-end processes and tools to effectively achieve their quality goals. This includes investing in test automation and focusing on the tactics and tools required to streamline the testing process to address code quality early in the development cycle. Fortunately, Visual Studio Team System, in conjunction with Team Foundation Server, offer application development teams the tools required to analyze, test, and manage the processes required to build and test high-quality code.

Key Points

- Create or refine your test processes within your organization.
  - ❑ Define a testing rhythm for your team.
  - ❑ Incorporate key testing methods at the appropriate time of the release cycle.
  - ❑ Track work items and bugs in Visual Studio Team Foundation.
- Invest in automated testing with Visual Studio Team Foundation.
  - ❑ Incorporate static code analysis.
  - ❑ Write automated tests against application code.
  - ❑ Use Visual Studio to accomplish scenario-based, functional, and load testing of your application code.
- Use metrics to understand application quality.
  - ❑ Leverage code metrics as a means of understanding code complexity and maintainability.
  - ❑ Incorporate team-wide metrics from Team Foundation Server to track and trend progress toward application quality.

Chapter 11
Improving Engineering Processes

If you're passionate about what it is you do, then you're going to be looking for everything you can to get better at it.

—*Jack Canfield*

Software development is an industry whose landscape has given rise to several different project management processes and methodologies, ranging from the rigidity of waterfall to the iterative nature of Scrum. As previously discussed in Chapter 1, "Code Quality in an Agile World," formal software engineering processes emerged in the industry in the 1960s to tame the project cost, time, and quality challenges that plagued the industry. Despite the different incarnations of software engineering processes and methodologies over the past four decades, the simplest goals of achieving a higher quality product and a more predictable time to market or deployment remains constant today. Achieving these goals requires the combination of great engineering practices and a repeatable project delivery rhythm that is well suited to your team's needs. Successful project teams recognize this and, as the quote suggests, continuously look for opportunities to gain efficiencies or implement processes that improve the quality of their work.

As project participants, many of us do not always look favorably upon some aspects of the software development process. This could be based on suboptimal project experiences in the past or the idea that formal project processes merely get in the way of writing more code. The reality is that software development processes are implemented to control the flow of software construction, as a means to increase efficiency and control costs, resources, and quality. This is somewhat analogous to the way speed limits are leveraged on highways to control traffic and prevent accidents or congestion. Without some level of governance over application development projects, our chances for shipping a high-quality product are severely limited. The challenge is, of course, applying the appropriate amount of process so that the outcome of your software projects actually improves.

At Microsoft, teams often establish the processes that work best for their respective culture, objectives, and project size, which actually works quite well for them. Since development projects generally range from large, well established applications like Windows and Microsoft Office to small, cutting-edge niche services like Zune, it makes sense to encourage organizational autonomy with respect to development processes. Across the many teams at Microsoft, there is no clear one-size-fits-all approach to delivering software. However, there are several best practices and common techniques that are applied broadly across teams and are independent of a specific process or methodology. Throughout the remainder of this chapter, we will review several of these practices and discuss how your team's existing processes could be augmented to include these techniques as a means to improve efficiency and product quality, regardless of the project's current methodology. By improving existing software development processes with these tactics, development teams will ultimately improve their efficiency at bringing their applications to market, while simultaneously improving the quality of the software they deliver, thus closing the loop on how solid code can be achieved without introducing heavyweight development processes.

Tactics for Engineering Process Improvement

Releasing high-quality software products is no accident. It is the result of the combined, focused efforts of software development teams that are composed of people from multiple engineering disciplines, like development, program management, and test. Teams that achieve the successes associated with releasing great software in a timely manner are keenly aware of the importance of the engineering rigor and processes that guided them to the result. They recognize that, without this rubric, releasing high-quality software products within a reasonable project timeframe would not be possible. Furthermore, they understand that the processes and practices they incorporate in one release may not be applicable to future releases and thus periodically self-evaluate and make necessary adjustments to their processes. It is this process of project execution, self-evaluation, and continuous improvement that allows software development teams to continuously evolve their ability to deliver high-quality software applications to market in a timely manner.

In subsequent sections of this chapter, we will review and evaluate several tactics for augmenting your organization's software development practices. Because there is such variation across organizations with respect to project processes, the focus of these recommendations will not align with a particular software development methodology. Instead, they will be presented in a way that assumes that a defined project management methodology exists and could be augmented to include some or all of these individual practices. Let us begin with some software project management basics.

Establish a Quality-Focused Project Rhythm

If your organization is actively developing software, it is likely that a well-defined software project rhythm has been established. In many cases, this process may model more traditional waterfall processes, and in other cases it may mirror more agile processes. In either case, it is critically important that a well-defined software project rhythm be established first and foremost. This rhythm should balance the cultural and business needs of the organization while focusing on delivering high-quality software in a repeatable and predictable way. It is certainly not the focus of this book to recommend one specific development model over another, but rather to illustrate how any existing model could be augmented to add more quality-focused development practices. So, for the benefit of conversation, let us assume that your organization has an established milestone-based project rhythm that resembles that of the one illustrated in Figure 11-1.

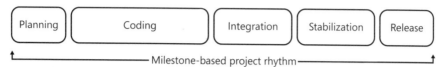

FIGURE 11-1 Generic milestone-based project rhythm.

In Figure 11-1, this typical software project rhythm is broken down into five major milestones that encompass the work required to ship any major or minor software release. These major milestones occur one after another, on a linear timeline, and each is defined as follows:

- **Planning**   The milestone typically reserved for requirements gathering, feature specification development, and application design.

- **Coding**   This is the milestone where the application code is developed and unit tested. This is also the time when testers write test cases in preparation for integration.

- **Integration**   The first of two testing milestones where all major test cases are executed and major bugs are discovered and fixed.

- **Stabilization**   The second of two testing milestones where deeper test analysis is completed and the build is further stabilized in preparation for release.

- **Release**   The shipping milestone where code is released to the user community, either through typical client distribution mechanisms or through the Internet.

In Chapter 1, we discussed the importance of injecting quality-focused practices into the engineering process earlier in the project cycle. We referred to this principle as moving quality upstream, and we demonstrated the importance of integrating more quality-focused engineering practices into the daily development and integration rigor of the project process. This principle asserted that, by incorporating certain quality-focused practices throughout the project life cycle, the quality of the software being produced will increase as the team advances through each milestone. For example, by incorporating certain design practices such as class prototyping or metaprogramming within the planning milestone, and engineering practices like automated unit testing in the coding milestone, the quality of the software being produced will be markedly better as the team reaches subsequent milestones. By contrast, deferring many of these practices until late in the development cycle increases the risk of delivering the software late and with an undesirable number of bugs and a generally low degree of quality.

Throughout this book, we have built upon the quality upstream principle and have enumerated the many design, development, and coding tactics that can be applied within each of these major project milestones. Quite obviously, it is important that application development teams implement a quality-focused, milestone-based approach to developing software that incorporates the practices mentioned throughout this book. As we progress through this chapter, we will discuss process improvement tactics that can be applied to your organization's milestone-based project rhythm. These tactics will focus on improving the day-to-day engineering processes that developers experience on almost every project and continue to build on the quality upstream principle. This will be accomplished by focusing on process changes and engineering protocols that will further help application development teams to achieve higher quality code. We will begin by discussing how to improve the quality of the code being stored in your team's source control repository.

Implement Source Control and Check-in Processes

It is probably reasonable to assume that most organizations that are building software products use some form of source control in which they store and manage their source code. If your organization is not currently doing this, please stop reading this book now and return only after you have established a source control database and uploaded all of your precious source code into it! As you have probably figured out, source control is very important and should be taken seriously by every application development organization. Source control provides a number of benefits to development organizations, including, but not limited to, version management, change history, and change rollback. Many potential software development tragedies can be avoided by simply leveraging a source control system.

There are several source repository products that are commercially available today for managed code developers. The most obvious Microsoft source control product is Visual SourceSafe, which has been available for a number of years and integrated with Visual Studio 2005 as well as prior versions of Microsoft integrated development environments. The successor to Visual SourceSafe is part of Visual Studio Team Foundation Server, which belongs to the Visual Studio Team System suite of client and server products. Team Foundation Server (TFS) goes beyond simple source control and also incorporates a host of different features for reporting and project tracking. Within TFS, the source control repository itself is referred to as Team Foundation Version Control (TFVC) and stores all code, as well as change history within a SQL Server database. Generally speaking, TFVC is a dramatic improvement over Visual SourceSafe and, in conjunction with Visual Studio Team System, has really enhanced the collaborative managed code development ecosystem.

In addition to merely establishing a source control repository within your organization, application development project teams need to also consider the way they govern the use of source control and their repository. Without clearly defined procedures and processes for managing and updating source code, the repository can quickly become disorganized and it is nearly impossible to manage different versions of software effectively. It is therefore very important that the day-to-day software development process enforce good source management behaviors so that only high-quality code gets checked into source and previous versions of the software are preserved appropriately.

Managing Source Control

Establishing a process for managing software versions and the associative source control for the version specific code is a difficult job that will require tedious version management planning and meticulous documentation. It requires coordination across the organization and will not be successful without support from every application developer or tester who is responsible to check code into source. It is an important aspect of managing the software development process and should not be taken lightly. That said, let us briefly review the scenarios that require vigilant management of source control.

In most software development organizations, there is more than one developer participating on a software project. In some cases, there may be dozens of developers working together on a project. Chances are they will need to work on the same source code, perhaps even at the same time. Additionally, within those same development organizations, there are likely to be multiple versions of the software being managed. Depending on the life cycle of the software, some versions may actively be getting patched or fixed as bugs are discovered, even as new versions of the same software are being developed. Finally, some developers may be experimenting with portions of the software for potential future versions that may not be actively being developed. Each of these scenarios is a prime example of a software development problem for which source control procedures should provide support. Let's consider some options for how to manage this.

At Microsoft, the scenarios illustrated above are fairly common problems. Without clear processes for handling these circumstances, there would most certainly be chaos in trying to manage different versions of the software. There would most certainly be an increase in the number of bugs getting introduced into the code. To address these challenges, many teams pursue a branching strategy for managing the different versions of source code. Branching allows files within version control to be forked, or branched away from the main trunk of the source tree so that multiple copies of the same file can be worked on at different speeds. These strategies usually involve multiple code branches with procedures for how the different branches are periodically merged with the main branch. Figure 11-2 illustrates how multiple code branches could be established for a specific software application.

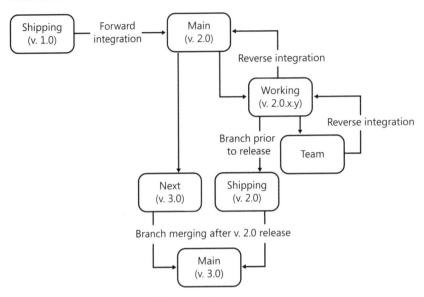

FIGURE 11-2 Source code branching example.

In Figure 11-2, there are five main source code branches to consider, which are referred to as the main, working, next, team, and shipping branches. For the purposes of this example, we can define each of these branches as follows.

- **Main branch**   This is the authority node, which contains the most current application source code that has achieved a certain quality bar. In other words, it represents the latest build that has passed a series of automated tests that have broadly examined the product for quality. Only code that has passed unit, functional, and integration tests would achieve the level of quality necessary to be reverse integrated into the main branch.

- **Working branch**   The working branch is home to the application source code actively being developed across the team. Code living in the working branch has not yet passed the quality bar to be reverse integrated into main, but it maintains a quality bar that is indicative of daily application builds.

- **Next branch**   This branch exists for the purposes of experimentation, prototyping, or for work being completed for a release that is further in the future than the current release. It is typically a fork of the main branch at a particular point in the current release cycle or a fork from the previous shipping branch.

- **Team branch**   The team branch allows teams, or even individual developers, to fork code from the current working branch and work on their specific features. This allows teams to maintain individual branches for specific features or for broad feature sets and reverse integrate into working when complete. This may prove useful in circumstances where new code dependencies or integrations are evaluated prior to integrating into the working branch.

- **Shipping branch**   This represents the version of the application that was actually shipped or released. Generally, as teams finalize their work in the working branch, the shipping branch for that release is created. This allows the code to be forked for the next release, while preserving a version of the application to which future bug fixes will be applied.

The diagram in Figure 11-2 depicts how these various branch types participate in the development life cycle. For example, the main branch represents the authority source repository. At any given time, source taken from main should be robust enough to be built and deployed with a reasonable level of quality. The main branch is periodically updated from the working branch, which is where day-to-day feature check-in occurs. This happens through reverse integration from daily builds that surpass a predefined quality bar. This process ensures that the main branch be kept free of dysfunctional code. For teams or features that may not be getting checked in on a daily basis, the team branch offers a method for forking code out of the working branch and reverse integrating back in when the feature is complete. Upon completion of the project, and after the final quality sign off has been attained, the shipping branch can be created as a means to archive the shipping version of the code for future bug fixes. Finally, prior to beginning a new release, the shipping branch (or main branch, since they are theoretically identical) is merged with the next branch to establish the new releases main branch.

> **Note**   TFVC allows development teams to maintain a source management process similar to the one mentioned above. This is accomplished through the branching and merging features within TFVC. A more detailed explanation of how to best accomplish this can be found in *Working with Microsoft Visual Studio 2005 Te*am System by Richard Hundhausen (Microsoft Press, 2005), or online at *http://msdn.microsoft.com/en-us/library/ms181423.aspx*.

This is just one example of how tactics for managing source code and software versions could be applied. There are certainly many other potential solutions for achieving similar objectives that could be more beneficial to your organization. The important point is to illustrate why source code management is so critical to maintaining high-quality code across multiple versions of the product and among multiple developers within a project. It is less important how you manage specific source control processes within your organization and more important that the proper attention be given to this engineering practice. Not only will a formal source control management process provide a well-defined way of managing your company's intellectual property, it will also provide teams the ability to enforce certain levels of quality within each branch and thus control the overall quality of the product across different versions. Subsequent sections of this chapter will build upon the concept of enforcing check-in quality criteria and recommend formal methods for governing code quality before the code is entered into the repository.

Establishing Check-in Procedures and Criteria

Once you establish the appropriate source control management process within your organization, it is important that you focus attention on how to manage the quality of the code being checked into the source repository. Oftentimes application development teams have no formal process for governing the quality of the code they check in. In some cases, simply getting the code to build on a developer's workstation meets the quality bar of adding to source control. In other, even more extreme cases, source control is simply used as a backup to a file on the developer's workstation. As we previously discussed, the source for your software application is critically important intellectual property, and development teams need to take the necessary strides to ensure that the code quality being checked into source will not accidentally degrade the overall quality of the application. The best way to prevent poor quality code or features from being introduced into the source repository is to establish check-in procedures and criteria.

Establishing a check-in process and associative quality criteria allows application development teams to enforce a certain level of quality in the code being checked into source control. This reduces the risk that certain classifications of bugs do not get introduced into the source repository, thus reducing the total volume of bugs likely to be found at the end of the development cycle. Additionally, these procedures also guarantee a certain level of product stability is always present within the repository, which is important for developers sharing the code. Accomplishing this, however, requires that engineering teams establish a process that all developers will adhere to, as well as certain criteria that define the quality bar for what features or bug fixes get checked into the repository. An example of what a hypothetical check-in process may look like is illustrated in Figure 11-3.

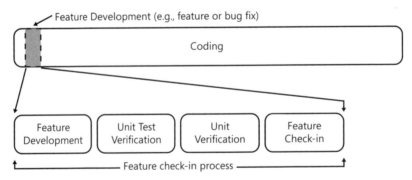

FIGURE 11-3 Hypothetical feature check-in process.

As depicted in Figure 11-3, a feature check-in process incorporates a series of steps or quality gates that application development teams should apply to their existing development process to ensure that code being checked into source does not introduce bugs into the application. This process can be applied to either feature-level development or bug fixes, and it guarantees that certain steps are taken to control quality. For example, during feature development, application developers and their test counterparts partner to develop the feature or bug fix code, as well as the automated test code. Once both code and tests are complete, the entire unit of work is handed off to the tester for verification on a test worksta-tion or a workstation that is independent from that of the developer. Upon verification by the tester, the feature can be cleared for check-in. Let us examine these steps in more detail.

Feature development   During the feature development phase, application developers will work to complete feature-level coding or a specific bug fix within their product. As part of the code deliverables, developers should collaborate with their test counterpart and also deliver specific unit tests that exercise the code and business rules that they are developing or changing. This will ensure that, as each feature gets worked on, developers continue to expand the automated unit test corpus that can be run against the feature code to main-tain code quality. In parallel to the application developer's efforts, the tester should be also updating the suite of tests that get used to determine the quality of the build. This will ensure that any changes the developer makes that would be considered high risk or build-breaking changes would be caught in the build verification testing procedures. In addition to these steps, developers and testers should seek formal code reviews from their peers to be sure that the newly written code adheres to any previously established guidelines or best prac-tices that the team requires. As previously established in Chapter 10, "Code Analysis," code reviews should be combined with code analysis tools like FxCop or the code analysis features within Visual Studio 2008. Once both feature code and test code are complete, the unit of work should move into the unit test verification phase.

Unit test verification   In this step, the developer and tester begin running unit test passes against the newly developed code and review the code for overall quality. Application developers should physically hand off the unit of work to their testing partner so that the complete work can be built and executed on the tester's workstation or within a lab environ-ment that is independent of the developer's workstation. This will ensure that the code can be independently built and deployed and all dependencies are accounted for within the unit of work. Visual Studio Team System can help facilitate this through the use of shelving, which allows a developer to temporarily set aside a set of pending changes for review by another developer or tester prior to check-in.

Note Shelving is a feature within TFVC that allows application developers to set aside, or "shelve," their work on the version control server without actually checking the code in. This al-lows the code to be safely stored on a central server within a personal source branch, which en-sures that the code is archived but not directly integrated with the working codebase. Once the work is shelved, it is preserved in source control for future use or can be shared immediately with other developers or testers.

Fortunately for application developers and testers, shelving opens up a number of different possible uses within the application development process. For example, it could be utilized for simple code storage or for sharing with another developer. It could also be leveraged for experi-menting with alternative feature ideas and storing each separately, or supporting the process discussed above whereby developers shelve a unit of work and hand it off to a tester to be built and validated locally on a different workstation. In either case, shelving is a very useful feature within the TFVC toolset, and it is highly recommended for allowing flexibility with storing unfinished code in the source repository but still preserving the quality of code in the working branch.

For additional information about shelving, as well as some of the other features within Visual Studio Team System (VSTS) and Team Foundation Server, I recommend reading *Working with Microsoft Visual Studio 2005 Team System* (Microsoft Press, 2005) by Richard Hundhausen. In addition to covering shelving, the book also covers numerous other aspects of managing projects with VSTS.

During this time, application developers and testers are likely to find and fix a few bugs before getting the complete set of unit tests to pass completely. This is a critically important step because any bug found during this process is one less potentially build-breaking bug introduced into the source tree. This process may seem slightly more rigorous than most application developers may be used to, but in the long run it actually saves a lot of time that would otherwise be spent squashing bugs in the integration and stabilization testing phase of the project. Once all unit tests are passing, the unit of work should then move onto the next phase, which seeks to evaluate the code in the context of the broader application.

Unit verification   The next step in the feature check-in process is to validate the unit of work against the complete application build and broader feature set. This implies that any automated test cases that evaluate code for potentially build-breaking bugs should be executed against the full build of the application. This process ensures that any changes introduced with this feature code will not break the build, which is to say, break major functionality of the application and not literally the build process. During this process, testers should be executing the broader set of build verification tests against the version of the application containing the new code. If no issues result from this test pass, then the tester should authorize the developer to check in.

Feature check-in   The final step in the feature check-in process is for the developer to check the code into the appropriate working branch within the source repository. This particular step assumes that the developer and tester have jointly met the previously established quality criteria for the feature. These criteria would have included passing all automated tests, performing a peer review of the application and test code, and any other specific rules that the team wishes to apply. Assuming that all appropriate quality gates have been passed, the developer would be authorized to check the code in by the tester.

Note In addition to simply establishing a check-in process with specific quality criteria, application development teams can also enforce certain rules and policies during the check-in process within Team Foundation Server (TFS). This is a very powerful feature within TFS that gives application development teams quite a bit of control over the quality of the code being added to source.

TFS offers certain check-in policy rules out of the box as well as an extensibility model for adding more custom policies. These policies can be defined by a system administrator and provide warnings to developers if they attempt to check code in that violates those policies. In addition to the tools available out of the box with TFS, a check-in policy pack is included with the TFS Power Tools, which can be found at *http://msdn.microsoft.com/en-us/tfs2008/bb980963.aspx#build*. The following are examples of some typical TFS check-in policies.

- The source intended for check-in must pass static code analysis rules.
- The code being added to source control must pass *x* number of unit tests before being checked-in.
- The source code must be reviewed by another developer prior to check-in.

The key point to remember is that TFS provides mechanisms to enforce the quality-focused policies that we have been discussing thus far. Additionally, it provides application development teams with flexibility for how they implement and enforce those policies. It represents precisely the toolset required to enforce the accountability for quality within the application development team.

If at any time during the development of this feature, other developers happened to check in newer versions of the same files being updated with this change, then the application developer of this new feature should perform the necessary code merging and re-execute the testing suites. This will ensure that the combination of these changes does not introduce quality issues with this new check in.

The previous example is just one possible solution to implementing a quality-focused check-in process for feature or bug fix development within your organization. As mentioned, establishing quality criteria for the source code being actively developed and checked in will help application developers and testers find and fix bugs earlier in the feature development process, rather than downstream during integration and stabilization testing phases. Discovering and fixing bugs early in the coding cycle not only increases the stability and quality of the code but ultimately saves time downstream during the integration and stabilization testing phases. It is important for application development teams to recognize the value in governing the quality of code at every step of the development cycle and establish the appropriate quality-control processes to ensure a successful project outcome. Creating these check-in processes and quality criteria is just one way to begin raising the bar on the quality of the code being produced on a daily or weekly basis. To build upon this process, application development teams should incorporate a daily build and release rhythm into their engineering rhythm as well. In addition to enforcing check-in criteria, this will further help them find and address bugs within the product earlier in the development cycle. We will explore this in more detail in the subsequent section.

Release and Test Code Daily

In addition to establishing a feature check-in process and associated quality criteria, application development teams should also incorporate daily builds and daily release testing. Adding these steps to the feature check-in process will further help development teams find and fix product bugs early in the development cycle, thus continuing to build upon the quality upstream philosophy. This concept was originally introduced in Chapter 1, when we evaluated the quality upstream approach that the Windows Live Hotmail team follows. As you may recall, the Windows Live Hotmail team incorporates a process of building and deploying its application each day once it surpasses a certain build quality bar. This is a process that allows the team to see the effects of recent code changes on the broader application immediately and to control the quality of the application very tightly. This helps the team maintain a high degree of quality with the daily builds, even when its release schedule is aggressive. Augmenting your organization's existing processes to incorporate these steps will also help your respective application development teams achieve the same result. Let us evaluate this process in greater detail.

In the previous section, we discussed a hypothetical feature development check-in process that included the establishment of quality criteria at each step. Within this process, we introduced the idea that application developers and testers collaborate on the development and testing of a unit of work prior to being checked into source control. The intent of this collaboration is to both parallelize the development of feature code and test code, while also encouraging joint ownership of the quality of the code being checked in. The result of this process assumes that units of feature work get introduced into the working branch of the source repository on a periodic basis. While this process works well at controlling the quality of code being produced by individual application developer and tester pairs, additional controls are needed to ensure that quality is also evaluated periodically across the larger team and the broader product. It is quite conceivable that developers across the team will write code that either interacts or overlaps with code being developed by other developers. Despite careful unit testing on the part of these individuals, there is a high likelihood that the testing will be somewhat isolated and not find broader product bugs. Therefore, it is important for application development teams to incorporate the use of Build Verification Testing (BVT) to ensure a certain level of quality across the product on a daily basis. In keeping with the spirit of previous examples, let us consider a hypothetical feature development and release process that defines a software development team's daily project rhythm. Figure 11-4 represents an example of this hypothetical build-and-release process.

In this example, you will notice that feature development is encapsulated into one part of the process. This part of the process is inclusive of the aforementioned quality criteria and related processes illustrated in Figure 11-3, shown previously. It assumes that the feature development portion ends once units of work are checked into the source repository. During the course of any day in the life of an application development team, several units of feature work or bug fixes are likely to be checked in as part of this process. After all work units are checked into source, a daily build should be executed against the latest code available in the source repository. This should happen on an independent workstation or build server that is managed within a test lab (we will discuss this process in greater detail in a subsequent section). Once a build has completed, it should be deployed to a test server for additional automated testing. The results of the daily testing should indicate whether the quality of the daily build is high enough to move forward with additional feature work or whether the development teams need to make immediate fixes so that the build can be declared success-ful. Let us evaluate this process at a deeper level and illustrate the importance both from a cultural and engineering perspective.

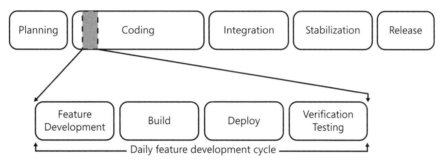

FIGURE 11-4 Daily build-and-release process.

> **Note** At Microsoft, the daily build process is engrained into the engineering culture. If a build breaks or BVTs fail on a daily build, it is generally treated as an "all hands on deck" issue, and forward progress ceases until the issues with the build are addressed. Historically speaking, there have long been rumors about how some teams treat the individuals responsible for build breaks. By all accounts, this is a label that most developers would rather not be adorned with.

Feature development   This process represents the period of time where individual units of development and test work, for a feature or bug fix, are being completed. As previously described in depth, feature development may take place over the course of hours, days, or weeks and culminates when all units of work have been unit tested and verified by a devel-oper and tester. As a best practice, a single unit of work should not take weeks to complete. Incremental units of work that make up a large feature should be validated and checked in periodically. The quality of the code being developed during this process is first validated in isolation by the individuals working on the feature, and then more broadly using automated test cases that search for potentially build-breaking bugs. At this stage, code quality has been primarily analyzed at the feature level, rather than across the broader application.

Build   The build is the complete, compiled application that represents the sum of all fea-ture development units of work that have been checked in within the past day. Building the complete application should be an automated process whereby the most recent code is obtained from source control, copied to a build machine, and compiled. This process should be repeated at a specific time every day so that a build rhythm is maintained and build quality remains high. All team members should be keenly aware of the designated build time and be available to support any issues that arise from build failures.

Deploy   Daily automated builds should be applied to a specific test server infrastructure that resembles that of the production environment. By installing builds on a daily basis, testers are able to validate deployment issues in parallel to application-specific issues as well. This will ensure continued high quality in application deployment processes, scripts, environmental dependencies, or configurations.

Verification testing   After the application completes the build and deployment steps, all core features of the product should be validated through the BVT procedures. These tests represent the highest priority automated test cases that adequately reflect the core functionality of the application. This suite of test cases should pass on a daily basis for all new features to ensure that no bugs have been introduced into the system that affects core functionality. Additionally, the BVT test cases should be updated with each check-in that occurs during the feature development process so that the corpus of high-priority test cases continues to evolve with the application.

As discussed, adding the additional steps of building, deploying, and verifying the quality of the application code on a daily basis will help promote a higher level of overall application quality, over and above that of the quality being verified at the feature level. With these steps, application and deployment bugs are discovered and fixed earlier in the release process, which provides a daily evaluation of end-to-end application quality. Additionally, this process also enables tighter control over daily application quality and project health, while also fostering a more rigorous engineering culture among the team members. By shining a light on the quality of an application development team's daily activities, individual team members will take more pride in the feature work for which they are responsible, and overall team results will subsequently improve.

By incorporating these processes and monitoring the results of daily builds and release testing, application development teams will get a better sense for how they are trending toward their overall project goals or future version objectives. At the same time, they will also continue improving overall product quality. To effectively execute on these processes, it is important that teams automate as much of them as possible. Automation will both alleviate the resource overhead of managing the various tasks as well as encourage repeatability and reliability of the overall process. In the next section, we will review one of the many ways that automation can streamline the daily workings of the application development process, beginning with simply automating the build procedures.

Automate Daily Builds

Incorporating quality-focused processes into your organization's day-to-day engineering rhythm is very important to the overall goals of delivering a functional and bug-free product. To that end, each process that gets added to your daily engineering rigor should be efficient, reliable, and repeatable so that quality objectives can be achieved without sacrificing unnecessary amounts of project time. One way to accomplish this is to automate as many of these processes as possible, which will help to maximize efficiency as well as reduce or eliminate human error. While some application development processes such as code reviews or project management will always require human intervention or coordination, many such as the application build process can be fully or partially automated using tools that are readily available to Microsoft .NET developers. Let's consider a hypothetical application build example and explore the tools available to automate the build process.

In a typical application build scenario, multiple steps are often required to ensure that a successful build occurs. These steps might include such tasks as requesting files from source control, compiling the code locally, running code analysis or automated testing, copying the code to a shared server environment, and perhaps even sending an e-mail to the team advising that the process is complete. These steps are represented visually in Figure 11-5.

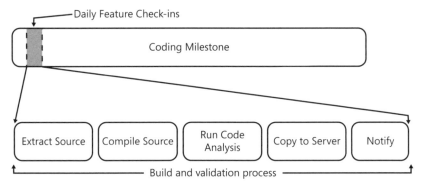

FIGURE 11-5 Hypothetical application build and validation process.

In many application development organizations, the build process happens at least once per day on any given project and often multiple times per day. This is not only a time-consuming effort but often very error prone if the steps are complex. Fortunately, it is an easily automatable process and one that pays repetitive efficiency and quality dividends after the initial engineering investment. Let's consider the array of options that are available to automate application builds.

NAnt   This is a free and open source build tool for Microsoft .NET applications. Originally released to the public in 2001, the tool was inspired by the freely available Java build tool called Apache Ant and was built to provide an extensible framework for automating complex build tasks. NAnt executes build tasks based on a set of instructions defined within an XML file, and because the framework is extensible, customized tasks can be developed and integrated directly into the build framework.

MSBuild   Officially known as the Microsoft Build Engine, MSBuild is the build environment for Visual Studio that can also be run as a stand-alone executable. Much like NAnt, MSBuild allows the build process to be described in an XML-based project that supports operations inclusive of build configuration, build tasks, inputs, and outputs. Because MSBuild is actually a build framework as well, it can also be extended to perform custom operations through the use of a managed code application programming interface (API). We will explore MSBuild in greater detail in a subsequent section of this chapter.

Team Foundation Build   This product was introduced with the Team Foundation suite and is a flexible and extensible build automation system that layers additional functionality on top of the existing MSBuild capabilities. In addition to offering an easy-to-use wizard interface to create initial builds, Team Foundation Build tightly integrates with some of the team-focused features of the Visual Studio Team Suite and streamlines many of the tasks, such as generating reports or updating project work items, which require customization work when using MSBuild.

In summary, there are several automated build tools currently available for managed code applications, which provide application development teams with several options for incorporating automated builds into their daily engineering regimen. Even though open source software has been an incredibly beneficial movement from an innovation perspective, many corporations will likely prefer to utilize build tools that are backed by support agreements such as MSBuild or Team Foundation Build. Fortunately, these are both excellent tools that are full-featured, extensible, and improving with each release of the Microsoft Visual Studio suite of products. Although it is beyond the scope of this chapter and book to discuss each of these products in depth, we will review MSBuild in greater depth in the next section.

Note Despite tackling a simple example of MSBuild in this chapter, this is a subject area that quite easily consumes an entire book. Constructing automated builds can be quite complex, and we definitely recognize that fact. That said, we simply could not provide a truly in-depth analysis in this chapter. For additional detailed information about MSBuild, we recommend reading *Inside the Microsoft Build Engine: Using MSBuild and Team Foundation Build* (Microsoft Press, 2008), by Sayed Ibrahim Hashimi and William Bartholomew.

Using MSBuild

MSBuild is a great command-line utility for automating your development team's daily application builds. It does not require Visual Studio be installed and is therefore ideal to use in test lab environments. Basic tasks such as building projects, copying files, and running code analysis tests are easily accomplished through the build project file. Additionally, MSBuild

provides an extensible framework for adding custom operations so developers can augment the build project to be customized to fit their respective needs. With a little ingenuity,
MSBuild can be leveraged to provide a very rich build experience for just about any managed
code development organization. Let us look at the basic anatomy of an MSBuild project, as
well as a simple example.

Project file   All elements and attributes of an MSBuild project are contained within a project file. An example of a project file is the .csproj file associated with any Visual Studio C#
application. Generally, the project file can contain any number of item collections, tasks, and
properties and represents the complete set of build directives organized within a single file.
The following illustrates the basic skeletal structure of an MSBuild project file.

```
<Project xmlns="http://schemas.microsoft.com/developer/msbuild/2003">
    <PropertyGroup>
      <!-- Properties -->
    </PropertyGroup>
    <ItemGroup>
      <!-Item(s) -->
    </ItemGroup>
    <Target>
      <!-Task(s) -->
    </Target>
</Project>
```

Items   Items represent the inputs of the build process. They can be represented as either
singular elements or as collections when they are of the same type, and they are created
within the project file as children of the *ItemGroup* element. The following is an example of
typical compile inputs.

```
<ItemGroup>
    <Compile Include="class1.cs" />
    <Compile Include="class2.cs" />
    <Compile Include="Properties\AssemblyInfo.cs" />
</ItemGroup>
```

Tasks   Within the MSBuild project, tasks are defined as the build operations of the project.
Tasks are represented as children of the *Target* element. They are also capable of accepting
parameters as well, which are represented as attributes of the *Task* element. MSBuild supports quite a few tasks by default, and custom tasks can be implemented by deriving the
custom task the *ITask* interface that is supplied to developers. The following represents a
WriteLinesToFile task, which is a default capability of MSBuild.

```
<Target name="AfterBuild">
    <WriteLinesToFile File="c:\temp" Lines="@(Items)" Overwrite="true" />
</Target>
```

Properties   These are the basic configuration parameters of the MSBuild project. They are
child elements of the *PropertyGroup* element and are used to describe such attributes of the
project as the project name, version, root namespace, and many others. The following repre-

sents an example of an *MSBuild* property. A complete list of properties has been purposely omitted for brevity.

```
<PropertyGroup>
    <AssemblyName>MyApplication</AssemblyName>
    <StartupObject>MyApplication.Program</StartupObject>
</PropertyGroup>
```

Although these elements represent the basic structure of the MSBuild file, there are several items and tasks available by default, as well as a number of default properties. Because it is out of scope for this chapter to list each one individually, it is recommended that application developers consult the definitive MSBuild Reference MSDN at *http://msdn.microsoft.com/en-us/library/0k6kkbsd.aspx*. The main point to remember is that Microsoft provides an initial set of functionality within MSBuild out of the box and allows application development teams to extend the framework to fulfill their specific needs. Now that we have reviewed the basic structure of an MSBuild project, let us look at a sample project file and the associative build process in greater depth.

In keeping with programming tradition, let us consider the bulid process of the simple yet well understood HelloApplication, which is a simple C# console application. For the purposes of this example, we will not focus valuable page space on the details of the application code but rather just discuss the basic structure so as to support the MSBuild example. In the HelloApplication, user input is received in the form of a first name and last name, and it is subsequently concatenated with a friendly message and output back to the screen. Within the application structure, there are three simple classes that provide the application functionality. Those classes include the following.

- **Program.cs**   Contains the main entry point of the application, which performs the main read and write functionality on the console window.

- **Person.cs**   Represents a simple person data structure that supports the *Program.cs* class.

- **AssemblyInfo.cs**   Default class that manages information about the compiled assembly.

When writing the HelloApplication, Visual Studio automatically created the appropriate MSBuild .csproj file for us, but let's assume we wish to add some functionality to the build process. We accomplish this by first unloading the project in Visual Studio and then editing the HelloApplication.csproj file directly. Next, we add some simple console messaging so that we can visually follow along with the build process. Finaly, we add an additional logging task where we will capture the list of files being compiled. Let us review an abridged version of the MSBuild file and review the changes.

```xml
<?xml version="1.0" encoding="utf-8"?>
<Project xmlns="http://schemas.microsoft.com/developer/msbuild/2003">
    <!-- Property Groups and properties ommitted for brevity -- >
    <!-- Add ItemGroup to define our log file -->
    <ItemGroup>
        <MyTextFile Include="logfile.txt"/>
        <MyLogHeader Include="Hello Application Build Log"/>
        <MyItems Include="*.cs"/>
    </ItemGroup>
    <!-- Compile Collection -->
    <ItemGroup>
        <Compile Include="Person.cs" />
        <Compile Include="Program.cs" />
        <Compile Include="Properties\AssemblyInfo.cs" />
    </ItemGroup>
    <!-- Before build directive -->
    <Target Name="BeforeBuild">
        <!-- Log a console message -->
        <Message Text="Begin Solid Code Chapter 11 HelloApplication Build." />
    </Target>
    <!-- After build directive -->
    <Target Name="AfterBuild">
    <!-- Log a console message -->
        <Message Text="Finished Solid Code Chapter 11 HelloApplication Build." />
        <Message Text="Writing simple log file." />
        <!-- Output files to a log -->
        <WriteLinesToFile File="@(MyTextFile)" Lines="@(MyLogHeader);@(MyItems)"
            Overwrite="true" />
    </Target>
</Project>
```

> **Note** As with all code associated with this book, the complete set of source will be available on the companion Web site, but, for the sake of brevity, we have only included an abridged version here to illustrate the specific additions being applied.

As you will note from the preceding MSBuild project code sample, the log file and compile inputs were specificed within the *ItemGroup* elements. Both our console output messages and file writing tasks were specified within the *Target* elements. Whenever a build is initiated, a log file called logfile.txt with a list of the compiled resources will be generated, and several output messages will be written to the console. To actually initiate the build, we launch the Visual Studio 2008 command prompt and execute the *build* command using syntax similar to the following. The results are illustrated in Figure 11-6.

```
Msbuild switches projectfilename
```

Specifically, the syntax required to execute the build is as follows.

```
Msbuild HelloApplication.csproj
```

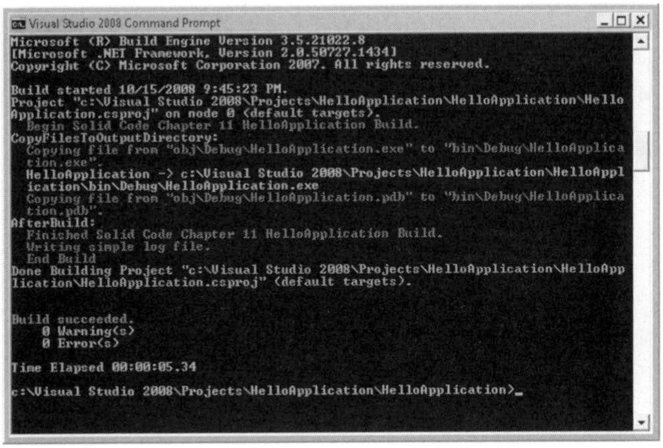

FIGURE 11-6 MSBuild console output.

Upon completion of the build, we note from the console output that the build was successful, and the messages specified in the build file were in fact output to the screen. Additionally, a physical log file called logfile.txt was written to the project's root directory, which contained the following log information.

```
Hello Application Build Log
Person.cs
Program.cs
```

Although this example has only focused on basic capabilities of MSBuild, we should once again emphasize that there is an incredible degree of flexibility with this build tool. In addition to the simple log file and console example above, application developers could quite easily automate common tasks such as obtaining the latest code from source, generating code analysis results, or sending e-mail when the build has failed or completed. Regardless of the build process requirements, the extensibility available within MSBuild can help application development teams fulfill their automated build needs. Additionally, for development teams that are leveraging the capabilities of Team Foundation Server and Visual Studio Team Suite, similar flexibility and extensibility is available with those tools as well.

Create and Enforce Quality Criteria

Thus far, we have focused many of our recommendations on quality- and efficiency-focused improvements that application development teams can implement within their respective organizations. For starters, we discussed how the appropriate source control processes and check-in procedures can help control the quality of code being applied to the source tree. Additionally, we reviewed how daily builds, releases, and testing can help teams find and fix product bugs early in the release cycle, which improves the quality of the application on a daily basis and decreases the number of bugs found during the testing phase of the project. As you have seen, each of these recommendations supports one central idea, which is to continuously increase the quality of the application code as early in the release process as possible, preferably before entering the integration and stabilization testing phase. Each of these engineering tactics will help application development teams to ratchet up the quality of the code during key points within the coding phase of the project. In addition to these tactics, it is also important to establish specific criteria across the application codebase, so that quality can also be improved within some of the key engineering focus areas previously discussed in this book, such as security, performance, and scalability.

In general, incorporating quality criteria into the feature development process helps teams to measure and maintain the health of their application code in specific engineering focus areas like security, performance, or scalability. Establishing and enforcing this criterion helps to ensure that focus is given to key areas of the application code, over and above that of basic functional code quality. For example, the code quality of a specific feature may be considered high when all functional test cases pass and the feature meets the necessary requirements. However, that feature may contain security vulnerabilities or be poorly performing, which ultimately affects the overall quality of the feature. To avoid this situation, application development teams must ensure that the quality bar they establish for their application code includes specific criteria for addressing issues within the following areas.

Security   This is perhaps one of the most important, yet most frequently overlooked, engineering focus areas, where code quality issues can produce disastrous results for applications, as well as their users. It is critically important for application development teams to understand their application's potential vulnerabilities, follow the security best practices outlined in this book, and continuously evaluate application code for security issues. It is not critical for security testing to be performed with the same frequency as functional testing. However, security testing should definitely be performed periodically throughout the development cycle. Security bugs are often quite challenging to find and sometimes very risky to fix once the application code reaches a certain completion state. Hence, discovering and fixing this style of bug early in the release process reduces potential code churn later in the development cycle. Establishing quality criteria for security within the team, which requires feature code to be free of security bugs prior to entering the testing phase of the project, is one way to ensure this class of bugs is caught early in the development process.

Performance   It is important for teams to embrace performance excellence and establish the appropriate performance goals for their applications. In Chapter 4, "Performance Is a Feature," we specifically discussed the risk and cost associated with fixing Web performance bugs after they have crept into a product release. It is incumbent upon application development teams to focus a portion of their development and testing efforts on setting performance goals, incorporating the best practices, and proactively measuring performance indicators during the feature development cycle. Ideally, application development teams should establish quality criteria for performance and hold themselves accountable to making sure performance quality is high prior to exiting the development phase of the project.

Scalability   Ensuring that your application is designed to scale appropriately should also be an area to focus specific attention on during the coding phase of the release cycle. Just like performance and security, quality issues in the area of scalability can be very costly and risky to fix late in the engineering release cycle. It is important that development teams make certain that their scalability designs are vetted with the appropriate testing during the coding period. This can be accomplished multiple ways, including leveraging such tactics as load testing daily builds, simulating hardware failure, or testing hardware load balancers. It is of course not critical that the testing be extensive, but it should evaluate key scale points of the application and ensure that major design flaws are not carried into the testing phase of the release cycle.

Although the three engineering focus areas we specifically mentioned will likely apply to a broad base of application development teams, there are other areas that deserve an increased quality focus also worth mentioning. For example, development teams that build international software should maintain a high degree of focus on globalization or localization quality. Alternatively, teams that develop software for government organizations should focus on ensuring a high degree of quality in the area of accessibility, which specifically improves the application usability experience for people with disabilities. In either case, it is important for development teams to identify the specific areas that are most relevant to their software applications and establish the appropriate criteria for maintaining a high degree of quality across the application during the coding phase of the development life cycle.

As you have seen, there are several key engineering focus areas that deserve special attention as applications are being constructed. Development teams should evaluate the set of focus areas that are most relevant to their applications and establish quality criteria to which they will hold themselves accountable to during the coding phase of the release cycle. Typically, this starts with setting simple goals for design reviews, test coverage, or bug counts in these specific areas. Once goals are established, application developers and their test counterparts should be held accountable to the established goals, prior to moving from the coding to the testing phase of the project. This implies, of course, that formal criteria and quality goals be broadly agreed to at the onset of the project to ensure that all stakeholders are bought into the process. Like the other tactics for improving quality that have been suggested in this chapter, this too will help to continue to focus on pulling quality upstream in the engineering process, which will ultimately lead to a much better product for your end users.

Summary

Early in this chapter, we discussed how process is applied to software engineering to help control the flow of software construction as a means to increase efficiency and control costs, resources, and quality. Oftentimes, these processes are imperfect and fail to achieve the core goals. In the same way that software engineering teams analyze code to find and fix bugs, they should continuously analyze their engineering processes, as well, and make necessary improvements. Successful teams often perform this self-evaluation at the end of each product development cycle and adjust their future processes to account for the inefficiencies or mistakes of the past. This practice promotes a continued focus on improving the quality of the team's output, as well as the efficiency of its working habits. The practices mentioned in this chapter, such as establishing a consistent milestone rhythm, managing and controlling the quality of code being introduced into source control, incorporating daily builds and release testing, and creating and enforcing quality criteria, are just a few examples of key process changes that will help improve the quality of the work being delivered by your team. Each of these recommendations contributes to the one central point, which is to continuously increase the quality of the application code as early in the release process as possible, which ultimately improves the overall quality of the final product being developed.

Key Points

- Establish a quality-focused, milestone-based project rhythm.
- Implement source control and check-in processes.
   - Establish a source management strategy.
   - Create and enforce source check-in processes and quality criteria.
- Release and test code daily.
- Automate daily application builds.
   - Leverage MSBuild or Team Foundation Build for automated application build processes.
- Establish and enforce quality-focused release criteria.

Chapter 12
Attitude Is Everything

Excellence is not a skill. It is an attitude.

—Ralph Marston

This book focuses on best practices and policies for writing solid code. In the areas of performance, scalability, defensive programming, security, memory management, and other key areas of managed programming, this book is a prescription to write quality managed applications. However, this book alone cannot guarantee that an application is perfect. Writing a perfect, or near perfect, application is about more than completing the software development life cycle, following proper naming conventions, implementing the dispose pattern correctly, or following the other recommended practices described in this book. Writing solid code is more than technical. It is also having the proper attitude as an individual, a team, and management. For example, some developers solve software problems with a less than scientific approach. They simply try a few solutions randomly. If a guess works, problem solved. Unfortunately, the resulting solution is probably just a Band-Aid hiding the real problem. Yet the application is running again. Both the customer and developer appear to be happy. But for how long? This is an issue of attitude and not a technical problem.

When programming, keep the holistic view of the application in mind. Customers don't view an application as a nuts-and-bolts proposition. A business person is interested in the application as a solution to a business problem. A gamer is interested in the quality of the game and not some algorithm that saves a nanosecond. A nanosecond the gamer won't notice, and you spent weeks researching and developing. Yes, an application is a composition of nuts and bolts. More importantly, you are creating a solution. It is that solution that should dictate product development and not technical fortitude. Many developers suffer from a syndrome best described as being unable to see the trees for the forest. Adhering to the software development life cycle, which is solution driven, will help balance customer expectations and the mechanics of product development. The remainder of the chapter includes other considerations that should improve attitude.

Passion

Passion. This word is important even for developers. I have found the best artisans to be passionate about their craft or some aspect of their current project. Would you hire a plumber who hates plumbing? What airline would hire a pilot who hates flying? If so, make sure your life insurance is paid in full before booking a flight on that airline. Passion translates into interest, curiosity, and focus, which are essential ingredients for a good developer. If you lack an interest in your work, you will have a tendency to sleepwalk. You cannot sleepwalk through programming. If you are an avowed geek, where anything that has ones and zeros is interesting, skip the remainder of this section. For the rest of us (the majority), choose to work on problems, projects, or technologies where you have a keen interest. Work in an environment that keeps you stimulated. It may be as simple as working with a team of smart developers. Using whatever means possible, find the passion in your work, or select something else to do.

I am presently managing a startup, which is developing an online debugger for Windows and other applications. The Chief Technical Officer is Oleg. The primary reason for that position, other than that he is an incredible programmer, is Oleg's passion. For most, debugging is forced behavior to be avoided whenever possible. However, Oleg is passionate about debugging. I am confident that Oleg takes crash dumps and debugging logs on vacation to read on the beach. Most importantly, this passion has translated into innovative, stable, and correct code. When there is a problem, I know Oleg will make time to investigate the problem and implement the best solution.

> **Tip** Be passionate about the technology, project, or problem.

Linear versus Iterative

Sometimes the quickest path is not a straight line. This definitely applies to the software development life cycle, which is an iterative, not linear, process. It may be simpler to code, test, and then debug in isolated and linear phases. But this approach is definitely harmful to your application. This is one circumstance where you should enjoy traveling in circles. My best advice—learn to multitask.

First, the linear approach will undoubtedly extend the development cycle. Without some degree of parallelism, the project is elongated. In the competitive and fluid business climate of the Web, unnecessarily extending the business cycle can be fatal. In addition, every day spent developing the project is an additional day of lost revenue. Even if you are not in management, marketing, or sales, lost revenue is important—especially for developers who hope to keep their jobs into the future.

Debugging while coding is essential. The goal is not simply to complete features like items on a checklist. You will complete the application but not be truly done. Actually, you won't even be close. It may take you an equal amount of time to resolve all the unaddressed problems in the code. Worse yet is that debugging at the end of a project is the worst possible time. Here are some reasons:

- Problems that could have been resolved earlier have had an opportunity to replicate in your code. Fixing bugs is about education and communication. Fix the bug early, learn from the problem, and communicate this to others on the team. This prevents others from repeating the same mistake in the application.

- Bugs are easier to resolve when you have recently worked in the relevant code. Later, when the code is cold, finding the proper resolution will inevitably take more time.

- Some bugs could require a redesign of some portion or the entire application. This is best discovered earlier and not later. Delaying that decision can be costly. You are in essence building your application on quicksand. The more code you write, the more code you will have to eventually rewrite.

"Bugs beget more bugs." Developers should start each morning by repeating this mantra during 15 minutes of meditation. Waiting to debug at the end of the project means you will have no idea how many problems truly exist in the application. Why? You will introduce new bugs while fixing the known bugs. In addition, correcting existing bugs will likely uncover bugs that were already there but unseen.

Ongoing bug fixes are an important barometer of the quality of the application. It could highlight systematic and technical problems beyond a simple fix. By delaying bug fixes, you could obfuscate the fact that you are creating a weak application. Reviewing bug fixes early on could uncover the presence of an inexperienced developer. Don't you want to know that before that developer contributes reams of code to the application?

Finally, you are setting false expectations with management and customers. Reporting on the completion rate of the features is misleading. If you are fixing bugs at the end, for the reasons already described in this chapter, you will have no clue when the project will actually be finished. You are more likely to be able to predict the next five winners of the Super Bowl than the correct end date of your project. This will set up a battle among you, the management, and the customers. The team will use shortcuts to get the project released, and the quality of the application will suffer.

> **Tip** Going in circles is sometimes the quickest path between two points.

Sales Are Good

For most of us, sales make the world go around. I cannot pay my mortgage, college tuition, or that Caribbean trip that I have planned with hypothetical money. This requires real money, which usually comes from sales to a tangible customer. Forget that at your peril.

I have heard, on more than one occasion and from a variety of sources, that the development team should drive deadlines. Bogus! Everyone should have a seat at the scheduling table for setting deadlines: management, sales, marketing, and you. The best schedule is a collaboration that balances technical with business and customer needs. If a company exhausts its available funds before the product is complete, who benefits? How useful is your product when competitors deliver a product with slightly less features a year earlier but captured the majority of the market share? Your competitors will be on that weeklong Caribbean vacation while you are on a one-day trip to the Air Force museum in Dayton.

Do not over-engineer. Over-engineering usually entails needless complexity and the implementation of features that almost assuredly the customer does not require. We all know developers, when asked to build a toaster, would deliver the space shuttle. Without a doubt, this would be the best toaster in the universe. However, customers only wanted to mildly burn bread. They never intended to fly their toaster to the moon—even though that is a cool feature. Fight the temptation to over-engineer. The additional complexity will introduce bugs (the kinds that are hard to find) and delay product release, and the code is most likely not maintainable. Plus, you will give your manager and peers heartburn. Over-engineering will exhaust available capital, which is rarely an unlimited resource.

> **Tip** The ultimate objective is a successful product.

Features

This section is best introduced with a passage from *Catch-22*. *Catch-22* is a book written by Joseph Heller that later became a popular movie.

"Can you ground him?"

"I sure can but first he has to ask me to. That's part of the rule."

"Then why doesn't he ask you to?"

"Because he's crazy," Doc Daneeka said. "He has to be crazy to keep flying combat missions after all the close calls he's had. Sure I can ground Orr. But first he has to ask me to."

"That's all he has to do to be grounded?"

"That's all. Let him ask me."

"And then you can ground him?" Yossarian asked.

"No, then I can't ground him."

"You mean there's a catch?"

"Sure there is a catch," Doc Daneeka replied. "Catch-22. Anyone who wants to get out of combat duty isn't really crazy."

This conversation takes place at a military base toward the end of World War II. Yossarian is a bombardier who should be rotated home after reaching a certain number of bombing missions. One problem is the base colonel keeps raising the number of missions required to return home much to the frustration of everyone. Similarly, when the feature set is not frozen, developer morale is affected. Particularly in the later phases of product development, this is a sure indicator of a lack of discipline and inexperience project management. Developer morale will suffer as the goal line is perpetually extended. Fatigue will occur, and the quality of product development will be affected. More bugs are created at this time than at any other time. In addition, feature creep makes meeting deadlines nearly impossible, which has an obvious adverse impact on the budget. The following is quote from the *Catch-22* movie.

Yossarian: If he raises the number of missions again, I swear to God, I'll help you kill him.

Dobbs: Really?

Yossarian: I swear.

Dobbs: Well, that's very reasonable of you.

View each new feature as a potential harbinger of the plague. That should provide the proper level of skepticism for assessing the benefit of adding a new feature. Each new feature is a harbinger of future bugs. Of course, this means extra development costs and missed deadlines. Now even that trip to Dayton seems remote. In addition, you are now spending more time on new features and related problems and less on your current code base. For this reason, the quality of your current code base will begin to suffer also.

There are two groups of developers. The first group lives in an infinite world where there is endless time to implement additional features. These developers have never seen a feature they did not like. You can also include some managers and marketing people in this group. The other group comprises developers who are overly ambitious and optimistic. They always commit to doing twice as much as necessary in half the required time. Developers like this never plan for a weekend, vacations, or even bathroom breaks. Of course, these people perennially miss deadlines. More importantly, their code is probably of lesser quality than anyone else on the team. They are often overcommitted and overwhelmed, which translates to poorly written code.

If developers have too much "I" in their vocabulary (such as the following statements) and not enough "the customer," be concerned. They are likely to add features that no one wants.

- That is a feature I would like.

- I find that to be very cool. Let us implement that.

- If I were the customer, this is what I would like.

Focus on key features. Prioritize the features to determine which features are the key features. Dedicate your resources proportionally to the high-priority features and lesser for low-priority resources. If you poorly implement the key features, the customer will never use the other features. Customers will switch to a competitor's product before then. Like most, I use Microsoft Outlook primarily to send and receive e-mail. There are plenty of other features, but those are the key features from the perspective of a user. If those features do not work, I would not use Microsoft Outlook, regardless of how great those other features might be. For those reasons, focus your efforts on the primary features and do not dilute your effort with additional features.

Tip Prioritize features and allocate resources accordingly.

Flexibility

Flexibility may be good when doing yoga, but it is bad in code. Pliant code can adapt to most any eventuality. However, pliancy infers complexity, and complexity is never a friend to stable bug-free code that is also maintainable. The best path to robust and stable code is straightforwardness. Your code should do a few things well and not a hundred things poorly. This requires prioritizing what is important to your customer and the project. This is different than prioritizing features, as described in the previous section. This prioritizing on customer goals, considering all options in your code, is of little importance if many of those options are not priority. In that circumstance, the practical result is to expand the code base. Of course, that extra code must now be debugged, tested, and maintained on an ongoing basis. Your customer is probably content with less flexibility and more stable code key features.

Commercial programming should not be approached as a math question from a school exam. My calculus professor graded a 95 percent correct answer as entirely incorrect. It was an all-or-nothing scenario. I had to invest the time and research for the 100 percent correct answer—regardless of how long that process took. That is okay in an academic environment, which is more ivory tower. Plus, as an undergraduate in college, my time is free. College professors did not mind wasting my time and frequently did so. However, commercial programming is more pragmatic. An 80 percent solution that solves 99 percent of the problem is acceptable—especially when, for that extra 1 percent of flexibility, you add measurably more complexity, reduce maintainability, and needlessly extend the development process.

Simple code is easier to debug. That probably sounds obvious but is often forgotten. The greatest challenge to simple code is reining in flexibility. The added flexibility is essentially noise that distracts the developer from focusing on the core functionality.

> **Tip** Keep coding simple and avoid non-core flexibility.

Solve Real Problems

Look beyond the symptoms to find the real problems. When customers are calling the support line nonstop and complaining about a problem in code that you wrote, it is tempting to fix the symptom and not the problem. That is frequently the quick solution. Of course the intent is always to return to the real problem later and find a resolution, but you never do. That is human nature.

When you fix the symptom, you can actually make the problem worse—sometimes much worse. Fixing the symptom hides the problem. If you subscribe to "out of sight, out of mind" as a motto, this is a perfect solution. However, the hidden problem may harm the application in more insidious ways, which highlights the fallacy of this approach.

A man goes to a doctor's office and says, "Doctor, it hurts when I raise my arm over my head."

The doctor replies, "Then don't raise your arm over your head."

The doctor resolved the problem based on the symptom. That was quick and easy. However, tomorrow the man could drop dead. He had an undiagnosed broken arm with internal injuries and was bleeding to death. But the doctor never knew. This is the classic example of treating the symptom and not resolving the real problem.

Don't *try* to fix a software problem. I have seen developers resolve a problem simply by trying a few things until the problem disappeared. However, this does not mean that the problem is fixed. Any observations made in this manner are anecdotal at best. A more scientific approach is probably advisable. If you are fortunate enough to fix the real problem with the "try" approach, consider yourself lucky. The stability of your application should not be based on luck.

Never make assumptions. Assumptions are almost always made from symptoms and not facts. By definition, if you had the facts, you wouldn't be making an assumption. Invest the time to investigate software problems beyond the obvious and obtain the facts. Because of the Web, you have almost an infinite repository of information at your fingertips. You will most likely find someone on the Web who had the identical or similar problem previously.

> **Tip** Solve problems, not symptoms.

You Are Responsible

Find a mirror and repeat: "You are responsible. You are responsible. *You* are responsible."

The designer, quality assurance person, and tester verify that an application is architected correctly, robust, stable, secure, and scalable, which is a valuable contribution to the project. However, this is short of a warranty for your code. Even if everyone else on the software team does his or her job competently, there is no assurance that the code is correct. Most of what is being verified at the functional level are return values, feature verification, or validation of customer expectations. These roles are not filled by developers, and most likely no one is looking at the code. Your code could pass a unit test and still be broken.

A quality assurance team does not provide a developer with an invitation to write bad code. If so, your bad code is likely to find itself in the release product, much to the dismay of everyone. The quality assurance person or the tester probably does not have a developer background. Even if they wanted, these are not the proper people to review and evaluate individual statements of code for software bugs. They do not have the experience. That remains your responsibility. You would be surprised how much bad code passes quality assurance and testing.

Software problems are also not the fault of the compiler, the operating system, or Microsoft. These could be the origins of the problem, but it is unlikely. Therefore, do not start there when trying to resolve a problem. Consider the problem to be yours. Your problems are easier to fix anyway. Why? You have control of your code base. If the problem is from Microsoft, they must fix it. They will set the timeline and resolution. You have no control in that scenario.

On more than one occasion, I have had this conversation, or something similar, with developers at work.

It starts with a developer walking into my office and announcing, "I have found a bug!"

With some interest, I say, "What kind of bug?"

The developer continues, "It is a bug from Microsoft."

I comment with some skepticism, "Are you sure about that?"

The developer adds, "The bug appears to be..."

"Stop!" I declare. "I will bet a lunch if the problem is actually from Microsoft and not you, the developer."

Of course, they always accept this challenge. The outcome is that I have won several free lunches. I have not lost the wager once. My experience is that the problem is always yours. Would you accept that wager?

Tip Accept the responsibility for your code.

Port Code as New Code

The body of available native code is extensive. It will be awhile before the breadth of managed code nears that of native code. Until then, there will be plenty of opportunities to port native code to manage code. Regardless of the level of familiarity with the native code, port the native to managed code as new code. It does not matter how many times the native version has been tested and deployed. Don't automatically trust that code. What worked in Microsoft C++ or Visual Basic 6 may not work well in the managed environment. This is particularly true about any code that involves memory management since that responsibility is now delegated to the Common Language Runtime (CLR).

All ported code should undergo the same rigorous testing as any other code. You should then run regression tests to confirm the health of the overall application after assimilating the ported code. Test not trust is the perfect policy when porting native code.

Furthermore, ported code often requires an extensive rewrite and may retain only a few vestiges of the original native code. Treat that code accordingly. It is not so much ported code but new code. As such, porting code to the managed environment is much more than translating individual lines of code. You are also changing the programming model and environment. That might necessitate other changes. Keeping the old programming model is a sure way to introduce the new code and a handful of software bugs to your application.

Tip Test ported code with the same diligence as the existing code base.

Refactoring

Visual Studio has amazing refactoring capabilities. This feature removes most of the drudgery of manual refactoring, making it almost a trivial task. I remember the mind-numbing challenge of updating variable names that were spread across dozens of source files. Even more, I remember the errors created from the tedium of refactoring a large application manually. Most likely I would abandon, revert back to the original, and enjoy a cup of coffee at the local café. Now even the most ambitious refactoring goals are simply a wizard away. In this quick-fix environment, it is easy to forget that automatic refactoring can touch a vast amount of code in an instant with unexpected results. With manual refactoring, you are present at every change. Worst case scenario: I may make an error every few minutes—almost all of them are noticed immediately. Automatic refactoring is a press of a button, and you can create hundreds of problems in an instant. None of them you see.

If the project has hundreds of source files, some not written by you, refactoring can be particularly a problem. Ironically, the more automatic refactoring may benefit you (i.e., the larger the project), the larger the possibility of abuse. This is the conundrum. For this reason, some companies have banned automatic refactoring altogether. I am not advocating something quite that drastic. However, I am advocating testing. For even the most innocuous refactoring, test and retest your application for improper changes that you may not be unaware of. If there are only a few changes, then ask to be prompted with each change. You will have the ability to review or reject each change, which is considerably safer.

No change is too minor to test. There are too many stories of the innocent change, the one that could not possibly harm an application, haunting a developer to the end of his or her days. If you change the name of a single variable, retest the application. If you change a class member from private to public, or vice versa, retest your application. If you change the [*fill in the blank*] in your application, retest the program.

> **Tip** Refactoring, even when trivial, requires retesting the application.

Priorities

Bob the developer has an important decision to make. Should he use a binary or XML formatter with Windows Communication Foundation (WCF)? This is a decision about speed and size (binary formatter) versus the importance of portability (XML formatter). Sally the developer is deciding between the complexity of AJAX and the simplicity of a traditional Web application. Do you want these decisions to be made by individual developers on an ad hoc basis or decided in a judicious manner with the appropriate stakeholders? I would recommend the latter. The priorities for product development can have a significant impact on the final product.

Decide on priorities as part of the design phase of the software development life cycle and communicate them to the team. This will prevent developers from making important strategic decisions without some proper guidelines. Macro priorities affect the overall application. For example, deciding whether XML or binary format is preferred for communication. Because most of your customers are geeks who value speed over a fancy user interface, you might decide to prioritize user interface responsiveness over aesthetics. Of course, security must be considered a priority. Nowadays, security trumps every other priority. However, don't assume developers are aware of this. There are also micro priorities that are organized, which are specific to a developer or module. For example, performance versus maintainability might be something that is decided on a per-module basis.

The following is a list of topics that should be considered when evaluating priorities:

- Security

- Performance or speed

- Scalability

- Maintainability

- Ease of use

- Size

- Complexity

- Robustness

Have a meeting with the team to specifically decide upon the priorities. Make sure the team members understand the rationale for each priority and not just the order. After the meeting, document the priorities and distribute to each team member. Throughout the product development life cycle, confirm that developers are adhering to these priorities. This should be part of the code review. Without this validation, priorities become optional and subject to each developer's whim. That will make the challenge of building a cohesive product even more difficult.

 Tip Set priorities in the design phase and confirm their adherence.

Be Realistic

Paul was the new man on the team. He was hired to manage quality assurance. His suggestions, although valid, were geared toward teams of hundreds of developers collaborating on millions of lines of code. We have six developers working on a few thousand lines of code. My unwillingness to build the infrastructure for a large organization was interpreted by Paul as a lack of commitment to quality. It was not a lack of commitment to quality but an acknowledgement of practical and pragmatic considerations.

First, there are always budgetary constraints. Most small companies do not have the budget of Microsoft, Autodesk, Intuit, or other large software companies. Pretending to be in that realm is a good way to exhaust needed capital before the product is complete. In that circumstance, all the quality assurance in the world will not get your product successfully to market. Second, a certain level of formality is required in large organizations or chaos will reign. However, a small company can dispense with some of that formality. One of the advantages of a small software company is being lean and mean. Don't lose that advantage pretending to be a big company.

I could easily create the perfect product in the infinite universe, with unlimited venture capital and unbound resources. However, because most of us live in the real world, this is not an option—even for a large software company or institution. Before the project starts, evaluate your financial position and define a budget. When the budget is finalized, you can then plan. The proper balance and allocation of resources among development, quality assurance, and testing can only be decided then. Hopefully, you will have the resources to implement the perfect product in an infinite universe. If not, you now have a realistic plan for success that can be executed.

> **Tip** Create a budget. From that budget, develop a plan to realistically complete the project.

Paradigm Shift

Embrace the new paradigm. .NET is not just another environment. C# is not just another programming language. This represents a seismic shift not only technically but philosophically in our approach to product development. Spend the necessary time to educate yourself in the best practices of this environment. Reading this book is a good first step. But go further. As a manager, you must be willing to make the investment in knowledge. The return on that investment will be exponential. The result will be a higher quality application that leverages the strengths and avoids the weaknesses of this environment. As mentioned previously, large applications ported to .NET from Windows "as is" will probably start with bugs. The environments are different and require a fresh perspective to programming and product development.

The .NET Framework is not Windows. Don't develop native Windows applications in .NET. Instead, write a managed application. For example, don't continue to use native APIs for methods available in the .NET Framework Class Library. Do not use unsafe code to avoid difficult porting decisions. Understand the technical and semantic differences between garbage collection in native versus managed environments.

C# is a fully object-oriented language, not a hybrid like C++. If the intention is to continue to write procedural code, keep C or C++ as the preferred language. In the managed environment, forget about the bits and the bytes. Managed languages, such as C#, create a safe envelope where developers can focus on engineering customer solutions and not low-level plumbing. C and C++ programming languages rely on developers to micromanage everything. From memory management to obtaining a device context to draw graphics in a window, you are involved in everything. In the managed arena, you fortunately subjugate much of this to the CLR.

I remember teaching Windows programming in C nearly 15 years ago. At that time, Window 3.1 was the current operating system. The first day was always spent teaching how to render a blank window. This is a window with no text, menu, icons, or anything—simply a blank window. Eight hours just for that. There was no discussion on how to create great business solutions. We were mired in too many low-level details to discuss anything else. Not surprisingly, software applications from that era are very complicated, hard to maintain, and not customer centric. In .NET, these details fortunately have been abstracted. As a developer, you have been freed from this minutia. In .NET, I can teach someone how to create a blank window in one minute. Most of the minute would be spent choosing the appropriate background color for the window. How about mauve? For this reason, you can focus on creating exceptional business solutions. Managed code frees the developer to be creative and not just a technician. This freedom will allow developers to create a new generation of applications.

> **Tip** In C#, write fully managed applications. Anything less compromises the objective.

Expand Your Perspective

While working in the trenches on a programming project, it is natural to be drawn to our peers for advice and consultation—whether discussing design issues, programming problems, or cracking the next level of the Xbox game in the lobby. This proclivity is understandable. There is a connection with our peers. We speak from the same dictionary. However, it is sometimes nice to communicate with others. No, this is not a social experiment about the interaction of technical and non-technical people. The advantage is a different perspective. Your peers are likely to have the same or similar perspective as you from being in the trenches together. Whether reviewing customer usability or a software problem, a fresh perspective can be helpful.

My fresh perspective comes from Andrea, who is not a computer person. However, Andrea is intelligent and can understand almost any concept. When I need a fresh perspective, I can talk with her about the project. Just having to explain a programming problem to her makes me think differently. Quite often, in mid-sentence of the explanation, there is a revelation. I am glad that she doesn't charge commissions for each revelation. Andrea would be a rich woman by now.

If in doubt, talk to the customer. Consider customers an equal partner on the project. Customers are a great resource for a fresh perspective. Importantly, they probably know the problem domain better than you. Not every customer is assessable for this type of conversation or wants to be involved at this level. However, if they are, you should take advantage of that. When I started programming years ago, developers never talked to customers. A them versus us mentality prevailed at that time. Sure the software products derived from that approach eventually worked. I wrote plenty of those applications. However, those products would have benefited from customer participation. Who knows customer expectation more than the customer? No one. Most important, this is a free resource—the best kind of resource. If managed correctly, a close relationship with a customer can be invaluable.

Tip Cultivate a relationship with resources not on your team—especially customers.

Appendix A
Agile Development Resources

In Chapter 1, "Code Quality in an Agile World," we discussed a number of agile development methodologies and resources available for application developers and their project teams. The following represents a partial list of books and Web sites that provide additional information about this topic.

TABLE A-1 Agile Development Resources

Resource	URL
Agile Project Management with Scrum	*http://www.microsoft.com/MSPress/books/6916.aspx*
Test-Driven Development in Microsoft .NET	*http://www.microsoft.com/MSPress/books/6778.aspx*
Extreme Programming Adventures in C#	*http://www.microsoft.com/mspress/books/6777.aspx*
Extreme Programming Series	*http://www.xprogramming.com/xpmag/books20011231 .htm#book0201708426*

Appendix B
Web Performance Resources

In Chapter 4, "Performance Is a Feature," we reviewed a number of tactics for improving the performance of Web applications. This is a broad subject area that requires more than a single chapter to cover the depth of information that is available. To supplement the information provided, the following represents a set of additional tools and resources available from Microsoft and other companies or individuals.

TABLE B-1 Performance tools

Tool	URL
Network Monitor	http://www.microsoft.com/downloads/details.aspx?FamilyID=f4db40af -1e08-4a21-a26b-ec2f4dc4190d&DisplayLang=en
Visual Round Trip Analyzer (VRTA)	http://www.microsoft.com/downloads/details.aspx?FamilyID=119f3477 -dced-41e3-a0e7-d8b5cae893a3&DisplayLang=en
Fiddler	http://www.fiddlertool.com
Internet Explorer Developer Toolbar	http://www.microsoft.com/downloads/details.aspx?familyid=E59C3964 -672D-4511-BB3E-2D5E1DB91038&displaylang=en
HTTPWatch	http://www.httpwatch.com
YSlow	http://developer.yahoo.com/yslow
Firebug	http://getfirebug.com
JSMin	http://javascript.crockford.com/jsmin.html
YUI Compressor	http://developer.yahoo.com/yui/compressor

TABLE B-2 Performance resources

Resource	URL
The PingER Project	http://www-iepm.slac.stanford.edu/pinger
Steve Souders' Web site	http://souders.org
Yahoo! Exceptional Performance	http://developer.yahoo.com/performance
HTTPWatch Blog	http://blog.httpwatch.com
Network Monitor Blog	http://blogs.technet.com/netmon
Limelight Networks	http://www.limelightnetworks.com
Akamai	http://www.akamai.com
Level 3 Communications	http://www.level3.com

Index

A

<Actions1> element, 233
activity diagrams, 24
Add element, 39
ADPlus (Autodump +), 223,
    231–236
  ADPlus_report.txt, 232
  configuration file, 232
  crash mode, 231
  hang mode, 231
  log file, 232
  Process_List.txt, 232
  Web applications and,
    233–234
ADPlus_report.txt, 232
agile methods of software
    development, 3–8
  eXtreme Programming, 5–6
  practices in Microsoft
    engineering culture, 7–8
  Scrum, 4–5
  Test-Driven Development
    (TDD), 6–7
algorithms, comments and, 186
anatomy of unit test, 249–252
application configuration files,
    52–65
  application configuration in
    practice, 65
  basics, 55–56
  configuration example, 57–58
  configuration settings basics,
    55–56
  configuration storage, 56–57
  custom, 60–65
  custom configurations, 60–64
  database connection string
    configurations, 58–60
  example, 57–58
  storage, 56–57
application failure, defending
    against, 109–111

application scalability, 98–104
  approaches to scalability,
    99–102
  database scalability, 102–104
application test code
  negative tests, 248
  positive tests, 248
applying runtime security,
    137–138
applying SD3+C strategy, 125
<appSettings> element, 55–56,
    58–59
AssertFailedException class, 250
AssertInconclusiveException
    class, 250
asserts, 250
  AssertFailedException class,
    250
  AssertInconclusiveException
    class, 250
  CollectionAssert class, 250
  ExpectedExceptionalAttribute
    class, 251
  StringAssert class, 250
  UnitTestAssertException class,
    250
attitude, 287–300
  being realistic, 297–298
  expanding your perspective,
    299–300
  flexibility, 292
  linear vs. iterative, 288–289
  paradigm shifts, 298–299
  passion and, 287–288
  porting code as new code,
    295
  priorities, 296–297
  refactoring, 295–296
  responsibility, 294
  sales and, 289–290
  solving real problems, 293
Autodump + (ADPlus), 223
  ADPlus_report.txt, 232

  configuration file, 232
  crash mode, 231
  hang mode, 231
  log file, 232
  Process_List.txt, 232
  Web applications and,
    233–234
automated code analysis,
    245–254
  anatomy of unit test, 249–252
  static code analysis tools,
    245–248
  testing with visual studio,
    253–254
  writing application test code,
    248–252
automating daily build-and-
    release process, 277–278
  Build process, 275–276
  Deploy process, 276
  feature development, 275
  MSBuild, 278
  NAnt, 277–278
  Team Foundation Build, 278
  Verification testing, 276

B

being realistic, 297–298
branches, source code, 268–269
  main branch, 268
  next branch, 268
  shipping branch, 269
  team branch, 268–269
  working branch, 268
Build process, 275–276
Build Verification Testing (BVT),
    241
build verification tests (BVTs), 12
BuildGreeting() method,
    251–252
BuildGreetingTest() method, 251
building perspective, 256

About the Authors

Donis Marshall

Donis Marshall is the chief executive officer at *Debuglive.com*. He manages a team of expert software developers creating the first entirely Web-based debugger for Windows applications. With 20 years of development experience and an in-depth background on Microsoft .NET technologies, he has authored several books, including *Programming Microsoft Visual C# 2008: The Language* and *.NET Security Programming*. As a trainer and consultant, Donis teaches classes and conducts seminars on .NET programming, debugging, security, and design and architecture.

John Bruno

John Bruno is a senior program manager at Microsoft with over 10 years of application development experience. He specializes in designing and building scalable Web-based applications and services using Microsoft .NET technologies. Since joining Microsoft, John has played key roles in launching multiple versions of Windows Live and has been responsible for the service architecture and developer platform of Windows Live Spaces, which is delivered to over 100 million users worldwide. His current focus is on bringing the next generation of Web-based services for Windows Mobile to the world. You can contact John through his Web site at *http://johnbruno.net*.

Best Practices for Software Engineering

Software Estimation: Demystifying the Black Art
Steve McConnell
ISBN 9780735605350

Amazon.com's pick for "Best Computer Book of 2006"! Generating accurate software estimates is fairly straight-forward—once you understand the art of creating them. Acclaimed author Steve McConnell demystifies the process—illuminating the practical procedures, formulas, and heuristics you can apply right away.

Code Complete, Second Edition
Steve McConnell
ISBN 9780735619678

Widely considered one of the best practical guides to programming—fully updated. Drawing from research, academia, and everyday commercial practice, McConnell synthesizes must-know principles and techniques into clear, pragmatic guidance. Rethink your approach—and deliver the highest quality code.

Agile Portfolio Management
Jochen Krebs
ISBN 9780735625679

Agile processes foster better collaboration, innovation, and results. So why limit their use to software projects—when you can transform your entire business? This book illuminates the opportunities—and rewards—of applying agile processes to your overall IT portfolio, with best practices for optimizing results.

Simple Architectures for Complex Enterprises
Roger Sessions
ISBN 9780735625785

Why do so many IT projects fail? Enterprise consultant Roger Sessions believes complex problems require simple solutions. And in this book, he shows how to make simplicity a core architectural requirement—as critical as performance, reliability, or security—to achieve better, more reliable results for your organization.

The Enterprise and Scrum
Ken Schwaber
ISBN 9780735623378

Extend Scrum's benefits—greater agility, higher-quality products, and lower costs—beyond individual teams to the entire enterprise. Scrum cofounder Ken Schwaber describes proven practices for adopting Scrum principles across your organization, including that all-critical component—managing change.

ALSO SEE

Software Requirements, Second Edition
Karl E. Wiegers
ISBN 9780735618794

More About Software Requirements: Thorny Issues and Practical Advice
Karl E. Wiegers
ISBN 9780735622678

Software Requirement Patterns
Stephen Withall
ISBN 9780735623989

Agile Project Management with Scrum
Ken Schwaber
ISBN 9780735619937

For C# Developers

Microsoft® Visual C#® 2008 Express Edition: Build a Program Now!

Patrice Pelland
ISBN 9780735625426

Build your own Web browser or other cool application—no programming experience required! Featuring learn-by-doing projects and plenty of examples, this full-color guide is your quick start to creating your first applications for Windows®. DVD includes Express Edition software plus code samples.

Microsoft Visual C# 2008 Step by Step

John Sharp
ISBN 9780735624306

Teach yourself Visual C# 2008—one step at a time. Ideal for developers with fundamental programming skills, this practical tutorial delivers hands-on guidance for creating C# components and Windows–based applications. CD features practice exercises, code samples, and a fully searchable eBook.

Learn Programming Now! Microsoft XNA® Game Studio 2.0

Rob Miles
ISBN 9780735625228

Now you can create your own games for Xbox 360® and Windows—as you learn the underlying skills and concepts for computer programming. Dive right into your first project, adding new tools and tricks to your arsenal as you go. Master the fundamentals of XNA Game Studio and Visual C#—no experience required!

Programming Microsoft Visual C# 2008: The Language

Donis Marshall
ISBN 9780735625402

Get the in-depth reference, best practices, and code you need to master the core language capabilities in Visual C# 2008. Fully updated for Microsoft .NET Framework 3.5, including a detailed exploration of LINQ, this book examines language features in detail—and across the product life cycle.

Windows via C/C++, Fifth Edition

Jeffrey Richter, Christophe Nasarre
ISBN 9780735624245

Jeffrey Richter's classic guide to C++ programming—now fully revised for Windows XP, Windows Vista®, and Windows Server® 2008. Learn to develop more-robust applications with unmanaged C++ code—and apply advanced techniques—with comprehensive guidance and code samples from the experts.

CLR via C#, Second Edition

Jeffrey Richter
ISBN 9780735621633

Dig deep and master the intricacies of the common language runtime (CLR) and the .NET Framework. Written by programming expert Jeffrey Richter, this guide is ideal for developers building any kind of application—ASP.NET, Windows Forms, Microsoft SQL Server®, Web services, console apps—and features extensive C# code samples.

ALSO SEE

Microsoft Visual C# 2005 Step by Step
ISBN 9780735621299

Programming Microsoft Visual C# 2005: The Language
ISBN 9780735621817

Debugging Microsoft .NET 2.0 Applications
ISBN 9780735622029

microsoft.com/mspress

For Visual Basic Developers

Microsoft® Visual Basic® 2008 Express Edition: Build a Program Now!
Patrice Pelland
ISBN 9780735625419

Build your own Web browser or other cool application—no programming experience required! Featuring learn-by-doing projects and plenty of examples, this full-color guide is your quick start to creating your first applications for Windows®. DVD includes Express Edition software plus code samples.

Microsoft Visual Basic 2008 Step by Step
Michael Halvorson
ISBN 9780735625372

Teach yourself the essential tools and techniques for Visual Basic 2008—one step at a time. No matter what your skill level, you'll find the practical guidance and examples you need to start building applications for Windows and the Web. CD features practice exercises, code samples, and a fully searchable eBook.

Programming Microsoft Visual Basic 2005: The Language
Francesco Balena
ISBN 9780735621831

Master the core capabilities in Visual Basic 2005 with guidance from well-known programming expert Francesco Balena. Focusing on language features and the Microsoft .NET Framework 2.0 base class library, this book provides pragmatic instruction and examples useful to both new and experienced developers.

Programming Windows Services with Microsoft Visual Basic 2008
Michael Gernaey
ISBN 9780735624337

The essential guide for developing powerful, customized Windows services with Visual Basic 2008. Whether you're looking to perform network monitoring or design a complex enterprise solution, this guide delivers the right combination of expert advice and practical examples to accelerate your productivity.

ALSO SEE

Microsoft Visual Basic 2005 Express Edition: Build a Program Now!
Patrice Pelland
ISBN 9780735622135

Microsoft Visual Basic 2005 Step by Step
Michael Halvorson
ISBN 9780735621312

Microsoft ADO.NET 2.0 Step by Step
Rebecca Riordan
ISBN 9780735621640

Microsoft ASP.NET 3.5 Step by Step
George Shepherd
ISBN 9780735624269

Programming Microsoft ASP.NET 3.5
Dino Esposito
ISBN 9780735625273

Debugging Microsoft .NET 2.0 Applications
John Robbins
ISBN 9780735622029

***Microsoft*® Press**

microsoft.com/mspress

For Web Developers

Microsoft® ASP.NET 3.5 Step by Step
George Shepherd
ISBN 9780735624269

Teach yourself ASP.NET 3.5—one step at a time. Ideal for developers with fundamental programming skills but new to ASP.NET, this practical tutorial delivers hands-on guidance for developing Web applications in the Microsoft Visual Studio® 2008 environment.

Programming Microsoft ASP.NET 3.5
Dino Esposito
ISBN 9780735625273

The definitive guide to ASP.NET 3.5. Led by well-known ASP.NET expert Dino Esposito, you'll delve into the core topics for creating innovative Web applications, including Dynamic Data; LINQ; state, application, and session management; Web forms and requests; security strategies; AJAX; Silverlight; and more.

Microsoft Visual Web Developer 2008 Express Edition Step by Step
Eric Griffin
ISBN 9780735626065

Your hands guide to learning fundamental Web-development skills. This tutorial steps you through an end-to-end example, helping build essential skills logically and sequentially. By the end of the book, you'll have a working Web site, plus the fundamental skills needed for the next level—ASP.NET.

JavaScript Step by Step
Steve Suehring
ISBN 9780735624498

Build on your fundamental programming skills, and get hands-on guidance for creating Web applications with JavaScript. Learn to work with the six JavaScript data types, the Document Object Model, Web forms, CSS styles, AJAX, and other essentials—one step at a time.

Introducing Microsoft Silverlight™ 2, Second Edition
Laurence Moroney
ISBN 9780735625280

Get a head start with Silverlight 2—the cross-platform, cross-browser plug-in for rich interactive applications and the next-generation user experience. Featuring advance insights from inside the Silverlight team, this book delivers the practical, approachable guidance and code to inspire your next solutions.

Programming Microsoft LINQ
Paolo Pialorsi and Marco Russo
ISBN 9780735624009

With LINQ, you can query data—no matter what the source—directly from Microsoft Visual Basic® or C#. Guided by two data-access experts who've worked with LINQ in depth, you'll learn how Microsoft .NET Framework 3.5 implements LINQ, and how to exploit it. Study and adapt the book's examples for faster, leaner code.

ALSO SEE

Developing Service-Oriented AJAX Applications on the Microsoft Platform
ISBN 9780735625914

Microsoft ASP.NET 2.0 Step by Step
ISBN 9780735622012

Programming Microsoft ASP.NET 2.0
ISBN 9780735625273

Programming Microsoft ASP.NET 2.0 Applications: Advanced Topics
ISBN 9780735621770

Microsoft®
Press

microsoft.com/mspress

Collaborative Technologies—
Resources for Developers

What do you think of this book?

We want to hear from you!

Your feedback will help us continually improve our books and learning resources for you.
To participate in a brief online survey, please visit:

microsoft.com/learning/booksurvey

...and enter this book's ISBN-10 or ISBN-13 number (appears above barcode on back cover).
As a thank-you to survey participants in the U.S. and Canada, each month we'll randomly
select five respondents to win one of five $100 gift certificates from a leading online merchant.
At the conclusion of the survey, you can enter the drawing by providing your e-mail address,
which will be used for prize notification only.*

Thank you in advance for your input!

Where to find the ISBN on back cover

ISBN-13: 000-0-0000-0000-0
ISBN-10: 0-0000-0000-0

9 0 0 0 0

0 000000 000000

Example only. Each book has unique ISBN.

Microsoft
Press

Stay in touch!

To subscribe to the *Microsoft Press* *Book Connection Newsletter*—for news on upcoming
books, events, and special offers—please visit:

microsoft.com/learning/books/newsletter